READING DIVERSITY THROUGH CANADIAN PICTURE BOOKS

Reading Diversity through Canadian Picture Books

Preservice Teachers Explore Issues of Identity, Ideology, and Pedagogy

EDITED BY INGRID JOHNSTON AND JOYCE BAINBRIDGE

UNIVERSITY OF TORONTO PRESS
Toronto Buffalo London

ISBN 978-1-4426-4673-5

Publication cataloguing information is available
from Library and Archives Canada.

University of Toronto Press acknowledges the financial assistance to its
publishing program of the Canada Council for the Arts and the Ontario Arts
Council.

University of Toronto Press acknowledges the financial support of the
Government of Canada through the Canada Book Fund for its publishing
activities.

Contents

Figures

Acknowledgments

This book and the national research on which the chapters are based were made possible by the contributions of the many undergraduate students and several instructors who generously participated in the studies described here.

We thank our colleagues, family members, and friends who played a significant role in enabling this book to be written and who offered helpful suggestions. We would like to acknowledge the thoughtful feedback offered by reviewers of an earlier version of this manuscript and all the help and support offered by Douglas Hildebrand and his team from the University of Toronto Press to ensure the publication of the book.

We also wish to thank the following publishers for their permission to use the picture book images incorporated in this book:

Red Deer Press for two images from *Josepha: A Prairie Boy's Story*, copyright © 1994 by Jim McGugan and Murray Kimber. First published by Red Deer Press, 195 Allstate Parkway, Markham, Ontario L3R 4T8.

Fitzhenry & Whiteside for the image from *Flags*, illustration copyright © 1999 by Paul Morin. Published by Fitzhenry & Whiteside, 195 Allstate Parkway, Markham, Ontario L3R 4T8, www.fitzhenry.ca.

Pemmican Publications for the image from *The Missing Sun*, illustration copyright © 1993 by Rhian Brynjolson. Published by Pemmican Publications, 150 Henry Avenue, Winnipeg, Manitoba R3B 0J7.

Pemmican Publications for the image from *Red Parka Mary*, illustration copyright © 1996 by Rhian Brynjolson. Published by Pemmican Publications, 150 Henry Avenue, Winnipeg, Manitoba R3B 0J7.

Finally, we would like to thank the Social Sciences and Humanities Research Council of Canada (SSHRC) for providing funding for these studies, the University of Saskatchewan for the generous grant they provided towards copy-editing costs, and all our universities for their support of our research.

READING DIVERSITY THROUGH CANADIAN PICTURE BOOKS

Introduction

INGRID JOHNSTON AND JOYCE BAINBRIDGE

Context of the Research Study

As Canadian teacher educators and researchers, we have become increasingly aware of the many geographic, cultural, and linguistic distinctions and similarities that exist across our country. We have questioned how preservice teachers across Canada understand multiculturalism, diversity, and Canadian identity, and how they are prepared to develop culturally sensitive curriculum and pedagogy for a diverse student population. We developed a multi-site, cross-Canada study aimed at illuminating preservice teachers' sense of national identity and their perceptions of the diverse needs of Canadian students. We were interested to know if preservice teachers in different provinces would be willing to bring into their classrooms Canadian literary texts that represented various aspects of diversity. In this book, we offer findings from each of the six research sites and consider their implications for Canadian teacher education and for teaching in kindergarten to grade 12 classrooms.

Diverse Canadian picture books from the 1990s onwards appeal to a range of readers, and many foreground questions of representation, identity, and power. In developing criteria for our selections, we were aware that not all multicultural picture books written and illustrated in this time period would address such complex questions. As Debra Dudek (2011) reminds us, "Some books represent multicultural themes at only a cursory level without engaging with more meaningful ideological tensions" (159). We sought to address these ideological tensions through a broad definition of diversity in relation to our picture book selection. We focused our attention on ethnicity, race, culture, language, religion, socio-economic conditions, gender, sexual orientation, and exceptionalities. Including books in our selections that addressed sexual orientation, same-sex families, and people with disabilities created both surprise and interest among some research participants. We explained that the books reflected the diversity of students and families that constitute contemporary school communities.

In our collection, we also included books that were situated in various regional contexts across Canada. The majority of diverse Canadian picture books speak to specific regional contexts and histories. We believed this was a significant component of the book collection, and that it was important for all preservice teacher participants to have the opportunity to see representations of their own locales and histories as well as diverse settings across the country.

In complex interactions between text and illustration, picture books invite and take up particular ideological positions and articulate varying understandings of difference. An engagement with the visual and verbal aspects of diverse Canadian picture books creates opportunities for preservice teachers to question white settler views of national identity and taken-for-granted perspectives on diversity, and to develop more culturally relevant pedagogies for their teaching.

The genre of the picture book, Perry Nodelman (1999) suggests, is a paradox: "On the one hand it is seen as children's literature's one truly original contribution to literature in general, a "polyphonic" form which absorbs and uses many codes, styles, and textual devices, and which frequently pushes at the borders of convention. On the other, it is seen as the province of the young child, and is therefore beneath critical notice" (70).

Shaun Tan (2010), an Australian picture book illustrator, elaborates on the power of the picture book for readers of all ages:

> The simplicity of a picture book in terms of narrative structure, visual appeal and often fable-like brevity might seem to suggest that it is indeed ideally suited to a juvenile readership. It's about showing and telling, a window for learning to "read" in a broad sense, exploring relationships between words, pictures and the world we experience every day. But is this an activity that ends with childhood, when at some point we are sufficiently qualified to graduate from one medium to another? Simplicity certainly does not exclude sophistication or complexity; we inherently know that the truth is otherwise.

This complexity of the picture book genre for our research purposes was further enhanced by our selection of Canadian texts that specifically addressed issues of diversity and multiculturalism. Official multiculturalism, which was entrenched through the Canadian Multiculturalism Act of 1988, constitutionally recognized the changing face of Canada as a result of immigration, and promoted an attitude of "tolerance and understanding" for all Canada's peoples. While this policy of multiculturalism has gained Canada an international reputation for respecting the rights and privileges of its diverse population, it has also been critiqued by researchers such as Bannerji (2000), Giroux (1991), Gunew (2003), and Mukherjee (1998) for its failure to address complex questions of identity. These critics contend that Canada remains a country in which much of the power rests in the hands of those of European descent and that the earlier national mythology of two European founding nations functions as a strongly embedded aspect of the country's historical memory. This metanarrative of nation, they suggest, authorizes stories that consciously or unconsciously suppress knowledge of difference and emphasize symbolic differences between "ourselves" and "others." Such a metanarrative forms the basis of critiques by Canada's Aboriginal peoples, who point to a denial of the role of First Nations in Canada's history.

As Edwards and Saltman (2010) explain, "Children's literature, and more particularly, the visual images in children's books can do the ideological work of extending hegemonic discourses within a society about collective identity, memory, and normative social practices" (12). The verbal and visual aspects of Canadian picture books, through their "word-image interaction" (Lewis, 2001, 94) suggest particular representations of what it means to be Canadian and offer a variety of approaches to multiculturalism and cultural difference. Through their ideological stances, picture books invite readers to take up particular subject positions, inviting them to "see" and understand their own subjectivity and the perspectives of others in specific ways. And, as Stephens (1992) reminds us, "In taking up a position from which the text is most readily intelligible, [readers] are apt to be situated within the frame of the text's ideology" (67). Often this ideological position is one that promotes a culturally acceptable view of who Canadians think they ought to be. In complex interactions between words and images, picture books invite readers/viewers to observe themselves reflected in the selected representations of the text; they can act as cultural texts that may promote a cohesive, harmonious, and exclusionary view of national identity, or serve as a counter-articulation to notions of a homogeneous and cohesive sense of nation (McKenzie, 2003).

Until late in the twentieth century, Canadian picture books, in common with other genres of Canadian literature, tended to privilege a dominant white Eurocentric perspective (Bannerji, 2000; Manning, 2003). Newer perspectives in Canadian cultural criticism have challenged former notions of a metanarrative in the literary field and interrogated notions of whiteness as the defining landscape of Canadian literature. This re-defining of Canada's unified story into a postmodern bricolage of competing traditions, histories, re-tellings and re-imaginings has emerged from a variety of sources, including writers and illustrators of European descent, immigrants of colour, and Aboriginal peoples. Their stories have helped to raise new questions and tensions that have the potential to disrupt any homogeneous notion of Canadian identity and to value what Bhabha (1994) terms "the migrant culture of the in-between" (224).

While there have been textual challenges to notions of a static Canadian identity, such challenges tend not to be apparent in the curriculum of most public schools, where literary text selections and English language arts teaching continue to promote a traditional view of Canadian citizenship. The majority of practising teachers in schools and preservice teachers in Canadian teacher education programs are of white European descent (Beynon, 2004; Carson & Johnston, 2001a); most have had few opportunities to question a white settler view of Canadian identity or to interrogate stereotypes of Canada's immigrant and Aboriginal peoples in the texts they read.

Significance of the Research Project

The curriculum of teacher education is traditionally structured around such commonalities as provincially mandated programs of studies, child development, learning theories, and the identification and measurement of expected outcomes. It is a curriculum of sameness that poses challenges for teacher educators who wish to address questions of difference and diversity with their preservice teachers. As Marilyn Cochran-Smith (2004) suggests: "In order to learn to teach in a society that is increasingly culturally and linguistically diverse, prospective teachers as well as experienced teachers and teacher educators need opportunities to examine much of what is usually unexamined in the tightly braided relationships of language, culture, and power in schools and schooling" (49).

An engagement with diverse Canadian picture books offers one avenue for these future teachers to understand how "learning to teach means coming to terms with particular orientations toward knowledge, power and identity" (Britzman, 2003, 33). Our study offers insights into how preservice teachers in different provinces across Canada were able to interrogate their own identities as Canadians and come to terms with difficult questions of race, culture, gender, and power in addition to how these explorations influenced their approaches to curriculum and pedagogy as they attempted to meet the diverse needs of their students.

Research Procedures

As a research team of eight university teacher educators and four doctoral students, we received national funding from the Social Sciences and Humanities Research Council of Canada to conduct multi-site case studies (Stake, 1995; Merriam, 1998) on preservice teachers' responses to diverse Canadian picture books. Our participants, 1108 in number, were preservice teachers (university students) who were enrolled in basic teacher education programs at Memorial University of Newfoundland, St John's; McGill University, Montreal; Lakehead University, Thunder Bay; University of Saskatchewan, Saskatoon; University of Alberta, Edmonton (Elementary and Secondary route programs); and Thompson Rivers University, Kamloops.

We conducted the research as teacher researchers engaged in practitioner inquiry (Cochran-Smith & Lytle, 1999; Richardson, 1994; Clandinin & Connelly, 1996), with data analysis and theorizing occurring simultaneously in the action-reflection cycles within the practitioner inquiry process. At the time of initial data collection, the participants were enrolled in literacy courses in a variety of teacher education programs at the six universities (see appendix A). Some preservice teachers were in an elementary route, preparing to teach kindergarten to grade 6; some were in a secondary route, preparing to teach grades 7 to 12; others were in specialized teacher education programs focusing on middle years education or on Aboriginal education. Some of the researchers taught the literacy courses themselves; others approached instructors for permission to conduct an in-class workshop, from which context students were invited to participate in the research.

At each research site, all preservice teacher participants had opportunities to engage in an identical workshop that consisted of reading and responding to the same selection of picture books, and of completing the same written survey instrument at the workshop's conclusion. All participants were invited to take part in focus group discussions or individual interviews about the picture books and their responses to them. Most participants also had the opportunity to develop lesson plans as part of their course assignments, and at three of the research sites were able to implement the lessons in their student teaching experiences. Several researchers had the opportunity to work with their participating students during their field experience placements.

Throughout the research project, we intended to challenge preservice teachers to negotiate a sense of national identity and to examine their views of "otherness" through reading and responding to the Canadian picture books used in the workshop. We hoped that the experience of participating in the study would enable the preservice teachers to develop criteria for the thoughtful selection of texts and curriculum materials for culturally diverse school populations. In addition, we hoped these preservice teachers would gain new insights into their own identities as Canadians and into possibilities for developing relationships with students from backgrounds different from their own.

The Workshop

For the study, we collaboratively made selections of eighty Canadian picture books to present in a workshop format to each class of preservice teachers. The picture books were selected according to the following criteria:

• Published in Canada since 1990
• Set in a variety of regions in Canada
• Written/illustrated by Canadians from a range of ethno-cultural backgrounds
• Offering a range of perspectives on what it means to be Canadian.

The selection of books for the workshop was not an easy or simple process. We wanted to present books that represent contemporary life in Canada rather than a mythic or fairy-tale view of the country. We did not select any books that could be categorized as trans-cultural (set outside North America); so, for example, none of Tololwa Mollel's books were included in the workshop, as many of them are set in Africa. We struggled to balance postmodern works such as Thomas King's *A Coyote Columbus Story* (1992) with more traditional stories such as Peter Eyvindson's *Red Parka Mary* (1996). We included bilingual language books such as Tomson Highway's *Caribou Song*, which is written in

Cree and English, and Jane Cooper's *Someone Smaller than Me* in Inuktitut and English. We selected award-winning books as well as books that had received positive reviews in educational journals. Many of the picture books we selected appear on recommended lists for teachers. In the end, we included:

- 22 books that had an Aboriginal focus
- 4 that had a Métis focus
- 18 that incorporated an immigrant experience
- 16 that focused on life in a specific geographic region within Canada
- 11 that contained languages other than English (Cree, French, Gaelic, Inuktitut, Spanish, and Chinese)
- 2 with a religious (Jewish) context
- 3 featuring a central character with a disability
- 3 incorporating same-sex parenting/sexual orientation
- 4 featuring specific ethnic or other differences.

Some books could not easily be classified as they overlapped the categories listed above; for example, they could be described as immigrant stories or as Canadian regional stories *and* have a second language in them. The complete list of books used in the workshop is presented in appendix B.

We introduced the workshop by reading aloud the picture book *Josepha: A Prairie Boy's Story*, by Jim McGugan (1994), and by providing a digital image of each illustration.

The story, narrated by a young primary-school boy, tells of the discrimination and difficulties encountered by his teenaged friend, Josepha, an immigrant from Eastern Europe in 1900. Josepha is adjusting to a new home and a new language. Because he doesn't speak English, Josepha is seated with the very young children in school, which creates a strong sense of shame and embarrassment.

Eventually Josepha makes some special friends among the primary-grade children, and when he has to leave school to work on the farm, the children are sad to see him go. Without a common language between them, the young boy decides on a gift he can give Josepha to show how important their friendship has been.

After the initial reading and viewing of the text and images in this picture book, we talked with the preservice teachers about visual and critical literacy and the potential of picture books for all ages, specifically, about how text and illustration work together and the benefits of

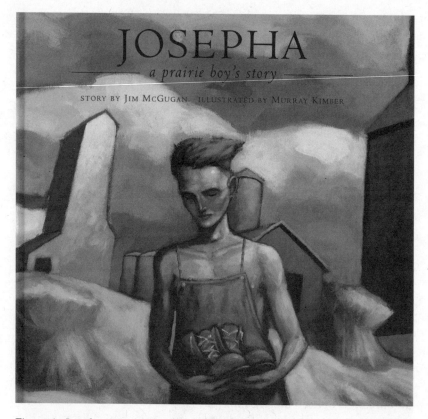

Figure 1. *Josepha: A Prairie Boy's Story* (McGugan and Kimber, 1994, cover)

a short text in certain teaching circumstances. The interactions of pictures and text created in contemporary picture books can be intriguing and challenging. They demand a high level of visual literacy, whereby readers must understand the tools, grammar, and principles of visual communication. Lapp, Flood, and Fisher (1999) use the term "intermediality" to describe the combined literacies needed in order to read effectively in the twenty-first century. They stress the importance of active reading based on visual communication to capture attention, reinforce knowledge, and stimulate reader responses. Bamford (2003) writes that "visual literacy involves developing the set of skills needed to be able to interpret the content of visual images, examine [the] social impact of those images, and to discuss purpose, audience, and ownership" (1).

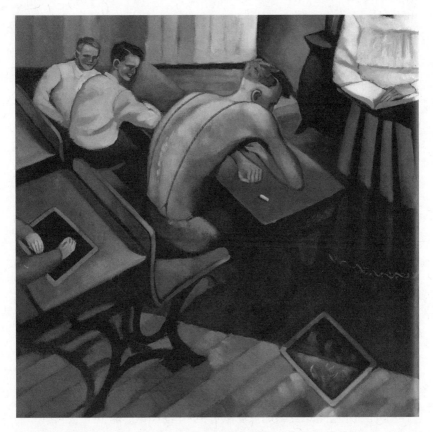

Figure 2. Illustration from *Josepha* (unpaginated)

Among those necessary skills, readers need to recognize issues of style (e.g., realism, expressionism, surrealism) that underpin the illustrator's fundamental relationship with the scene and characters depicted. Readers also need to understand that layout is a particularly important element of the picture book. Artists and book designers use layout features to communicate with their audience and they pay special attention to the use of single-page or double-page spreads; the inclusion of borders; where the page turn comes in relation to the text and the meaning conveyed; the design of the last page; the end papers; and how the gutter will be used to maximum effect.

Pictures are often incorporated into books to support beginning readers' constructions of meaning. But increasingly we recognize that illustrations are an alternative means of developing meaning – introducing clues and cues not provided in the text. Good picture books call on the pictures as much as the text, not only to tell the story, but also to deepen the meanings created by their readers. The pictures set a tone, an atmosphere, establish feelings, depict setting, and indicate much beyond what words can convey. In *Josepha: A Prairie Boy's Story* (McGugan, 1994) the illustrations heighten the intensity of the prairie light and heat during the fall season, and with that, the intensity of the feelings of the characters: a teacher, a little boy, and Josepha, a teenaged immigrant who does not speak English. The slope of a shoulder, a towering grain elevator, the broad expanse of the prairie, and the dust from a cart that rumbles along a rutted track all connect with readers in ways that words alone could not. The meaning created becomes deeply etched in memory and emotion.

We presented to the preservice teachers Freebody and Luke's (1991) four-resources model for thinking about critical literacy and its place in language arts education. Freebody and Luke maintain that readers take up four roles: code breaker, text participant, text user, and text analyst. They argue that successful reading means being able to accomplish all four of these roles simultaneously. Important to critical literacy is the reader's fourth role, that of being a text analyst, which means having "conscious awareness of the language and idea systems that are brought into play when a text is used" (13). The role of text analyst involves being able to recognize the ideological perspective of a text and having the capacity to stand outside that perspective and critique it.

From a critical literacy perspective, reading is seen as an act of coming to know "the world" as well as "the word" (Freire, 1983) and serves as a means to creating a fairer and more just society for all people regardless of race, culture, class, sexual orientation, gender, or language. The purpose of critical literacy teaching is to empower teachers and students to move literacy beyond a simple decoding of text to personal and social action (Cadiero-Kaplan, 2002).

We additionally provided a historical context for the books by explaining how Canadian picture books have changed over time, reminding the preservice teachers that fifty years ago picture books were seen as being for very young children only, and few were published in Canada before the mid-1970s. We explained that the relatively few Canadian picture books published in the 1950s, 1960s, and 1970s generally assumed an audience that was mainly white, European, and middle class, and the content reflected this assumption, as did most of the American and

British books readily available to Canadian children during those times. We suggested that, in more recently published Canadian picture books, attention is paid to presenting a diversity of perspectives.

In small groups, the participants browsed through a random selection of books. We asked them to keep in mind the following questions:

(a) What do these books appear to suggest about what it means to be Canadian?
(b) Would you use these books in your classroom? Why or why not?

These questions provided opportunities for discussion about issues of Canadian identity and the potential role of picture books in elementary and secondary school curricula. We felt these discussions would help to focus the preservice teachers' interactions with the books and assist them in responding to our survey.

Data Collection and Analysis

In the written survey, participants provided demographic information on their family backgrounds and home languages, their experiences of reading Canadian literature, their responses to the picture books, and their understandings of issues of Canadian identity, representation, and stereotyping in relation to the texts. Follow-up audio-recorded conversations with volunteer preservice teachers explored these issues in more depth. Focus groups were also held in which discussion centred on questions of Canadian identity formation as represented in the picture books and on participants' own understandings of what it meant to them to be "Canadian." The interviews and focus groups also explored the significance of these understandings for the participants' own teaching and considered the potential of contemporary Canadian picture books for teaching and curriculum development in elementary and secondary English language-arts classes.

As is evident in several of our book chapters, data were also collected at some research sites from email conversations between the researcher and the preservice teachers during their coursework and practicum placements. In addition, lesson plans incorporating the selected picture books were collected from a number of participants either as they were preparing for a practicum placement or during the placement itself.

Survey results, student assignments, notes developed from the transcripts of individual interviews and focus group discussions, email conversation transcripts, and field notes of school classroom observations were analysed qualitatively for emerging themes. These themes were filtered through our research objectives of exploring questions of Canadian identity formation as represented in the picture books, considering the participants' own understandings of what it means to them to be "Canadian" and the significance of these understandings for their own teaching. Following our initial data analysis of our own case studies, we came together to analyse and discuss regional similarities and differences in the responses of our student teachers and to share thematic findings across all the sites in order to clarify emerging local and national themes and trends. All preservice teacher participants mentioned and quoted in our book chapters have been given pseudonyms. Given the time lapse in transcribing data from the two years of the study, it was not always possible to return interview and focus group transcripts to participants for their verification.

Theoretical Framework

This study is underpinned by post-structuralist notions of identity as contingent and indeterminate (Bhabha, 1994; Giroux, 1991) and by research on critical multiculturalism (Shor, 1996; McCarthy, 1998) that involves deconstructing traditional knowledge and power boundaries. The study is also grounded in transactional theories of reading, mainly in the work of Iser (1980) and Rosenblatt (1978). These two theorists focus on how readers draw on their personal literary and life experiences to create meanings through reciprocal relationships with texts and images, allowing opportunities for readers to take account of the cultural and social contexts of texts. Picture books, through the interplay of text and image, offer particularly rich contexts for readers to engage with and to interrogate subjectivity, representation, and ideology. Each chapter in the book presents data from the study framed by these theoretical lenses while focusing on particular aspects such as critical literacy, visual literacy, identity formation, Aboriginal education, space and time, imaginative engagement with a text, pedagogy, and political and social change.

Objectives of the Book

This book is not about diversity teaching per se, but rather about how diverse literature, broadly defined, may promote cross-cultural interest and understanding. The chapters in this book offer significant insights into how teachers and teacher educators can address vital questions of diversity, multiculturalism, and citizenship with their students through the medium of contemporary literary texts. The stories of preservice teachers' responses to the picture books, highlighted throughout the book, illuminate how participants reflected on their own cultural locations in the world, their beliefs and understandings and assumptions about difference, and the students they were about to teach. The stories also allowed participants to question what it means to be Canadian in the twenty-first century and to consider their resistances to the difficult knowledge of difference, marginalization, and historical inequities they encountered in the books.

The book is written for teacher educators; researchers and graduate student scholars investigating picture books, children's literature, and diversity education; librarians; and consultants and other personnel within departments of education who are engaged in book selection, curriculum development, and policy development and enactment.

Overview of Chapters

Chapter 1, "Picture Books and Pedagogy: From Possibilities to Practice" by Joyce Bainbridge (University of Alberta) and Beverley Brenna (University of Saskatchewan) describes the varied responses of preservice teachers in Alberta to diverse picture books in terms of critical literacy and the participants' sense of social responsibility as preservice and beginning teachers. Their responses to the picture books revealed tensions that were in direct conflict: a desire for supporting social justice in the classroom; caution in regard to engaging students in controversial texts; and concern about using an age-*in*appropriate medium. These tensions directly affected the pedagogical decisions the preservice teachers were prepared to make. The chapter explores the preservice teachers' comments and responses, and contextualizes their concerns in a broader discourse of pedagogy.

In chapter 2, "Who Does This Text Think I Am? Exploring Questions of Subjectivity through Diverse Picture Books," Ingrid Johnston and Farha Shariff (University of Alberta) take a psychoanalytical stance on identity, focusing on the responses of preservice teachers to the picture books and their notions of what it means to live and teach in a multicultural society. Drawing on examples from the Alberta case study, the chapter considers how particular picture books challenged participants' sense of self and taken-for-granted views about Canadian multiculturalism and exposed their fears and uncertainties about encountering difference in the classroom. The chapter explores how these textual encounters might be considered as a *mode of address* that created "a space of difference" between the reader and the text, allowing for resistances and the development of human agency.

Chapter 3, "Historical and Contemporary Perspectives on Cultural, Social, and Political Issues in the Canadian West," written by Lynne Wiltse while she was at Thompson Rivers University, British Columbia, focuses on preservice teachers' responses to picture books relating to historical injustices: the internment of Ukrainian Canadians in the First World War and Japanese Canadians during the Second World War, the role of Chinese immigrants in the building of the Canadian Pacific Railway, and residential schooling. The chapter shows how the picture books became an impetus for preservice teachers in central British Columbia to explore links of the cultural, social, political, and geographical aspects of the past and question their own identities around themes of social justice, land claims, and power relations.

In chapter 4, "Prairie Spaces Recreated: Aboriginal Education and Canadian Picture Books," Angela Ward (University of Saskatchewan) describes how non-Aboriginal and Aboriginal preservice teachers in Saskatchewan interpreted diversity through their experiences with the picture books in the study. Some of these participants tried to create decolonized spaces where their students could reconcile current and historical views of Aboriginal peoples, while others were more resistant to reconstructing their identities as teachers in Aboriginal contexts.

In chapter 5, "Imagining the Possibilities: The Pedagogical Potential of Diverse Canadian Picture Books," Mary Clare Courtland and Ismel Gonzalez (Lakehead University) describe how preservice teachers' engagement with picture books in the study disrupted and challenged their unexamined beliefs about literacy and diversity. As evidenced in their lesson plans, these Ontario participants expanded their understandings of Canadian multiculturalism and identity and their perceptions of the themes, issues, and pedagogical potential of picture books.

Chapter 6, "Very Far Away: Traversing the Distance between Imagination and Actualization," by Teresa Strong-Wilson and Heather Phipps (McGill University), considers what is involved in traversing the distance between imagination and actualization, demonstrated when predominantly white preservice teachers designed culturally sensitive and critical lesson plans around children's literature by Indigenous authors. These student teachers' negotiations with the Indigenous texts, as demonstrated in their lesson plans, ranged from emotional critical engagement to avoidance and to a refusal to engage.

Chapter 7, "Connecting Visual Literacy and Cultural Awareness through Picture Book Illustrations," by Anne Burke (Memorial University), focuses on the artistic and visual aspects of picture books in the study and describes how preservice teachers in Newfoundland and Labrador explored the spaces between image and text to reveal themes of diversity, cultural heritage, and historical disruptions. The chapter emphasizes the importance of visual literacy in diverse picture books for developing global and cultural awareness in classrooms.

In chapter 8, "Generative Ways to Promote Political Activity and Social Change with Picture Books," Roberta Hammett (Memorial University) demonstrates how engagement with the picture books, classroom and focus group discussions, and the creation of lesson plans raised awareness of multicultural issues, revealed concerns about ways to address diversity in the English language arts classroom, and challenged traditional views of national identity. Thus, the research activities served as generative ways to promote potential political activity and social change in classrooms.

An Afterword offers a synopsis of our findings and final reflections on the study.[1]

NOTE

1 In each chapter, we have cited the picture books with the author's name followed by the illustrator's name in italics (where applicable).

1 Picture Books and Pedagogy: From Possibilities to Practice

JOYCE BAINBRIDGE AND BEVERLEY BRENNA

Through images as well as words, diverse picture books can help educators to support and encourage acceptance and understanding among their students, as well as offer an opportunity for learners to see aspects of their own lives represented at school. Picture books also provide an appropriate vehicle for helping students of all ages to become more critically literate, and an increasing number of picture books are now intended for an audience of older readers. Picture books by illustrator/authors such as Shaun Tan (Australia), Anthony Browne (UK), and George Littlechild (Canada) demand the application of sophisticated reading strategies including "critical viewing," whereby readers examine images for the messages they contain beyond the textual storyline. Such critical literacy expectations require readers to be especially active in their construction of meaning. Because picture books are now designed for a wider age range of readers and broader reading purposes than in the past, it is important that preservice teachers consider the potential of picture books for inclusion in classroom activities across the grades.

This chapter explores the varied responses of preservice teachers at the University of Alberta to the selection of diverse Canadian picture books described in the Introduction. From a social constructivist stance, we attempted, in the study, to encourage a spirit of inquiry and to hear our participants' own stories and perspectives as well as listen to each other's ideas through the context of focus groups. These stories and perspectives are important elements of conversations whose purpose is the broadening of personal responses to diverse picture books as well as the facilitation of perceptions related to these books as curriculum resources. As already described, the picture books were selected because of their representations of cultural diversity. Many of the titles reflect particular ethnicity in regards to their characters, while others focus on marginalized sexual orientations, social class, characters with disabilities, and particular depictions of gender.

Critical Literacy

Teacher educators know that literacy is complex and that teaching literacy is also complex. In teacher education programs, it is especially important to avoid presenting literacy teaching as a set of simplistic step-by-step routines and recipes. Duffy, Webb, and Davis (2009) maintain that professional literacy educators need three kinds of knowledge: "declarative" (knowing *what* to teach), "procedural" (knowing *how* to teach), and "situational" (knowing the overall purposes for literacy, and being able to "rethink ideas and practices, transform knowledge to fit situations, and change what they are doing when, in their judgment, there is a need to do so"; p. 192). Situational knowledge, with its emphasis on transformation, suggests critical reflection; it can be seen as a way of exploring how a teaching and learning event is constructed and how effective it is, but it can also involve critical literacy in terms of "reading" the learning context as well as exploring classroom resources. Through considerations of power structures, critical literacy can foster and support the development of a critical social consciousness. Here, we use the term "critical literacy" to describe one of the aims of literacy instruction: to help students to consciously interrogate all texts, whether in books and the media or on the Internet, so that their understandings reflect the social, political, and power relations embedded in the discourses they sample. The employment of a critical literacy stance offers readers a kind of control over texts, promoting an understanding of textual perspectives that can lead towards personal and social transformation. The outcomes produced through critical literacy experiences with texts can offer new insights related to self and others.

In critical literacy, textual meaning is essentially a process of construction. One constructs meaning, "imbuing a text with meaning rather than extracting meaning from it" (Cervetti, Pardales, & Damico, 2001, 5). Textual meaning is constructed in the context of social, historic, and power relations. In this study, we aimed to stimulate critical discussion about the picture books, and to challenge preservice teachers to think about their selection of texts for classroom use and the identities and needs of their future students.

Lewison, Flint, and Van Sluys (2002) reviewed definitions of critical literacy and synthesized them into four dimensions of reader activity:

- disrupting the commonplace (seeing the everyday through new lenses for understanding experience);
- interrogating multiple viewpoints (standing in the shoes of others to understand experience and text from our own perspectives and the viewpoints of others);
- focusing on socio-political issues (stepping outside the personal to explore how socio-political systems and power relationships shape perceptions, responses, and actions); and
- taking action and promoting social justice (identifying how power is manifest and seeking to redistribute some of this power).

Although these dimensions are not sequential, Lewison, Flint, and Van Sluys found that educators generally focus more on the first two or three dimensions than on the last one. To be truly critical, a consideration of action towards equity and social justice must be in place. Note, however, that action can mean a change in attitude or the development of new understandings. In this chapter, we use Lewison, Flint, and Van Sluys's (2002) definition of critical literacy as a framework for presenting the findings of our research.

Encountering Diversity in Picture Books

The preservice teachers involved in the research were in one of two programs: the elementary route (K–6) of a generalist BEd or the secondary route (7–12) of a BEd with a minor in English education. Over the two-year period of the study, all the preservice teachers attended a workshop presented over two class sessions within their program of study. In total, 206 elementary-route and 166 secondary-route preservice teachers responded to the survey we distributed at the end of the workshop sessions. Two to three weeks after the workshop, fifteen volunteering elementary-route and eight secondary-route preservice teachers participated in interviews or focus groups.

At this research site, the researchers were not teaching the courses in which the workshops were conducted; therefore, contact with the preservice teachers was limited. The course instructors, however, taught the courses from a syllabus that was consistent across sections, and all the instructors expressed particular interest in issues of diversity,

critical literacy, and the use of picture books across the grades. Assignments in the classes varied from course section to course section, with
some preservice teachers preparing lesson plans and others integrating
the use of diverse picture books into alternative assignments. In addition to limited contact with preservice teachers during courses in ses-
sion, we were not able to follow our study participants into their field
placements, but relied on their reports and stories through email and
face-to-face meetings and interviews.

The preservice teachers themselves came from a range of backgrounds, but could be described as mainly white and middle class. For
almost all of them this was their first experience with an English language arts education course, and very few had taken university courses
that dealt with multiculturalism, issues of diversity, Aboriginal education, children's literature, or drama. Most of the preservice teachers
were from the Edmonton metropolitan area, with little experience of
living in provinces other than Alberta. Very few had lived outside Canada, though many had parents or grandparents who were immigrants.
A few of the preservice teachers had been raised in homes where English was not the only language spoken.

During the workshops, the preservice teachers approached the use
of diverse picture books with both excitement and a sense of unease,
and their reactions to the books were varied in terms of interest. Some
of them handled the books with eagerness, staying at the end of class
to finish reading particular selections or to browse through a few more
of the books. Many of them spoke informally about their excitement at
discovering such rich resources. One preservice teacher spoke about
her intention to share some of the titles with her five-year-old son.
Another individual said:

> I loved *Tiger Flowers* just because it was so relevant; I liked *Mom and Mum
> are Getting Married!* – I don't remember picture books from my childhood
> addressing anything so controversial, and it seems to me that picture
> books have grown and evolved along with society, which is nice … inter-
> esting to see some of the native work, for example, one where the top part
> was in English, [the] bottom part in Cree [*Caribou Song*].

Other participants remained aloof from the workshop, and a few were
observed texting with cell phones throughout the latter half of the ses-
sion. Some preservice teachers were ambivalent about using the books.
Keith commented, "I don't see the need [to address an issue through

literature] if it's not in the curriculum – certainly not in my first few years of teaching. I don't plan on stirring the pot."

During the closing remarks in the workshop, about half of the participants continued picking up picture books, their interest piqued. Others packed up their belongings and left as soon as possible, perhaps hurrying to lunch or to other classes.

Of those preservice teachers who were interested in the picture books, what insights did they gain from them, and what plans of action were they developing with regard to the introduction of these books into their own classrooms? Further conversations with individual volunteers offered answers to some of these questions, but other questions remained unaddressed. What causes interest or disinterest in issues of diversity, and how does this translate into classroom teaching, where a large percentage of the children in schools have non-white cultural roots? Our findings related to this study represent voices heard; however, it is important to note that there are many other voices unheard, voices that may ring just as powerfully on the school landscapes we are currently seeking to build and whose silence here is both provocative and disconcerting.

Considering Diverse Picture Books

The findings of the study suggest that many of the elementary preservice teachers were, like Keith above, reluctant to use potentially controversial texts in their future classrooms, whereas the secondary preservice teachers expressed concern regarding the use of an age-*in*appropriate medium – picture books – with senior grades. Simultaneously, preservice teachers preparing for teaching at either level, elementary or secondary, expressed a desire to support social justice in their classrooms – a sentiment seemingly at odds with their conventional attitudes towards the potentiality of particular texts. In this chapter we explore these tensions and consider the implications of our preservice teachers' responses to the books in terms of their developing pedagogy, where pedagogy refers to instructional strategies related to curriculum planning and classroom practice.

The preservice teachers recognized and discussed the importance, hypothetically, of including in the curriculum the issues the picture books evoked in terms of critical literacy: interrogating multiple viewpoints, focusing on socio-political issues, and disrupting the commonplace. These attributes were apparent within the preservice teachers' responses to the selected texts and illustrations, exemplified in the following statements:

> I think it is important to read literature to my students that deals with many different issues so students have an open mind.
>
> It's important to educate children about their background. Educating children in ... multiculturalism is critical to critical thinking and learning.

However, potential controversies were quickly cited as a rationale for steering clear of many of the books, as opposed to any personal motivation, and thus curricular planning was prevented from moving past the initial stages of design. Jackie, an elementary participant, commented:

> Multiculturalism is very important to me and I have confliction about it because I think [about] what I want to do and what is best for me to do in my first year of teaching ... I'm going to be conflicted because social justice, social issues and equality are very much part of who I am, but depending on the situation where you're in, that may not be welcomed and so trying to have that represented to children, which I feel is important, but yet doing it in a way and in a manner where I am under a microscope my first years of teaching, well ...

A different tension was expressed by one of the secondary participants: "I won't use picture books. I feel the students will feel extremely patronized by them – no matter how complex the issues they raise." These preservice teachers opted not to employ particular books rather than consider what might be done to successfully include the "more controversial" picture books in classrooms. Greg, keeping in mind his prospective status as a beginning elementary teacher, said of George Littlechild's *This Land Is My Land* (1993): "If I had it my way, if I wasn't under scrutiny of parents or principals or administrators I would probably go ahead and teach it."

Many of the elementary route participants expressed particular discomfort with the issue of sexuality presented in *Asha's Mums* (Elwin & Paulse; *Lee*, 1990). Some of them were aware that specific areas of the country have, in the past, challenged such books. Other preservice teachers in the study mentioned *Mom and Mum Are Getting Married!* (Setterington; *Priestley*, 2004) as a text they would be reluctant to use in classrooms. Rather than exploring possible responses to parental concerns regarding the use of the book and identifying ways it might support individual students and existing curricula, they allowed the potential controversy in regard to the book's perspective on same-sex marriage to limit their openness towards including the book in classroom activities. They also tended to focus on potentially negative parental responses towards this particular book rather than anticipate positive responses.

Interestingly, the elementary-route preservice teachers gave greater consideration to the potential responses of parents than did their secondary counterparts, an attitude mirrored by teachers in the field. Heffernan (2004) identified his own teaching journey in seeking and using social-issues texts in his third-grade classroom, reporting his initial "complicity in perpetuating the status quo by choosing safe, happy books" (4). Many elementary-route participants expressed concern about introducing Littlechild's *This Land Is My Land* (1993). The book is certainly not a "safe, happy book." It is an autobiographical account of Littlechild's struggle to become a recognized and respected artist. He tells about the discovery of his Aboriginal ancestry and about how he came to meet and know his biological family members. Certain aspects of the content may be uncomfortable for some readers – both of Littlechild's parents died of alcoholism on "skid row" and his grandparents were sent to residential schools. It is not hard to see why some preservice teachers would not want to deal with the many issues the book might raise with their students. However, our participants' comments also foregrounded the question of how much our preservice teachers know and understand about the topics/issues raised in such books. Stephanie, for example, commented: "I don't know much about residential schools so I can't comment on some of the books that were at my table." Fay was an exception in this regard, as she was clearly aware of the importance of using such books, as well as cognizant of the influence of context on how these books might be used. She was open to finding "a way in":

> With a book like "Asha's Moms," it depends where you live. I mean if it's urban Vancouver, it's different than if it is somewhere rural like Chase. It's important to be aware of that context. And not that I'm shying away from something, but if it's not appropriate for the community that you're in, then why put your job in jeopardy? ... So, rather than in your face, here's a gay couple, you have to find another way to introduce it that has a subtle approach.

Some of our preservice teachers demonstrated their willingness to explore these books during practicum placements when they carefully selected multicultural picture books for classroom use. They found ways to incorporate these books into various strands of the curriculum. There were many success stories, but also some disappointments. Lynette told us:

> I brought *Asha's Moms* into my practicum classroom, my Kindergarten/ Grade 1 class, as part of celebrating families … I had a book about a single mother in there as well and a boy being raised by his grandmother or something like that. My teacher sort of said that she was fine with it but, you know, maybe I could just go talk to the principal … and he had a problem with it. He went on the Internet and pulled up the information based on what had happened in Surrey. He said this book is too controversial and he asked me what my point was, what was I trying to do in the classroom with this book. I said I have kids in this classroom that are in foster care, that live with one parent or another, that have, you know, a mom and a dad and a step mom and a step dad and there's a lot of variations of families now and there's a lot of them in that classroom. He sort of said well, you know, I don't really know that this is appropriate and I just don't want a parent coming and getting all upset about this sort of thing. So he requested that I not use the book, and that was the end of the situation.

It's easy to understand why the principal might take this stance; he knew the community and the families in it, and he wanted to be cautious about what he encouraged a student teacher to take on. Lynette was disturbed by the school principal's reaction, but she let the matter drop. She was aware that she did not hold any real authority on the issue and she had no way to demonstrate to her principal that the book could be a valuable resource in her classroom. However, it continued to be a source of discomfort for her and she later reflected that she would like to "follow up" on this situation when she eventually had a job in a school. She commented that a situation like this one could negatively affect her future as a teacher, and she realized that even as a certificated teacher she would have to be very thoughtful about how she handled certain books in her classroom.

Employing a framework of critical literacy in teaching implies some risk taking, as bumping up against taken-for-granted assumptions, or disrupting stereotypes, can be uncomfortable, and may cause tensions for particular people. It became clear to us during this study that teacher educators need to consider all aspects of preservice teachers' experiences and the risks they take in schools when the curricular focus involves discussions of social justice issues, and that this consideration involves the classroom pedagogy component of teacher education. In terms of critical literacy, teacher educators need to be prepared to guide their preservice teachers through potentially difficult terrain. We believe that diverse Canadian picture books provide one operative framework for such discussions, as they give preservice teachers an opportunity to think through situations ahead of time and to be more prepared for taking measured and thoughtful action in their own schools in the future.

Belief Systems

Santomé (2009) writes that "educating" means "helping students to construct their own views of the world by providing them with key information about present and past events that explain the potentials and limitations of social, cultural, political, and scientific development" (76). He illustrates how schools can be powerful agents in helping students to reflect on the negative influences of society in terms of power differentials. Universities can offer a similar function in terms of promoting diversity and multiculturalism. The provision of opportunities to explore how actions are shaped by belief systems and how books can affect those belief systems is necessary if preservice teachers are to engage in any real sense with ideas related to the controversies particular texts may evoke.

As we spoke with the preservice teachers in our study, we noted how they frequently reflected societal stereotypes in their thoughts and actions. Stereotypes are generalizations about others, both unwarranted and unfounded on the basis of available evidence, and they "reduce a complex phenomenon to simple (or simplistic) explanations that are generalized to a whole category without acknowledging individual differences" (Fleras, 2010, 74). In and of themselves, stereotypes can be harmless, but they can also be a foundation for discriminatory practices. Stereotyping is particularly problematic when negative images of minority groups are reinforced. Fleras asserts that members of a dominant group tend to be less concerned with negative stereotyping because, through the protective layer of privilege surrounding members of a dominant group, these individuals have the power to resist or neutralize stereotypes directed at themselves. Maddie, one of our preservice teachers, demonstrated her own embeddedness in societal stereotypes when she expressed her thoughts on what an "inner city school" meant to her: "I did my [practicum] at an inner city school. It was very, you know, lower social status ... a lot of ethnic diversity, so multiculturalism was sort of a norm, versus I had a friend who taught in [a more affluent neighbourhood] and listening to her experiences versus mine, I'm like, "You're crazy. You have it so good you don't even know it.'"

Maddie lived out of a belief system that equated low socio-economic status with ethnic diversity as well as with a heightened potential for difficulties in terms of practicum teaching. Cochran-Smith (2004) writes: "Many White middle-class teachers understand diversity as a deficit to be overcome and have low expectations and fears about students who are different from themselves, especially those in urban areas" (6). The picture books in our workshop inspired the preservice teachers to explore such values and beliefs in conversations that challenged their existing assumptions. Through group discussions during the workshop, the preservice teachers had the opportunity to reflect on their ideas regarding "good" and "bad" teaching contexts, deconstructing the notion that, for example, teaching in an affluent neighbourhood is somehow devoid of diversity and provides a more positive experience than teaching in a lower socio-economic area.

A study conducted by McDaniel (2006) indicates that preservice teachers "overwhelmingly ignored stereotypes in picture books," supporting the idea that "preservice teachers need opportunities to think about, reflect on, and understand their own views, as well as the reality of their future school settings, deciding (before they enter the classroom) how they might handle particular situations" (153). The identification of stereotypes in literature is a first step in textual analysis, and it can lead towards either a critical literacy approach in terms of pedagogy, or to censorship, where particular books are denied classroom entry.

Some of our preservice teachers demonstrated an understanding of stereotyping, an aspect of characterization that we explored in terms of the presence of particular dominant ideologies regarding gender, culture, and ability. One person commented: "The *Mom and Mum Are Getting Married!* book is stereotypical of lesbians. One is the man and one is the woman. The images are extremely stereotypical and specifically the image at the dinner table."

This was a comment endorsed by a small number of other participants in our study. Many of the preservice teachers were, however, especially unaware of the potential for stereotyping in "well intended" contemporary literature such as Setterington's book.

Many of our participants demonstrated a lack of clarity regarding what constitutes "reality" within a cultural or ethnic group, or they accepted without question the prevailing images portrayed in media or common in the general social milieu in which they live. "I think sometimes stereotypes are confused with culture. A lot of the Aboriginal literature we read had to do with legends and mythical animals, which can be seen as stereotypical representations. But really it is their reality." In their comments about children's literature, we noted that other preservice teachers held confused or contradictory notions about stereotyping. Notions of what stereotypes are, and how they may appear in texts, are important criteria for preservice teachers to explore during a study of children's literature. Consider the examples below in light of understandings that may have supported or prevented critical reading.

> Modern story books (last 10 yrs) seem not to use stereotypes. I see many stereotypes shattered. In *M Is for Maple*, every character (minus 3) was white. Also, the book played into stereotypes of Canada as large spaces, nature, and hockey. Although various names [of people] were mentioned, most of the book dealt with Canada in terms of landscape.

The preservice teachers often held an "us/them" attitude towards visible minorities that was at odds with the social justice agenda they claimed to espouse. The notion of difference embedded in "us and them" implies that "they" are different from "us" and "they" are "the other." When the preservice teachers used the term "we" it generally denoted "mainstream white English-speaking Canadians." Although some of the preservice teachers performed out of a belief system that marginalized minority cultures and ethnic groups, some of these beliefs were stirred up or shifted through interactions among the study participants as they explored the multicultural picture books.

Rick demonstrated some criticality in his response to *This Land Is My Land* (Littlechild, 1993), yet his position as a member of dominant white society was evident in his comment: "I was hoping to see more books that portrayed more urban Aboriginal culture ... that they are not just in their own far off land hunting, or with the fox, or with nature, but that Aboriginals are living with us."

Rick's perspective was echoed by other preservice teachers when they spoke about the minority groups represented in student populations in schools as "others," different from "us" (for example, immigrant children, English language learners, and Aboriginal children). In this context, the preservice teachers were often ready to censor a book rather than explore possibilities for engaging in critical dialogue about it.

One study participant, Karen, took a different stance when she noted the book *How Smudge Came* (Gregory; *Lightburn*, 1995), saying it "showed how people with special needs are treated differently. It's interesting because she isn't labelled as having Down Syndrome in the story, but you can tell from the illustrations."

Karen's comment about *How Smudge Came* opened the door for her peers as they discussed the stereotyping of characters with disabilities in the more "traditional" content of classic literature, something few of the participants had previously considered. Brenna (2011) writes about the treatment of characters with disabilities in children's literature, and maintains that historical patterns suggesting characters with disabilities must be "cured" or "killed" within the course of a story have recently shifted, making room for contemporary patterns that may be almost as troubling. It used to be rare to have characters with disabilities depicted as protagonists in stories, but now that such characters are appearing, they seem doomed to reside in white middle-class homes without displaying other characteristics that imply diversity. In our study, simply reading a picture book where a viable protagonist disrupted the commonplace was not enough to engage the critical attention of the preservice teachers. Critical literacy is a stance that can be difficult to teach and to learn, and we believe it needs to be taught explicitly within the context of curriculum and pedagogy courses, along with the application of teaching approaches associated with social constructivism, such as learning within the zone of proximal development (Vygotsky, 1978) and scaffolding learner development (Bruner, 1986).

A few of the preservice teachers in our study were a little dubious about the authenticity of the content of some of the books in relation to socio-political issues. Azia commented: "The themes in some of these books were too positive, which somewhat overlooks the conflict that often comes with issues of diversity. In *Mom and Mum Are Getting Married!* did all of the extended family attend the wedding and show support for the same-sex couple?"

Some of the participants had mixed feelings about the books, perhaps considering how they would present the books to their prospective students. Preservice teachers like Michael, in thinking about *Shi-shi-etko* (Campbell; *La Fave*, 2005), identified common stereotypes within the stories depicted in the books: "Aboriginal people were given a positive portrayal in a way that was actually a negative stereotype, especially in *Shi-shi-etko*. The 'noble savage' portrayal."

Here Michael was attempting to address the passive image of Aboriginal people living idyllic, pastoral lives in close community with each other in spite of the realities of residential schools. He goes on to discuss a contrasting negative stereotype in regard to *Shi-shi-etko* when he comments: "It doesn't match today's criminal justice statistics either, so now what? How do we teach that?"

Shi-shi-etko thus became a vehicle that assisted Michael in considering how he would approach these books with his students, keeping in mind commonly held beliefs about Aboriginal people and about Canada's history as well as current events and social justice issues.

Pedagogy

In addressing issues related to teaching and to curriculum, we use the term pedagogy to reflect the theory of teaching as well as the goals of education and the ways in which these goals can be achieved. Paulo Freire (1983) introduced the term "critical pedagogy" when he referred to his own teaching of adults. Critical pedagogy attempts to help students question and challenge dominant beliefs and practices in order to achieve critical consciousness. In critical pedagogy, the teacher's own philosophical beliefs about instruction are taken into consideration as well as the student's background knowledge, experience and environment, and the learning goals (which are set by the student and teacher). Critical pedagogy is a continuous process of unlearning, learning, and relearning, especially in relation to students who have been, and continue to be, marginalized by traditional schooling. A goal of identifying students who may not be comfortable on the school landscape is a first step in considering what resources and teaching strategies are most pertinent.

Demonstrating Critical Literacy

Keeping in mind Lewison, Flint, and Van Sluys's (2002) four dimensions of critical literacy (disrupting the commonplace, interrogating multiple viewpoints, focusing on socio-political issues, and taking action and promoting social justice), we can say that commonplace thinking was disrupted when conversations about the diverse picture books offered new ways of examining traditional beliefs. Participants' comments regarding the depiction of particular cultural groups were noted, as well as comments about books they termed "controversial" yet whose themes arise within classroom contexts. Even a consideration of the genre of the picture book as a resource across the grades disrupted commonplace thinking for many, and the inclusion of these picture books in classroom teaching provided an opportunity to dislodge the dominance of stereotypical texts and images within the resources traditionally used in unit plans.

At the same time, multiple viewpoints emerged during book discussions, especially related to parental response and authority in curricular planning. In addition, some of the picture books offered diverse lenses on issues that the preservice teachers identified as important in contemporary classrooms. One book that emerged as effectively engaging multiple viewpoints is the book *Caribou Song* (Highway; *Deines*, 2001), where text is presented in both English and Cree, and the story is told from the perspective of a Cree family. The preservice teachers also noted where multiple viewpoints were lacking, such as in *M Is for Maple* (Ulmer; *Rose*, 2001), where most of the characters were identified as "white." Individual participants reported having different favourites in terms of the diverse picture books, and this offered a chance to examine how some texts speak to readers in ways other texts do not, which promotes the need for a varied collection of classroom resources.

We discovered that when diverse picture books, and the issues that surround their use in schools, are introduced to preservice teachers, university instructors have the opportunity to assist their students in examining, through dimensions of critical literacy, their own belief systems, as well as the manner in which these belief systems may operate. Through attention to the first three dimensions of critical literacy listed by Lewison, Flint, and Van Sluys (2002), disrupting the commonplace, interrogating multiple viewpoints, and focusing on socio-political issues, preservice teachers may identify and reconsider their own positions regarding particular social issues in light of changing times and contexts. This then encourages "taking action and supporting social justice," offered as a fourth dimension of critical literacy by Lewison, Flint, and Van Sluys. Rather than erecting a barrier to the use of diverse picture books, scholarly discussions at the university level may provide preservice teachers with strategies for taking action in promoting social justice while at the same time considering their career safety as beginning teachers.

Supporting the Use of Controversial Texts

While the elementary- and secondary-route preservice teachers appeared to have similar views about supporting social justice in the classroom, their fears regarding controversy and the use of appropriate media appeared to differ in degree. The elementary-route preservice teachers largely considered the topic of diversity a "difficult" or "controversial" issue. Their definition of "controversial" incorporated any materials that presented non-mainstream or non-European points of view. As already described, they expressed particular concern over books presenting same-sex parenting. It appeared that very few of the elementary preservice teachers were aware of the number of students in schools who are from families with same-sex parents.

When exploring contemporary picture books such as *Asha's Moms* (Elwin & Paulse; *Lee*, 1990) or *Mom and Mum Are Getting Married!* (Setterington; *Priestley*, 2004), we noted the iterative formula of the storylines – a didactic reassurance of the positive aspects of change within a family structure – and that when change occurs within a family, it is possible for those changes to be affirmative ones for the family members involved. While the perspective of the stories involves same-sex parenting or gay marriage, the texts re-signify the common theme of family life. This theme provides justification for the use of these texts within standard curricula dealing with family changes and it provides an underlying pedagogical perspective for teachers including these texts in classroom programs. At the same time, this theme can open up space for dialogue about family constellations, and for developing understandings of "the other."

Some of the participants in our study were aware of real problems in the current educational and political climate, and they recognized that introducing controversial materials into elementary classrooms could be fraught with difficulty for a beginning teacher. The current climate does in fact create a "censorship-in-advance" mentality that may translate as anti-educational. In contrast, some of our secondary-route participants were more prepared to take risks regarding issues of culture and representation in books. In fact, one of the secondary-route participants chose to incorporate picture books into her high school teaching practicum as a means of introducing controversial topics with her teenage students. She explained her decision to use picture books to deal with sensitive issues in the following terms:

> I think when you look at controversial issues such as maybe *Asha's Moms*, how is that child really different than me? I think that's not harmful for kids to think about that. But I can understand the point where parents could get very upset. But issues about differences within our own country, about different beliefs and understandings, I don't see that as controversial.

Both elementary- and secondary-route participants were apprehensive about responding to sensitive issues in their classrooms, especially as student teachers and beginning teachers. We realize that preservice teachers often hear in education classes about avoiding lawsuits and about the perceived power parents can have in influencing a teacher's educational decision making. Resulting fears may thus be derived from a number of influences. The secondary-route preservice teachers acknowledged, however, that controversial issues would be part of their lives as teachers of English language arts. Many of these research participants saw the picture books in our workshop as a means to addressing sensitive issues in a concise and somewhat non-threatening manner.

While the elementary-route preservice teachers were able to see the literary merit of bringing multicultural picture books into their teaching, many of the secondary-route participants remained doubtful of their value for adolescent readers. For these participants, the picture books we brought to them in our workshop presented two challenges: one in the form itself and the other in the content. For those participants who were more comfortable with the genre of picture books, the perceived challenges for their teaching were the controversial nature of some of the books in raising issues of race, class, power, and sexual orientation and having to deal with the "difficult knowledge" of exclusion and marginalization with their students in school.

A few of the participants had an opportunity to use the selected picture books from the study while completing their practicum placements. They reported success, especially with books such as Trottier's *Flags* (*Morin*, 1995), Skrypuch's *Silver Threads* (*Martchenko*, 1996), and Fitch's *No Two Snowflakes* (*Wilson*, 2001) that deal with racial and cultural differences. However, some of the preservice teachers met with resistance in the schools, particularly with the books dealing with same-sex families, and preservice teachers such as Lynette, whose story we related earlier in this chapter, felt deeply concerned at the lack of a proactive stance on the part of school administrators. What the preservice teachers had not yet considered was how these power structures might change over time and that, in years to come, they themselves could emerge as administrators and have further opportunities to engage in self-reflective behaviours regarding the introduction of controversial issues on school landscapes.

Age-Appropriate Media and the Value of Picture Books

The secondary-route preservice teachers participating in the study were completing a minor in English language arts. A number of them expressed cynicism about the value of picture books for the secondary students they might one day teach. For many of them, this hesitation was related to their lack of experience with or exposure to any picture books in their past teaching or in their studies in junior/senior high school. It was clear that very few of them had considered picture books as appropriate pedagogical materials for secondary classrooms. Some of the comments reflecting these perspectives include:

> I'm not sure I'd know how to make it applicable to junior/senior high school classes.

> I find it creative and fun to look at these books. It's also harder and more complex than I imagined. I didn't realize all that could be taken away from a picture book, but this workshop exemplified that they could be used, and in a highly analytical way.

> It's interesting how the things that we take as amusements for children are really vehicles that cover the same thing as in "adult" novels.

In a number of cases, the preservice teachers saw picture books as primarily appropriate for English language learners or for "struggling" readers. Commenting on whether he would use Canadian multicultural picture books in his teaching, Kalin explained: "I'm not really sure. I'm still struggling with ways to work it into an academic stream class. They would be very useful in ESL or non-academic streams."

Overall, and not surprisingly, the elementary-route preservice teachers had a clearer understanding of the pedagogical value of Canadian multicultural picture books compared to the secondary-route teachers. They understood the impact and importance of visual images and were also aware that young readers must be able to relate to a book and see something of themselves in it. They understood that Canadian books were likely to have more relevant content and would speak more directly to the reader and impart something of Canadian identity than non-Canadian books. They also took the presence and use of Canadian picture books for granted. However, they were relatively uncritical of the content of the books. Very few of the preservice teachers from either the elementary or the secondary route of the BEd program commented on the issues raised by·the books (other than sexual orientation and Aboriginal issues) or the representations of Canadian identity found in the books.

Considering Diversity and Representation

It is perhaps surprising that the majority of our study participants had not considered socio-cultural factors such as Canadian identity, diversity, and representation in the books they would select for use in their prospective classrooms. One participant commented: "Mmm, honestly before this course I didn't really think about the idea of multiculturalism and having diversity in books. But now that I've taken this course, I have realized that it would be useful to include a wide range of diversity in the books that I'm using in class."

Few of the participants had considered the issue of book selection at all, and many of the preservice teachers assumed that an appropriate collection of books would be ready and waiting for them in their classrooms. Given the absence of teacher librarians from most schools in Alberta, as in many other parts of Canada, and given that most teachers purchase their own books for their classrooms, this is an unreasonable expectation. This issue in itself provided a foundation for stimulating some critical thinking about books and what they represent. In general, when considering book selection, the elementary-route preservice teachers felt it was important to have books that are "age appropriate" and "well illustrated" with a "high interest level." The actual content and the ways in which Canadians (or anyone else) are represented in the books were not considered.

Within the body of comments made by the preservice teachers there was a taken-for-granted notion, reflective of the official rhetoric that Canada is a multicultural country and that "diversity" is a "good thing." But the data collected in the study suggested that most participants had not thought deeply about their own location in this context, nor were they reflective about the nature of the diversity of the Canadian population. For example, some participants appeared to conflate "immigrants" with "refugees" and did not appear to be aware that immigrants come to Canada from many different backgrounds and circumstances, not all of them traumatic. These attitudes unconsciously reveal some simplistic categorizations and stereotypes that may emerge as a result of understandings of "official multiculturalism" in relation to questions of migration and citizenship. However, the "us" versus "them" attitudes demonstrated by some participants offer an opportunity to deconstruct preservice teachers' notions of how they identify with the status quo in a manner that may affect classroom decision making.

Freire (1998) writes: "We have a strong tendency to affirm that what is different from us is inferior. We start from the belief that our way of being is not only good but better than that of others who are different from us. This is intolerance" (71). The diverse nature of the picture books used in our study did evoke some resistance in comments from a few participants, but we can only assume that these remarks reflected the somewhat cursory format of a written survey instrument rather than a particularly deep ideological stance. However, a number of the comments did intrigue us:

> Those who immigrate here have a greater appreciation for Canada – however they should learn how to drive before getting a licence!!!

> People who are immigrating are usually coming from something worse so they appreciate much more what they find here.

> I didn't find anything I could really relate to [in the books]. I'm from a very nuclear family and grew up in Vancouver.

Some of our preservice teachers had to be "coaxed" into reading the picture books during the workshops, and would have preferred not to look at the books at all. This resistance signalled to us a lack of awareness of the relevance and importance of the books, as well as communicating a strong unwillingness to engage with the issues the books raised. An examination of the multicultural picture books through group discussion offered an opportunity for the preservice teachers to air views that, once spoken, could be further reflected upon by the group. In this way, discussants had a chance to re-construct and revise ideas that initially seemed to make sense, but which, in light of discussion, seemed incomplete or flawed.

Particular Books and Their Influences

In general, the books in the multicultural collection were new to the preservice teachers. We discovered they had little experience with contemporary picture books, and especially with Canadian books, either in their field placements or in their personal lives. Even participants who had children of their own seemed to be unfamiliar with Canadian books. As a result, there was a sense of apprehension when they first picked up the books and began to browse. After a while, it became clear that some participants had found a book they related to, or found interesting or unexpected. There was some excitement at discovering new books and many of the preservice teachers expressed affection for particular ones. They indicated they were eager to use these books in their future teaching, and for some of them, memories of their own childhood experiences were evoked. This speaks to the power of "seeing oneself" or seeing familiar places in a book, but in considering the books as a classroom resource, their own responses to the books seemed to take precedence over the realities of contemporary Canadian society. Their personal relationship with a book appeared to hinder serious reflection on the background experiences their future students might possess. Although many participants were enthusiastic in wanting to present their own experiences and favourite books, they were reluctant to step outside their comfort zone, or to explore what might be most relevant to their prospective students. Janine said: "The book I love is called *Tiger's New Cowboy Boots*, and being from Western Canada myself, as I go through this I see pictures of the mountains and I see pictures of the different evergreens and stuff ... I can make real life connections to this book." Keith, who had grown up in the inner city of Toronto, commented on *A Big City ABC* (Moak, 2002): "When we were in class I almost stole this book ... It was a book that totally rung home for me because like the first page, A, is for the Art Gallery of Ontario. You kind of go through the book and I was like totally remembering my childhood." Keith went on to talk about how he'd "hung out" around the art gallery after school and climbed on the sculpture that was on the first page of the book. The illustrations captivated him and "took him back" to his childhood.

A number of preservice teachers commented on *If You're Not from the Prairie* (Bouchard; *Ripplinger*, 1993). They felt the book captured their own experiences of growing up in rural Alberta or Saskatchewan, and it brought back fond memories for them. The illustrations by Henry Ripplinger depict wide skies, pure white snow, deep golden grain, and wooden grain elevators beside a railway track. In this book, time stands still as children walk along country trails, play with friends and family in the snow, and travel on the school bus. Yet, the images in *If You're Not from the Prairie* represent only Canadians of European background. Like many adults, the preservice teachers in this study carried romanticized notions of childhood and growing up, and so this one book was identified as being very special to many of them. Rod said: "I think a large part of why I was drawn to it was just the images it conveyed and the memories it brought back from being a child in Canada in the winter."

The resulting discussions regarding particular books offered a chance to express differing opinions on books, an aspect of critical literacy that is important in terms of reader response. In addition, these discussions provided the preservice teachers with an opportunity to experience how their peers were engaged by certain texts, reinforcing the artistic merit and multigenerational aesthetic value of the books.

Reflections

Connelly and Clandinin (1988) offer an intriguing definition of the word "curriculum." They indicate that its Latin root means "race course" (4), an apt metaphor illustrating the perspective of many beginning teachers who consider the employment of a standardized curriculum as both a race against time and a "safe route" to follow with their students. Yet using a pre-made curriculum has its share of problems. Without diagnostic instruction, teachers are unaware of exactly what students require at any particular time, and they are also unaware of where student interests lie. As well, society's marginalized populations are not typically in a position to develop curricula, and accordingly, pre-made curricula may not reflect the student diversity that teachers encounter in their classrooms. Santomé (2009) writes: "A culture of debate must be fostered in our classrooms. By so doing, we will allow the diversity that already exists in our lives to enter into the curriculum" (78).

The preservice teachers in our study seemed likely to make pedagogical decisions based on their limited previous experiences with picture books as well as with controversial issues, resulting in quick assumptions that limited their ability to consider alternatives. While the desire to broaden curriculum often leads away from pre-packaged materials towards the use of resources such as multicultural picture books, we discovered that this response to diversity is not without challenges. The preservice teachers involved in this study were aware of aspects of curriculum design that suggested potential difficulties in terms of pedagogy, including the approach Lynette took in attempting to establish her administrator's support, and in going further to investigate how administrators deal with issues related to parental requests to ban particular books in schools. However, by opening up topics related to the use of diverse picture books, these preservice teachers had the

opportunity to further consider their role as curriculum decision mak-
ers in taking action and supporting social justice. Such considerations
involve exploring the strategies that teachers can use when introducing
potentially controversial texts into their classrooms.

One important set of supports for teachers and administrators are
provincial curricular documents. In some aspects, provincial curricula
may support diversity with respect to school resources; in other aspects,
there remains room for improvement in future drafts of these documents. Teachers, even preservice teachers, need to be thinking about
matters of equity and social justice, realizing that they themselves have
important roles to play in curriculum revision. Santomé (2009) believes
that "the curriculum can become a space that brings us together, not one
that divides – one in which the right to be different while still mutually
respecting our legitimate rights is made possible" (78).

Phelan (2005) gets to the heart of something we have also perceived
regarding the comments of the preservice teachers: we often educate
prospective teachers in "method" without offering the possibility that
simple application of knowledge may not be the equivalent of ongoing
thoughtful inquiry and discernment. As teacher educators interested
in the preparation of preservice teachers, we believe that one of the
implications of this study involves the important message that teaching
is very much an "in the moment" craft. Rather than a solitary wisdom
that comes from an accumulation of facts, three other things are critical for students to develop within their preparation years: a positive
philosophy about children and diversity, a willingness to engage in curriculum making, and an openness to the ever-changing face of "best
practice" according to current research.

Our findings support McDaniel's (2006) concern that educational
institutions are merely perpetuating the status quo. In response, we
underscore the importance of introducing preservice teachers to the
potential of diverse Canadian picture books in their classrooms, emphasizing a richly planned route for children's learning rather than running
the "race course" of standardized curriculum. The route we suggest
includes a consideration of diversity as well as pedagogy, leading to
support for critical-literacy approaches to classroom texts. By facing
their fears and assumptions through the supported context of university course work, preservice teachers can address early the selection
processes and criteria they will apply regarding classroom resources.
Considerations of diverse picture books as classroom resources may
assist preservice teachers in critically devising their upcoming journey

into school curriculum while keeping in mind their professional interests as well as student diversity.

Bell (1997) writes: "Social justice involves actors who have a sense of their own agency as well as a sense of social responsibility toward and with others and the society as a whole" (3). Our research study has demonstrated that positive academic encounters with diverse Canadian picture books can inform and strengthen preservice teachers' sense of social responsibility in terms of respect for diversity and can reinforce the merit of picture books as valuable resources for use across the curriculum and across the grades.

2 Who Does This Text Think I Am? Exploring Questions of Subjectivity through Diverse Picture Books

INGRID JOHNSTON AND FARHA SHARIFF

I never "am" the "who" that a pedagogical address thinks I am. But then again, I never am the who that *I* think I am either.

Elizabeth Ellsworth

Overview

As teacher educators, we are particularly interested in the potential of contemporary Canadian picture books to engage teachers and students in complex reflections on questions of national identity, diversity, and their own subject positions in the world. In this chapter we focus on the responses of secondary-route preservice teachers at the University of Alberta to the eighty Canadian picture books selected for the national study. We follow the findings explored in chapter 1 by considering how these texts challenged participants' sense of self and taken-for-granted views about Canadian multiculturalism, and exposed their fears and uncertainties about encountering difference in the classroom. We draw on data from 166 surveys and 20 lesson plans completed by these preservice teacher participants over the two years of the study, and on insights gained from personal interviews with eight of the participants to suggest how these textual encounters disrupted readers' socially constructed subject positions and challenged their liberal humanist notions of self and other.

Initiatives to Prepare Preservice Teachers for Diverse Classrooms

Our picture book study was conducted as part of ongoing research initiatives in the Faculty of Education at the University of Alberta to prepare preservice teachers for the realities of teaching in diverse classrooms. Recent census data from Statistics Canada (Mahoney, 2010) shows that Canada has one of the highest foreign-born populations in the world; only Australia and New Zealand have higher proportions. According to these statistics, by 2031 between 29 and 32 per cent of the Canadian population could belong to a visible minority group and at least a quarter of the population could have been born outside the country. These changing demographics have already resulted in more diverse urban school classrooms in Alberta, with larger numbers of immigrant and refugee students, along with increasing numbers of students of Aboriginal heritage. This ethnocultural diversity in schools is not, however, well represented among the preservice teaching population at the University of Alberta, which has one of the largest teacher education programs in the country. The majority of the preservice teachers in our program are Canadian-born and of European heritage and many of them feel unprepared for engaging with issues of diversity in schools (Carson & Johnston, 2001a).

For the ten years previous to our picture book study at the University of Alberta we had worked with colleagues in our Faculty of Education on preservice teachers' attitudes towards questions of multiculturalism and understandings of teacher identity (Carson & Johnston, 2001b; Johnston, 2006). In our large-scale surveys, interviews, and focus-group discussions with our student teachers, we drew on Bakhtin's (1981) notions of the tensions between authoritative discourses and internally persuasive discourses to consider how our student teachers were negotiating their sense of personal and professional identities. Discourses that are externally authoritative in teacher education include prescribed teaching quality standards, subject matter disciplines and the views of experienced teachers – what Deborah Britzman (1998) has termed the "commonplaces of teaching." Internally persuasive discourses, by contrast, such as student teachers' biographical experiences, family, culture, race, politics, gender, and sexuality, are often the unacknowledged discourses that come to the fore in the biographical crisis they encounter when confronted with difference in the classroom. Tensions between these authoritative and internally persuasive discourses may leave student teachers confused and uncertain about how to position themselves as teachers in relation to difference.

We found in this earlier research that many of our student teachers offered technical solutions to questions of difference, considering it as an aspect of classroom management they would have to "deal with." Many of them considered the curriculum they were preparing to teach as "culturally neutral." They often had little awareness of their personal beliefs and biases, responded with platitudes to complex issues of diversity and offered resistance to personal stories of racism and injustice that appeared to threaten their own perceptions of themselves as fair and equitable teachers. For many of these preservice teachers, diversity proved to be a "slippery signifier" that they saw as including race, culture, class, religion, gender, sexual identity, and disability. They felt challenged to address these issues in order to meet the general expectation that public schools are "expected to respect" diversity. Respecting diversity became one of the most authoritative and personally persuasive discourses that they were being asked to attend to that required them to face the "unknown other." This fear of otherness and difference led them to unconsciously resist efforts in our teacher education program to encourage a deep reflection on their own biases and world views.

Engaging Preservice Teachers with Picture Books

Building upon these previous research findings, we hoped that a project to ask our preservice English language-arts teachers to read and to respond to issues of diversity in Canadian picture books might provide new opportunities to engage them in reflections of encountering the other. We began with a pilot study at the University of Alberta which then expanded to a national study as discussed in the introduction to this book. We collectively selected eighty multicultural picture books and planned a workshop for introducing the texts to the student teachers during the regular English education or literacy courses at each site and collected data through surveys, interviews, focus group discussions, course assignments, and email conversations with those who agreed to participate.

As an inherently political enterprise, the subject "English" is concerned with issues of representation of the world outside the classroom, dealing with ideas about society through the study of language and of selected texts. Language and literature are inextricably linked with notions of citizenship, society, and the ways we get along with one another in the world.

Alberto Manguel (1993), the Canadian writer and critic, reminds us that literature, in addition to its personal potential, also has political and social power:

Words, literature, books, because of their very nature relentlessly challenge the right of those in power, ask unsettling questions, put in doubt our assumptions. Literature may not be able to save anyone from injustice, but something about it must be effective if every dictator, every totalitarian government, every threatened official tries to do away with it, by burning books, by banning books, by censoring books, by taxing books. (xi)

Erin Manning (2003) offers a similar reminder about the power of reading literature. Reading, she suggests, "is not just a tranquil act of deciphering, but an exposition of the irreducibility of the other as text, as world, as human being." The practice of reading, she believes, "inaugurates a politics-under-deconstruction. Reading is an interpretive gesture always to come·that challenges my subjectivity-in-process ... Reading can also be formulated as a proposal for an encounter with the other. The text is the other to whom I turn not for comprehension, but for the challenge of exposing my own difference" (151).

Seen in this way, our preservice teachers' responses to the multicultural texts in our study can be considered as acts of imagination with the potential for challenging, transforming, and renegotiating who they believe themselves to be as Canadians and as teachers.

As with all literary texts, picture books, through their ideological stances, ask readers to take up particular subjectivities, and as John Stephens (1992) reminds us, "in taking up a position from which the text is most readily intelligible, [readers] are apt to be situated within the frame of the text's ideology" (67). This ideological position may be one that promotes a culturally acceptable view of who Canadians think they ought to be or may subvert such expectations. Picture books, with their complex interaction of words and images, can act as cultural texts that may promote a cohesive and exclusionary view of national identity, or serve as a counter-articulation to notions of a homogeneous sense of nation.

A number of the picture books in the study addressed issues of Canadian multiculturalism and diversity from a predominantly Eurocentric viewpoint; some portrayed a view of identity through the eyes of recent immigrants or second-generation Canadians; others focused on specific Aboriginal experiences of Canadian life and history, questioning the taken-for-granted stories of Canada's colonial past; several books pointed to Canada's history of marginalization and discrimination in stories about the internment of the Japanese in the Second World War and the mistreatment of early Chinese immigrants who built Canada's railroads, while others focused on Canada as the land of freedom for runaway slaves and a haven of tolerance and diversity. A large proportion of the books addressed issues of race, culture, gender, and sexual orientation, either overtly or implicitly. The themes that emerged from our study findings relate to these differing representations and ideological perspectives on Canada and point to ways in which the pre-service teachers located themselves and others on shifting borderlands of national identity.

Responding to Issues of Identity in the Texts

Many of the secondary-route participants in our Alberta setting commented on the importance of place as represented in the picture books for articulating their own sense of identity. Place was referred to as geographic location, as a sociocultural space for identity exploration, and as critical or reflective discourse. Some participants articulated their sense of comfort with a "white landscape," selecting books such as *If You're Not from the Prairie* (Bouchard; *Ripplinger*, 1993), with illustrations that focus on a predominantly "European" representation of the Canadian landscape. As Manning (2003) reminds us, art represented in this way "offers a primarily linear rendition of space, inviting us to enter into an apparently coherent construction of the Canadian landscape" (14). This particular spatial perspective was challenged by several Aboriginal participants who questioned power relations between "mainstream, white Canada" and other groups, pointing out that much of the Canadian landscape represented in this particular picture book was disputed territory. One participant commented, "My sense is that Canada believes that we are all in search of certain justices, but only as long as it is not too uncomfortable," pointing to the ongoing disputes among the federal government and Aboriginal peoples over treaty and land rights.

Some participants in the study focused on the idealized portrayals of Canada in several of the picture books, choosing to view Canadian identity through the lens of official multiculturalism with its promotion of Canada as accepting and open to immigration and diversity. They offered comments such as "Canadian identity is multiculturalism. It is the acceptance of different people regardless of age, colour, sex, gender, ability, belief or religion" and "being a Canadian to me means being tolerant and aware of other cultures and backgrounds within Canada." These preservice teachers' responses to the picture books reflect an uncritical liberal humanist view of national identity that expresses superficial support for the acceptance of diverse identities in Canada.

However, their use of phrases such as "being tolerant and aware of other cultures" suggests that they saw multicultural identities as a form of "otherness" that had few personal implications for their own lives.

Several other participants challenged even such traditional notions of multicultural acceptance. Their comments suggested a biased and racist viewpoint on ways in which the portrayal of multiculturalism in the texts disturbed their own sense of Canadian identity. One preservice teacher commented that "we need to remember our culture too, not just focus on others," emphasizing her belief in the primacy of a European culture in Canada, with "other cultures" relegated to the margins. Another expressed a similar belief in a binary that positioned "Canadian" on one side of the divide and "immigrant" on the other with her comment that "people who immigrated to Canada hold different values and beliefs that may be very different from Canadian values of those who call themselves Canadian."

Several other participants expressed a sense of personal exclusion and discomfort with the selection of picture books that focused on the experiences of Canada's immigrant and Aboriginal population. One preservice teacher commented: "I didn't find that many of them [the picture books] would relate to mainstream society," while a second suggested: "Most of these books don't reflect my experiences of growing up in rural Canada." We assume that many of these preservice teachers had attended schools that were largely monocultural, embedded in social structures that shut out understandings of difference and offered curricula that failed to acknowledge the backgrounds, experiences, and viewpoints of Canada's diverse population. As a result, students came to university misinformed and unaware of the rich histories and diverse racial, cultural, and linguistic experiences of Canadians outside the so-called "mainstream."

David Schoem has commented in his book *Inside Separate Worlds* (1991): "The effort it takes for us to know so little about one another across racial and ethnic groups is truly remarkable" (4). The life stories of young people from different ethnic and religious backgrounds portrayed in his book point to the chasms that have existed between the lifeworlds of these youth. As Schoem writes:

> We have systematically limited our visions of the world. We have narrowed our personal life experiences in our society, and limited our intellectual horizons by placing boundaries on what our schools and universities allow us to know. We allow ourselves to see and understand social and

historical events from just one point of view ... Our schools don't teach us about different groups and how they see the world; we learn but one truth, one vision of our past and future. (4)

This limited and often myopic view of the world and of viewpoints other than one's own was not shared by all participants. In particular, a number of first- and second-generation Canadian student teachers in the study had much more open-ended responses to the picture books from those presented in the previous two paragraphs. Their focus was on the potential of several texts to "re-story" some of Canadian history to include the previously absent experiences of Canada's immigrant population who suffered racism and discrimination because of their race, culture, or language. For example, one participant's survey comment made reference to the picture book *Ghost Train* (Yee; *Chan*, 1996), which relates a poignant Chinese ghost story about the dangers of building Canada's railways: "It's important to acknowledge the part that Chinese immigrants played in Canada's history." Another selected the same text as the focus of her lesson plan for teaching a grade 10 class, explaining that "students should understand relevant issues surrounding immigration past and present and how some immigrants were treated unfairly and exploited." And another respondent referred to the book *Flags* (Trottier; *Morin*, 1999) in which a young girl's neighbour, Mr Hiroshi, a Japanese Canadian, is taken away from his home during the Second World War with her comment: "The book *Flags* reminded me of Canada's shameful treatment of Japanese Canadians."

These participants' varied experiences of engaging with the picture books and their responses to both the literature and our survey questions inform our understandings of the complexities of racial, ethnic, gender, and language identities. Carl James suggests that accounting for our experiences "can alert us to the contextual and relational nature of identities, and to the various players and events that contribute to their process of becoming" (James & Shadd, 2001, 3). Through understanding other people's experiences, James considers that we can "gain insight into the ways in which social structure shapes and mediates identities, experiences, and interactions: how it excludes some people and prevents many of us from truly knowing about each other, and how through our attitudes and actions within that structure we reinscribe difference and maintain inequity" (4).

The picture books in our study presented mediated forms of these diverse experiences, offering an invitation to the study's readers to engage in a journey of discovery about the lives of Canadians, past and present, and to reflect on their own lives, experiences, and values. We were interested to see how responses to these invitations were taken up in such different ways by our participants.

Preservice Teachers' Responses to Mode of Address

In reflecting on our findings from the Alberta study with secondary-route preservice teachers, we were reminded of the work of Elizabeth Ellsworth (1997) on the concept *mode of address*, and we became interested in considering how dissonances in preservice teachers' responses to the texts could be articulated through this particular concept. Ellsworth explains that in films, mode of address refers to the way a film addresses its audience and can be articulated in the question "Who does this film think you are or want you to be?" (22). Films, she contends, have intended, imagined, and desired audiences and are designed to evoke predetermined responses and ways of understanding from these audiences, who have already been located by filmmakers within assumptions about culture, race, socio-economic status, age, and sexuality.

Drawing parallels and intersections between film and other texts, Ellsworth further describes "mode of address" as being about the need to address any communication or text to a particular "someone" and the desire to control, as much as possible, how and from where that person reads the text. "It's about enticing the viewer/student into a particular position of knowledge towards the text, a position of coherence from which the film/curriculum works" (28). In other words, there is an intention to achieve an exact fit, or what Ellsworth calls full understanding, between a film or curriculum text's mode of address and the response of the viewer/student. Such a fit is, however, never fully achieved. As Ellsworth explains: "The viewer is *never* only or fully who the film thinks s/he is." In addition, "the film is never exactly what *it* thinks it is. There is never one unified mode of address in a film" (26). As the viewer/student's reading of the film/curriculum constantly and inevitably passes through the uncontrollable stuff of desire, investments, history, and preconceptions, the interaction between the viewer/student and the film/curriculum becomes a messy, unpredictable event in which differences in meanings, experiences, histories, conscious and unconscious desires, investments, and subject positioning always interfere with the goal of achieving exact fits or full understanding between a film/curriculum's mode of address and the viewer/student's response.

These differences create what Ellsworth calls a "volatile space between the outside (i.e., the film/curriculum/society) and the inside (the viewer/student/individual psyche)" (42). In order to achieve genuine understanding, she suggests, we need to recognize this gap as "a space of difference" (38) between the learner and the text, a space that allows for resistances and the development of human agency.

How, then, did the preservice teachers in our study, the vast majority of whom were born in Canada and were of European ancestry, with English as their first language, respond to the mode of address posed by the picture books? What kinds of volatile spaces opened up as they encountered the question "Who does this book think I am?" How did their responses articulate their personal and professional histories and sense of identity, conscious and unconscious desires, investments, and subject positioning?

All the picture books, through the interactions of text and images, asked readers to consider particular representations and ideologies of what it means to be Canadian. As teacher educators, we hoped that the images, stories, and languages portrayed in our picture books might serve as a type of new knowledge for our preservice teachers, that might challenge them to reflect on their preconceived notions of what it means to be Canadian. We purposely selected texts that reflected this diversity of identities and specifically represented a range of contemporary views on being Canadian. Our survey, conducted after participants had spent time reading the books in our workshops, included two specific questions that asked participants to reflect on Canadian identity:

1 How would you describe "Canadian identity" as it is presented in the picture books you read in the workshop?
2 What does "Canadian identity" mean to you?

We have attempted to articulate the student teachers' responses to these questions in relation to Ellsworth's "mode of address" under the following headings: spatio-temporal responses; viewing Canadian identity as the invisible other; resistance to difficult knowledge.

Spatio-temporal Responses

Particular spaces of difference emerged in relation to student teachers' interest in texts that depicted physical landscapes and spoke of strong affiliations to notions of "the land." One respondent offered a comment that "people have that really strong sense of place in relation to where they've grown up and that it is the best place to be." A second participant explained: "Canadian identity really talks to me about landscape ... I feel people in Canada have a really strong sense of place and ... seem to really strongly connect with where they grew up"; and a third commented: "Canadian identity to me means a connection to the landscape, to my family's personal history."

As mentioned earlier, these references to a personal sense of "place" and "landscape" as symbolic of Canadian identity were mostly articulated in relation to a small number of the picture books such as *If You're Not from the Prairie* (Bouchard; *Ripplinger*, 1993) and *A Mountain Alphabet* (Ruurs; *Kiss*, 1996), which portray a European landscape devoid of Aboriginal or non-white immigrant populations. There was little acknowledgment from the student teachers that much of the land described in these picture books was the traditional territories of Canada's First Nations peoples, despite the inclusion of a number of provocative texts that specifically address the power of the land for Aboriginal Canadians. For example, *This Land Is My Land* (Littlechild, 1993) is an autobiographical account of the power of the land for the author's family members and the struggles they endured through many generations; *Shi-shi Etko* (Campbell; *La Fave*, 2005) describes an Aboriginal girl's last week at home as she enjoys the beauty of the trees, water, and mountains before being sent to a residential school; and *Caribou Song* (Highway; *Deines*, 2001), written in Cree and English, shares the story of the land, peoples, and customs of two brothers following the caribou in northern Manitoba.

In relation to our participants' apparent lack of interest in these Indigenous texts, Clare Bradford (2007) has argued: "As colonial narratives of exploration, adventure, and settlement produced and reinforced the givens of Western cartography, alternative modes of mapping the world – the spatio-temporal cartographies of Indigenous peoples – were rendered invisible" (147). The gaze and desires of the colonizers mapped the world according to their own interests. As a result, Bradford suggests, "the imperial map of the world was deeply implicated in the expansion of western capitalism, whose relentless push towards new forms of production and new markets has continually reshaped the way space is used and represented, affecting time–space relations, the material practices associated with production and consumption, and processes of urbanization" (148).

For immigrants, notions of "land and landscape" become complicated by indistinct borders and boundaries, which are often blurred by the mingling of diasporic identities and negotiations between cultures. Many of the texts in our study addressed these narratives of boundary crossings and culture clashes for new immigrants to Canada. Yet very few participants in our study commented on the conflicting notions of place experienced by immigrants in books such as *A New Home for Malik* (Steffen; *Stopper*, 2003), in which a young boy from the Sudan learns about the possibilities of a new life in Calgary, or *A Gift for Gita* (Gilmore; *Priestley*, 1998), in which a girl from India comes to understand the complex meanings of "home" through her growing attachment to her new life in Canada. Most of the preservice teachers in the study resisted the invitation offered by these texts to question their own taken-for-granted understandings and subject positions in relation to the significance of the land for a diverse population.

Canadian Identity as the Invisible Other

A more explicit resistance to notions of Canadian identity as articulated in the picture books was apparent in responses that focused on a perceived "lack" of an identifiable Canadian identity. One participant suggested in the survey that "Canadian identity means what we are not" and another commented, "What it doesn't mean is a better question." Other responses had similar connotations: "The intriguing thing about Canadians is their constant insistence to describe themselves by saying what they are not. To me it seems we are so preoccupied by juxtaposing our identity in sharp contrast with the US or the Brits. This in itself makes our culture interesting – as we are the 'invisible other.'" Another respondent articulated a similar concern with the notion of absence of identity in Canada: "We compare ourselves to other countries by saying what we're not rather than what we are. So, you know, we're not a melting pot like the U.S. We're not this, we're not that, but you're left with – what are you then?" One participant, trying to explain her difficulties in defining what it means to be Canadian, said:

> The question isn't right for Canadians. What are you? Their identity is so much of what Canadians are not. We're, I don't want to say we're not Americans although that's what, something that comes up a lot. I think very peaceful, accepting … but in a way they're true because there is no Canadian … um even Aboriginal people but I think that's why I left it blank – it's too hard.

For these student teachers, Canadian identity was conceived of as a lack, an absence reflected only as a shadow of a more clearly defined American identity.

Resistance to Difficult Knowledge

While these previous respondents focused on a perceived lack of a coherent identity, others offered specific resistance to the depiction of Canadian diversity in many of the picture books. One complained that the representations in the picture books "did not reflect my experiences growing up in rural Alberta," while another commented: "As a white, middle-class girl, I felt incredibly under-represented by the literature in the workshop. While I totally appreciate diversity (you can never get too much of it) it is easy to marginalize who we are not concentrating on."

Such resistance to representations of difference in the books pointed to these preservice teachers' discomfort with a changing Canadian demography and their apprehension of having their sense of self challenged as they saw themselves represented as "other" in the picture books they read.

The picture books in this study that addressed issues of sexual orientation and same-sex marriage were considered as "controversial" by most of the preservice teachers. For a small number of the participants, these picture books were perceived as valuable texts for engaging their students in discussions around the need for more inclusivity of differing lifestyles. One such respondent selected *Tiger Flowers* (Quinlan; *Wilson*, 1994) for her lesson plan for a grade 10 class. The book describes the experiences of a boy called Joel who is grieving over his uncle Michael's recent death from AIDS. In her lesson plan, the preservice teacher explained why she selected this text:

> I believe that students need to be introduced to controversial issues and themes in literature, especially ones that address Canadian society. We are preparing students to be contributing members of society and school issues should reflect real-world issues and concerns. A picture book allows me to gently introduce controversial subject matter, like AIDS, by presenting it in a non-threatening medium that does not place a value judgment on the subject but allows my students to respond individually. By using a picture book, it allows students easy access to a difficult topic.

In contrast, most of our participants in the study expressed a sense of discomfort with teaching picture books such as these that might be considered as controversial by parents and the school community. Several were unsure about including *Tiger Flowers* in their classroom selections, explaining that they felt unprepared to deal with representations of an "uncomfortable" illness such as AIDS and the implied references to Michael's homosexual relationship in the picture book. Other preservice teachers noted that they would not include books that address issues of same-sex marriage. Their comments focused particularly on the picture book *Asha's Moms* (Elwin; *Lee*, 1990), which highlights the difficulties children of gay and lesbian families encounter when teachers are not aware of their family structure, and *Mom and Mum Are Getting Married!* (Setterington; *Priestley*, 2004), whose simple story relates the excitement of a young girl about the forthcoming wedding of her two mothers, Mum and Mom. Several preservice teachers echoed the sentiments of one young man in our study who commented: "*Asha's Moms* – the lesbian one. About the girl with two moms ... Like it depends if I was teaching in – you know – the gay village in Toronto, sure why not. But if I'm teaching at Peace River ... Yeah, no."

For some participants, a number of the Aboriginal books were also considered to be controversial as teaching texts. Several respondents commented that books about the treatment of Aboriginal peoples in residential schools, such as *This Land Is My Land* (Littlechild, 1993), would not be appropriate to teach in rural settings because they would not "fit into" the existing community mores. As one participant commented, "It's too much. Like the boarding, the Red Horse Boarding Schools, treatment of natives." And another said, "I can see this book creating a huge uproar in certain areas of the province where acceptance [of diversity] is not something that is valued by parents."

This fear of difference provoked by texts that confronted student teachers with complex questions of race, culture gender, sexual orientation, and discrimination may be seen as resistance to Britzman's notion of difficult knowledge that threatens the coherence of the self. Following Lacan, Britzman (1998) uses the term "passion for ignorance" to evoke the pressures of the refusal to learn stemming from the resistance to learning. "Such passion is made when the knowledge offered provokes a crisis within the self and when the knowledge is felt as interference or as a critique of the self's coherence or view of itself in the world" (118). She further comments: "To consider the vicissitudes of learning from difficult knowledge, educators must begin by acknowledging learning as a psychic event, charged with resistance to knowledge. The resistance, she claims, "is a precondition for learning from knowledge and the grounds of knowledge itself" (118).

Learning "from" Knowledge

We hoped that these participants' varying resistances to the mode of address offered by many of the picture books might have opened up Ellsworth's "space of difference" between the text and the psyche of the readers, presenting them with a challenge to begin a transformation that might lead to new learning. Deborah Britzman (1998) explains how confronting new knowledge that threatens our sense of who we think we are is a kind of "learning from" knowledge, rather than a "learning about":

> The learner must be willing both to confront outside knowledge as a mode of address that demands the learner's transformation of memory and to tolerate psychic or existential time, the time of the belatedness of understanding. Learning from demands both a patience with the incommensurability of understanding and an interest in tolerating the ways meaning becomes, for the learner, fractured, broken, and lost, exceeding the affirmations of rationality, consciousness, and consolation. (118)

This kind of learning, Britzman explains, requires a modification within, where the self must interfere with itself and reassess its previous investments. New knowledge is first confronted as a criticism of and loss of the learner's present knowledge if the knowledge offered is felt as non-congruent with the self, if it seems to threaten the ways the world has been perceived (128).

On reflection, we considered that the expectations of many student teachers in our study were based on assumptions they had of what their classroom experience *should be* as well as on their past classroom experiences. The ideologies and representations of difference in the picture books challenged them to confront the experiences of marginalization represented there and to come face-to-face with their own preconceived values about race, culture, disability, gender, and sexuality. These experiences highlighted a conflict between their taken-for-granted simplistic notions of a "multicultural" Canada and what is actualized in classroom settings today.

We saw the picture books as creating a space-between, what James Donald (1991) has termed "the idea of another locality, another space, another scene, *the between perception and consciousness*" (5) that highlights the lack of fit between the modes of address of the texts and the psychic effects of feeling for the student who encounters them. Donald argues that this space of difference between curriculum and student understanding is "characterized by oscillation, spillage and unpredictable transforma-tions" (1992, 2). We hoped that this research with our student teachers might have allowed for such unpredictable transformations.

Providing opportunities for our participants to encounter spaces of difference through the mediation of picture books allowed us as researchers to gain new insights into "how the learner comes to identify and dis-identify with difficult knowledge" (Britzman, 1998, 119). Such difficult knowledge was embodied by many of the texts in our study. As Bradford (2007) explains:

> The language of children's books performs and embodies ideologies of all kinds, since children's texts purposively intervene in children's lives to propose ways of being in the world. Settler society texts for children thus constitute an important and influential body of postcolonial works that construct ideas and values about colonization, about postcolonial cul-tures, and about individual and national identities. (6)

We have learned that asking our preservice teachers to engage with these questions of difference and identity, even in seemingly simple picture books, may be complex and often fraught with tensions for both teacher and learner. We saw how our preservice teachers' responses to reading the diverse picture books moved along a continuum. For some, the texts evoked an emotional identification with issues of place, race, gender, and culture and with the marginalization experienced by many of the characters; for others, the books raised an intellectual awareness of difference that they saw as reflective of Canada's multicultural poli-cies; still others resisted portrayals of difference in the texts by argu-ing that these representations were not reflective of their own lives or experiences or were too controversial for them to consider as relevant for their teaching. Our study offered the potential for participants to reflect on these responses and to reconsider how they might address difference in their own lives and teaching. But, as Ellsworth suggests: "The workings of power and social positioning in the pedagogical rela-tion – especially a pedagogical relation with all good intentions – can be delicate and seemingly intangible" (6). Her caution reminds us that we can never know for sure whether our research enabled preservice teachers to bring new insights into their teaching through an enhanced understanding of difference or whether it entrenched their fears and uncertainties about encountering difference in the classroom.

3 Historical and Contemporary Perspectives on Cultural, Social, and Political Issues in the Canadian West

LYNNE WILTSE

In the fall of 2007, the Centre for the Study of Canada (CSC) at Thompson Rivers University (TRU), where I was conducting my part of the study at the British Columbian research site, hosted a conference, *Still the "Last Best West" or Just Like the Rest? Interrogating Western Canadian Identities*. I presented a paper, "Preservice Teachers' Responses to Representations of the West in Canadian Picture Books," which drew on preliminary data from the first year of the study. It was the nineteenth-century immigration poster, featured on the pamphlet advertising the conference, that provided the inspiration for this chapter.

The call for papers on the conference poster read as follows:

> From the 19th century immigration poster from which this conference adapts its title to the travel brochures of today, Canada's Western provinces have long been embedded in many and often disparate, even contradictory, identities ... This conference aims to examine some of the cultural, social, and political ways in which the provinces – individually or collectively – have informed the wider imagination.

The conference brochure called to mind *Josepha: A Prairie Boy's Story*, the Canadian children's picture book chosen by researchers to introduce the study to the preservice teachers in our workshops (see introduction to this book). Set in 1900, this story describes the challenges Josepha, an immigrant from Eastern Europe, encounters in his new homeland. The Canadian government used the catch phrase "The Last Best West" in an effort to attract prospective immigrants to settle in the Canadian prairies during the surge of western settlement from 1896 until the start of the First World War. It struck me that (barring the language factor), the

Figure 3. Pamphlet advertising *The Last Best West*, 1909 (Museum of Civilization, public domain)

immigration poster advertising ranching, grain raising, mixed farming, and so forth could have been used to attract Josepha's family to the Canadian West. For Josepha and his family, the reality did not prove to be as marketed. The narrator of the picture book, a young boy, describes Josepha's home and his family's struggle:

> You saw their home when you passed by at night from selling grain in town. A lonesome soddy standing on the rise, wee and frail and blackened. Supper in the gloom to save kerosene. Until next harvest. Or next. Pa said their storehouse was nothing but empty. And not a wonder, Pa said. For Josepha was the bairn of city folk, a main street shopkeeper's son. And Pa said Old Country or no, shopkeepers didn't make farmers. Farmers made farmers. (McGugan; *Kimber*, 1994, unpaginated)

The conference poster invited the reader to consider whether we as Canadian westerners were still the "Last Best West" or Just Like the Rest. The question – just like the rest? – was a pertinent one, as tentative study findings were pointing to the difficulty of articulating Canadian identity and the significance of regionalism. However, in relation to the first part of the question, *Josepha* called forth other questions: Was it ever the last best West? Or, for whom was it the last best West? It certainly was not for Josepha's ilk. How did other immigrants fare? And, what about native Canadians, who had been displaced from their land to make space for the "homes for millions"? Several months later, as tentative ideas for this chapter began to take shape, a headline in the *Globe and Mail* newspaper caught my attention: "Warning: The boom out West is both a lure and a trap." It struck me that, although specifics had shifted, the warning could have been written one hundred years ago, as a caution to Josepha's family. Jeffrey Simpson (2008) began his article with the comment that "fundamental shifts produce winners and losers. In Canada, fundamental shifts in worldwide energy and agricultural prices bless the West and curse most of the rest … Even more people will migrate to these provinces; even more of the country's wealth will be generated there" (A27). Simpson's comment suggests that perhaps we can still think of a "last best west," set apart from the rest of Canada; however, whether we are considering the past or the present, not everyone within the West could be considered "blessed" or "winners."

As presenters at the conference, we were asked to consider how the multiplicity of identities in the West link to the past, inform the present, and shape policies and decisions that, in turn, will affect the future. Since many of the picture books in the study collection featured the Canadian West, I was readily able to situate this request within the research project for the purpose of the conference presentation. However, as I continued with the second year of the study, I noted with interest how many of the teacher candidates were making connections between the past, the present, and the future as they responded to various texts. In her book *From Nursery Rhymes to Nationhood: Children's Literature and the Construction of Canadian Identity*, Galway (2008) emphasizes this relationship between the past, present, and future in literature for children: "This connection between the past and the present makes the manner in which a nation communicates its history to children, who represent the present and the future, particularly significant" (115).

Study Details

Before turning my attention to interrogate the "last best west" claim, I will provide brief background information about the teacher education program and the preservice teachers in the study at Thompson Rivers University. The two-year after-degree elementary program (K–6) enrols two cohorts of approximately thirty students each year. At the time of the study, the program was competitive, and the students were of high calibre.[1] Many came from Kamloops and the surrounding area (and had completed their undergraduate degree at TRU), with a small number from elsewhere in British Columbia and other Canadian provinces. There was a broad age range; most of our preservice teachers had a good deal of life experience and many were parents. As is typical in an elementary education program, our students were mainly women, although we had on average close to half a dozen men per cohort. In terms of ethnic diversity, the majority of the students were of European ancestry; however, representative of the local community, our student population comprised two other ethnic groups in particular, Aboriginal Canadians and Indo-Canadians.

The teacher candidates who participated in this study were in my language and literacy curriculum and pedagogy course. Data collection procedures included observations from workshops conducted in class, surveys, transcripts from audio-recorded individual interviews and focus group discussions, teacher candidates' lesson plan assignments, and email correspondence from those preservice teachers completing field placements. While all teacher candidates completed the surveys and lesson plans, volunteers only were interviewed or took part in the focus groups. For the purpose of this chapter, I have drawn on the following data sources: individual interviews, focus group conversations, and lesson plans. Due to the very small size of the program, I was able to conduct individual and focus group interviews with relative ease; many of the preservice teachers were keen to participate in this part of the study. I was also able to make connections to other courses the preservice teachers were taking, as appropriate. As there is a significant First Nations population in Kamloops and the surrounding region, Aboriginal issues featured prominently in various courses (for example, their social foundations, First Nations, and social studies courses).[2]

Due to variations in programs from site to site, not all researchers in this study were able to engage the preservice teachers in completing and teaching lesson plans; for that reason, I will explain this data source in more detail. As part of their coursework, teacher candidates were required to develop a lesson plan, using one or more of the picture books presented in the workshops, appropriate for exploring a selected topic with elementary students. The purpose of the assignment was to provide teacher candidates with an opportunity to consider how particular concepts, themes, and issues of identity are portrayed in diverse Canadian picture books. Sample topics included: historical revisioning; representations of Aboriginal peoples; rural/urban representations; the importance of place; dealing with controversial issues through picture books; varying representations of immigrants to Canada; difficult issues in Canadian history; language issues; and visual aspects of picture books. As the language and literacy course was linked to the first practicum, the hope was that the preservice teachers would be able to teach their lessons while in the field. In many cases this proceeded as planned; however, in other instances this was not possible due to various factors such as grade-level appropriateness or topic suitability.

"M": Multiculturalism or Myth?

Although the demographics of the research participants in the Kamloops site provide a contrast to those in the study's other sites, it is important to note that the responses of teacher candidates at the BC site to questions related to what it means to be Canadian were not atypical. Nodelman and Reimer (2000) explain how university students in a Canadian children's literature course responded to the request to consider distinctly Canadian aspects of their experience:

As happens in most discussions of Canadian identity, their ideas tended to focus around key features of Canadian history and geography. Our immense mountains and prairies ... made us especially reverent of nature. Our British roots made us more reticent and polite than Americans. Our two founding European nations and multicultural history of immigration made us more tolerant of ethnic difference. (15)

In her book *Re-mapping Literary Worlds: Postcolonial Pedagogy in Practice*, Johnston (2003) examined the reactions of high school students to postcolonial literature. She makes the point that "for many students in contemporary classrooms, the national fiction of Canada as a humane, nonracist, multicultural nation has permeated the construction of their own personal identities" (118). Similarly, a selection of teacher candidates' comments made during focus group interviews reflects harmonious images and stereotypical symbols of national identity:

We have multiculturalism, not the melting pot.

We're more open minded; everyone's accepted.

Canadians are thought of as being nice, and friendly, and open.

You have your choice, you have your life, and you have your freedom to do what you want – I think that's what Canada is.

When I was abroad, what I was very proud of is that we were seen as peacekeepers.

We've got our resources: the water, the fresh air, the land.

Do these images of Canadian identity correspond to how Canada is represented in Canadian literature for children? Galway (2008) notes that "throughout the process of attempting to articulate a sense of national identity, these children's writers exhibit a set of some commonly-held notions of what Canada and its inhabitants represent ... There is a prevailing image of Canada as a land of natural beauty and rich resources waiting to be developed, and a place that represents freedom, opportunity, and independence" (177). Although Galway is referring to Canadian children's literature written between 1867 and 1911, a sampling of the titles in our study show that many contemporary texts feature the nature and the positive aspects of what it means to be Canadian: *A Mountain Alphabet* (Ruurs; *Kiss*, 1996); *Suki's Kimono* (Uegaki; *Jorisch*,

2003); *From Far and Wide: A Citizenship Scrapbook* (Bannatyne-Cugnet; Zhang, 2000); *If You're Not from the Prairie* (Bouchard; *Ripplinger*, 1993).

However, Galway (2008) goes on to acknowledge that "such an ideal view of a nation is difficult to live up to. Freedom is tempered by government policy, diversity is not uniformly embraced, and certain linguistic and ethnic groups are excluded from the mainstream" (177). In like vein, Johnston (2003) further notes that this "fabulation is one not shared by all Canadians. For many Canadians of colour, for example, living in Canada has meant living with racism and with experiences of exclusion" (118). In my study, other comments made by participants suggest that this idealistic perspective of a nation is indeed hard to live up to. For example, after hearing several of his classmates describe positive aspects of Canadian diversity and multiculturalism, Leonard (one of the research participants) expressed his view that "we get brushed with a rather nice stroke of paint, I think. But, in my opinion, the 'm' in multiculturalism stands for myth. We have a horrible past. We've done terrible things to our minorities, just like everybody else." Correspondingly, a classmate commented: "I grew up thinking Canada is this great multicultural place, and that we're so accepting and loving of all of these other people from different places. But when I took Canadian history, I realized that there have been some difficult things in our past that we shouldn't necessarily forget, and that it's really important to bring those issues across to children" (Katy).

Using Picture Books to Teach Difficult Historical Issues

One way of introducing children to difficult subjects is through the use of Canadian picture books, as evidenced in the following statement from a teacher candidate's lesson plan:

> I love the idea of introducing difficult or controversial issues through picture books. I would definitely use books such as Trottier's *Flags*, Skrypuch's *Silver Threads* or Yee's *Ghost Train* to introduce units in social studies dealing with internment or immigration. I could see myself using Littlechild's *This Land Is My Land* to introduce the Aboriginal point of view to a class about land claims or Canadian history.

Johnston, Bainbridge, and Shariff (2007) make the point that "picture books have the potential to articulate varying understandings of Canadian identity, offering a double form of representation in the liminal spaces between words and images. They may promote a cohesive and exclusionary view of national identity that can marginalize or exclude diverse immigrant and Aboriginal perspectives, or serve as a counter-articulation to such notions of a homogenous sense of nation" (75). In this chapter, then, preservice teachers' responses to picture books that relate to particular historical injustices of the Canadian West – the role of Chinese immigrants in the building of the Canadian Pacific Railway (CPR); the internment of Ukrainian Canadians in the First World War and of Japanese Canadians during the Second World War; and Aboriginal issues, for example, residential schooling – will be examined. Their responses reveal the potential of these books to interrogate "notions of a homogenous sense of nation" and to explore the links among past wrongs, contemporary realities, and future possibilities.

Remembering Wrongs: Chinese Railway Construction Workers

In the Canadian Museum of Civilization's online exhibit *The Last Best West: Advertising for Immigrants to Western Canada, 1870–1930*, the significance of the railway in helping to promote government land in western Canada to would-be immigrants is noted. In the 1880s, thousands of immigrants from China worked on building the CPR. This railway enabled immigrants such as Josepha's family to settle in the Canadian West. Unlike Josepha's family, some of these settlers experienced the "last best west" as advertised. For the Chinese who came to Canada to work on the railway, what they encountered was anything but the "best."

Several teacher candidates chose *Ghost Train* (Yee; *Chan*, 1996), a historical account of the dangers Chinese Canadians faced in building Canada's railways, for their lesson plan assignments. Katy, who wanted to make sure that children had the opportunity to learn about "difficult things in our past that we shouldn't necessarily forget" selected *Ghost Train* so she could "have students explore the poor treatment the Chinese immigrants faced in building Canada's railway. I was really interested to deal with the issue in the classroom through Paul Yee's book." Unlike Katy, who had not been introduced to negative aspects of Canadian history as a young student, Paula chose the same book because it reminded her of own schooling:

> I chose *Ghost Train* because it sparked a memory of my own in-school experience. During Social Studies when we were learning about the Great Canadian Railway being built, I remembered how I felt when I found out

that so many lives had been lost, and the poor treatment of the Chinese immigrants who had been made all kinds of promises. The book triggered an emotional response, and I wanted to explore that with students.

Given the following excerpt, it is hardly surprising that *Ghost Train* affected Paula's emotions so strongly, and reminded her of the false promises that had been made:

> Walking through the train now, Choon-yi found it filled with men. Their clothing was torn and dirty, stained with mud and blood ... Choon-yi's eyes welled with tears. The men talked of their families, about how they longed to see them. They talked of hopes and dreams, about what they had planned to do with their earnings. They talked of work, about how each day had been a question of life or death. (unpaginated)

In a chapter entitled "Teaching for Hope," Werner (2008) makes the point that when students are learning about difficult issues in social studies, it is important to focus "not only on the informational content of issues, but also on their emotional content ... Emotions have to be shared – listened to and discussed – in order to be understood and harnessed for learning" (250). Lacy alludes to the significance of reaching students' affective domain in her lesson plan write-up:

> *Ghost Train* deals with an extremely important aspect of our history, and one that is difficult to discuss because of how the workers were treated and the effect their deaths had on their families back in China. It is a topic that is crucial for students to be exposed to because it helps readers to empathize with the Chinese workers and their families and realize that immigrants to Canada were not accepted with open arms or on equal ground in terms of rights and respect. This is something that we seem to still be struggling with today.

Mary, who used *Ghost Train* in a unit on this topic for her practicum in an upper elementary classroom, also makes it clear that, although students are learning about historical discriminations, issues such as racism continue to exist in Canadian society:

> Through this series of lessons, students will learn about the history of our Chinese Canadians and their role in our country's growth. They will learn about the extent racism played in the mistreatment of Chinese immigrants building the railway and continues to play in our society today. They will

be able to think critically about the outcomes that these historical issues have had on our past, present and future.

Learning from Past Mistakes: Internment Camps

Ukrainian Canadians' internment was part of the confinement of "enemy aliens" in Canada during and after the end of the First World War, lasting from 1914 to 1920. About 5000 Ukrainian men were interned in twenty-four camps and related work sites; their belongings were confiscated and they were forced to do hard labour. In *Silver Threads* (Skrypuch; *Martchenko*, 1996), set on the prairies, the author makes use of her grandparents' experiences as immigrants in early-twentieth-century Canada to tell the story of a young couple that escapes a life of poverty in their Ukrainian village to move to the Canadian frontier. When the First World War breaks out, the husband is arrested as an "enemy alien" and interned for years. Although most of the research participants knew nothing of this aspect of Canadian history, a number of teacher candidates saw this picture book as a way to expose students to this little-known topic. For example, Tanya chose *Silver Threads* for her lesson because "it is important for students to understand the hardships that immigrants faced in Canada. I also believe that students should be shown the progress that Canada has gone through in terms of the way immigrants are now treated." Yes, there has been progress; yet, many immigrants to Canada still face various challenges. Tanya does take this into consideration, as she furthers her point: "Canada, as a multicultural country, still experiences high volumes of racism. If students are not aware of this, then it may be harder for them to accept people who do not seem to be in the mainstream of today's society."

Flags (Trottier; *Morin*, 1999), a story about Japanese internment, proved to be one of the most oft-selected books in the study collection. Set on the Canadian West Coast during the Second World War, *Flags* describes the friendship between Mary, who was visiting her grandmother for the summer from the prairies, and the next-door neighbour, Mr Hiroshi, who grew a variety of irises, called flags, in his garden. When Mr Hiroshi is interned with other Japanese Canadians, Mary promises to look after his garden. Although the details of the internment camps are not addressed directly in the text, an author's note provides the historical context. In the note, Trottier explains what happened to the people of Japanese ancestry who had settled on the West Coast following the bombing of the American base at Pearl Harbor by the

Japanese air force during the Second World War: "The homes and businesses owned by the Nikkei (people of Japanese ancestry) were seized. Families were relocated to isolated camps or split up and sent to different places. Far from the coast, it was believed they would not be able to act as spies for Japan" (unpaginated).

Leonard had strong personal reasons for selecting this book for his lesson plan assignment, as can be seen in his explanation: "The reason I chose *Flags* for my lesson is because I grew up in the Slocan Valley where thousands of Japanese Canadians were interned in the 1940's. David Suzuki was a little boy when he was forced to live in the encampment in Lemon Creek just 15 minutes from where I grew up." In contrast, Anna, who knew very little about the internment of Japanese Canadians chose *Flags* because the timing of her lesson coincided with Remembrance Day: "I thought that the theme of Japanese internment would really tie in well with a lesson on Remembrance Day. I found that the kids were really inspired to learn about that piece of history. As for myself, I didn't even really know anything about Japanese internment before I read the book ... But, the lesson was right after Remembrance Day and led into a discussion about war." Unlike some of their classmates, these teacher candidates were able to teach the lessons during their field experience. Leonard described how he used *Flags* in his lesson:

> My chicken coop served as a house where two families lived during their imprisonment (strong word used very intentionally); it wasn't much bigger than a small shed. I can remember the yellow numbers stencilled onto the building – 103/104 – they still send shivers down my spine. So, in my lesson I had a space that size and had ten kids come and sit in that space so they could kind of conceptualize the living space.

Although having students partake in activities of this nature has been critiqued as problematic (see, for example, Boler, 1997 or Todd, 2003), in conjunction with class discussion sparked by the picture book, Leonard felt that his students benefited from the lesson: "I think it opened up a lot of their eyes. We started talking a lot about acceptance, and understanding, and my big question of what makes us different. That's what I thought the students got out of the lesson."

Anna explains that she used *Flags* as a platform to challenge students' beliefs:

> I told them that *Flags* has a really strong message that they should start thinking about, as it has to do with your beliefs. I made up a quiz with a

few questions that may be considered somewhat controversial. For example, I asked, "Do you always believe what the government says is right?" And, we returned to the questions after I read the story and we talked about what happened to the Japanese Canadians during and after the war.

As these examples demonstrate, particular groups of immigrants to Canada faced hardships, racism, and injustice in the "last best west." Canadian picture books such as those mentioned in this part of the chapter can be used to bring these issues from our past to present-day students; the lessons learned have contemporary implications. Anna describes her students' reactions: "They couldn't believe what happened to Japanese Canadians; they were aghast. The class was like, "That is absolutely wrong. Why did we let that happen?'" And, Leonard explains: "This book allowed me to go into that avenue of what happens if we're not open, and if we're not accepting of differences. Then, we're going to be in trouble for the rest of our lives." Sadly, this message leads all too well into what follows. The suffering experienced by the original inhabitants of this land will be the focus of the next section. Given the magnitude of the injustice, the local context, and the reality that the effects of what happened in the past are still very much felt in the present, these issues will be discussed in more depth.

"Filling in the Blanks": Aboriginal Issues

O is for Ojibwa
just one of the tribes
that spanned this vast country
before settlers arrived.
We're Canadians all,
but we must never forget
that our land was their land
and we owe them a debt.

Unlike "the *Patriotic Primer's* representation of native Americans as merely another group of new arrivals" (Bradford, 2007, 2), the excerpt from *M is for Maple* acknowledges "our land was their land," allowing for the construction of Canada as a "settler society" rather than a "nation of migrants" (2). Focusing on Canada, the United States, Australia and New Zealand, Bradford defines settler societies as "those where colonizers (settlers) exercised racial domination over the autochthonous inhabitants of the lands they invaded, and where

Indigenous peoples continue to seek recognition, compensation, and self-determination" (4). Bradford explains that each of these settler nations developed its own myths of foundation. For the purpose of this chapter, I will mention only the Canadian myth: "a conviction that its dealings with Indigenous people were benign and fair" (5). Aboriginal issues in Canada constitute one of the ways in which the M in *M is for Maple* could more appropriately signify myth. Pursuing the "our land was their land" theme, I was intrigued by the connection between George Littlechild's (1993) *This Land Is My Land*, one of the books in our study, and Nodelman's (2008) "At Home on Native Land," a chapter in *Home Words: Discourses of Children's Literature in Canada* (Reimer, 2008). The title for Littlechild's book plays on Woody Guthrie's song *This Land Is Your Land*:

> When I was a boy I was taught the song "This land is your land, this land is my land." When I got older I thought it was very strange to be singing about the ownership of the land. Whose land was this? Did it belong to anyone? The first people in this land were the Indians. We prefer to be called First Nations or First Peoples, because this was our homeland first. (16)

Nodelman (2008) explains how multiculturalism allows "people of differing backgrounds their differences while nevertheless sharing the same space, our home here in Canada" (114). What non-Aboriginal Canadians share is a history that happened elsewhere; but for Aboriginal Canadians, their history "occurred nowhere else but on the land we all now occupy together" (114). As a non-Aboriginal Canadian scholar writing about Aboriginality and property in Canadian novels for youth, Nodelman explores these tensions:

> It seems, then, that the mere existence of Aboriginal peoples is a threat to what appear to be some key aspects of the multicultural ideologies that are supposed to work to bind Canadians together. If those ideologies are to maintain their power generally – and if they are to include Aboriginal nations among the diverse cultures that define the country as a whole – then ways must be found to circumvent or confront the question of history. (114)

Indeed, that "this history still matters and is not yet over" (Nodelman, 2008, 114) is echoed in Bradford's point that the colonial "past enters the present in the form of relations of power, systems of government, modes of representation, and myths of national identity" (4).

In this section, some of the ways in which this occurs will be examined though the medium of Aboriginal children's literature. The following interview excerpt, which features Erica – white, middle class, born and raised in the lower mainland of British Columbia – provides a starting point for the discussion:

> As a young child, I often chose to read historical settings, like *Little House on the Prairie* from pioneer days, and I really romanticized the whole First Nations culture. I was very unaware that there was a difference between then and now. In high school, I had very few Aboriginal friends, so nothing bridged me to reality. I guess you could say I was very much infatuated with the old days.

Books like *Little House on the Prairie* (Wilder, 1953), written from a white perspective, enabled Erica (and countless other readers) to remain infatuated with the past. In addition to historical fiction, retellings of Aboriginal myths and legends by white authors constituted the foundation of Canadian children's literature about Aboriginal peoples for many years (Bainbridge & Fayjean, 2000). And, "despite contemporary debates about the appropriation of voice" (Wolf & DePasquale, 2008, 90), non-Aboriginal authors continue to write children's literature on Aboriginal content, although to a lesser degree. Wolf and DePasquale (2008) further this point: "Against this heavy colonial and neo-colonial history, Aboriginal authors writing picture books for children have had to adapt and redefine this Western literary form to tell their own stories" (90). In *The Truth about Stories*, Thomas King (2003) explains that what native writers discovered was that the North American past that had been created by the dominant culture "was unusable, for it had not only trapped native people in a time warp, it also insisted that our past was all we had" (105–6). For Erica, this time warp was not problematic as a child; however, when she decided to become a teacher, Erica acknowledged that her childhood impression of First Nations culture had little to do with contemporary reality:

> But when I decided to get into the field of education, I realized I'm likely going to teach in a small community with First Nations students. It started to make me aware of what has happened since then, and to think about the First Nations who were in my mind growing up and the real children who would be in my future classrooms. I had to fill in the blanks. So, with this project, I gravitated towards a lot of the books with First Nations content.

Were there books in our study collection that could assist Erica and other preservice teachers to "fill in the blanks" when it came to Aboriginal issues? Drawing on their study of Canadian Aboriginal picture books by Aboriginal authors, Wolf and DePasquale (2008) explain that, "unlike adult fiction, which tends to foreground such issues as poverty, poor health, substance abuse, lack of educational or employment opportunities, and other inequities still all too prevalent in many Aboriginal communities in contemporary Canada, children's fiction notably avoids the portrayal of these realities" (91).

Rather, with picture books for children "the pressures to produce ... positive images of Nativeness come from the history of colonization and a desire to counter the contemporary stereotypes of the drunken, lazy, or promiscuous Indian, or the historical ones of the bloodthirsty warrior, Noble Savage or seductive Indian maiden" (Wolf & DePasquale, 2008, 92).

Several contemporary books in our research project collection present "positive images of Nativeness," for example, *Morning on the Lake* (Waboose; *Reczuch*, 1997) describes a canoe trip for an Ojibway grandfather and his young grandson, while *My Kokum Called Today* (Loewen; *Miller*, 1993) celebrates the relationship of an urban Aboriginal girl and her grandmother, who lives on a reserve. While these representations play an extremely important role in countering negative stereotypes, they fail to address either ugly historical issues (for example, residential schools) or the challenging contemporary problems that have resulted from these past experiences. Two of the books in the collection deal with the horrific topic of residential schools in strikingly contrasting ways. *Shi-shi-etko* (Campbell; *La Fave*, 2005) tells the story of the last few days of a young girl's life at home with her family before leaving for residential school, whereas in *This Land Is My Land* (1993), Littlechild depicts the devastating effects of the residential school in a chapter entitled "Red Horse Boarding School."

As we could see the former Kamloops Indian residential school from our classroom window at the university, it is not surprising that many of the teacher candidates were drawn to these books. Erica, for example, noted that what she "liked about *Shi-shi-etko* was the local context of the book, and the fact that the author grew up not far from here." Karina enthused: "My teacher mentor was ecstatic that I was going to use *Shi-shi-etko* in my practicum, because he will be teaching *My Name Is Seepeetza* (Sterling, 1992) at the end of the year and that is also about a residential school in the local region." Another teacher candidate who chose *Shi-shi-etko* for her lesson with grade three students describes the book's potential for tackling the topic of residential schooling:

Shi-shi-etko offers a respectful and sensitive way for students at this grade level to consider such a great human tragedy in our recent history. Students require a critical understanding of the cultural destruction that resulted from residential schooling, because Aboriginal healing will, as Campbell [2005] points out in the preface, require resources and support for many more generations. (Monica, lesson plan)

The text itself, though, fails to deal directly with the harsher aspects of residential school, corresponding to the "general expectations of age appropriateness surrounding ... the picture book form, which is typically aimed at the youngest readers, and particularly from the assumption that children's innocence should be protected" (Wolf & DePasquale, 2008, 92). That this makes *Shi-shi-etko* more suitable for use with young students than *This land Is My Land* can be seen in Erica's explanation:

Shi-shi-etko was much more gentle; it doesn't discuss the horrors of the residential school. It talks more about her roots and her family and the place that she came from. That's another important way to look at the topic, right? This might be accepted a little bit more easily than *This Land Is My Land*. *Shi-shi-etko* could connect with a lot of children: tell me about your grandmother; tell me about your summers; tell me about how you feel before you come to school. Whereas with Littlechild's book, like, what could they tell me about skid row right now?

Certainly, Littlechild's autobiographical account of the struggles his family endured over several generations provides an exception to the expected in children's literature. Despite her comment, Erica sees a place for *This Land Is My Land* in the elementary classroom, albeit with older students. As a volunteer judge for the Regional Historica Fair competition, Erica met Philipa, a grade 4 student who won an award for her project, "Locked Up Indians."[3] As Philipa had interviewed both her grandmothers about their experiences at two different residential schools in the interior of British Columbia, Erica saw Littlechild's book as an ideal reference:

Well, I'm fairly certain that somebody would have introduced *This Land Is My Land* to her knowing the topic. I think this would have gone beautifully with her presentation, having to deal with her two grandmothers having such differing experiences with residential schooling. I think that this could have helped her bridge between the two. I think books like George Littlechild's *This Land Is My Land* have their place in saying this is an important issue, let's talk about it now.

The following year, I had the opportunity to interview Philipa as part of another research study involving students' Heritage Fair projects.[4] I asked her about "Locked Up Indians":

> Before I did my project, I didn't realize residential school was that big of a deal. But, as soon as I chose the topic my dad's like, "Wow." There are a lot of people around here to interview about residential school, but I decided to interview both my grandmas, because both of them went to different residential schools … I learned that they had to cook and clean and they were separated from their parents and punished for being different. They weren't allowed to speak their native language.

Undoubtedly, *This Land Is My Land* would have been an excellent resource for Philipa as she did research about residential schools for her project. Littlechild informs the reader:

> For many years, up through the 1960s, the government took Indian children away from their families and forced us to live in boarding schools. In these places we "Red Indians" as we were called were educated in the white man's way. The teachers forced us to learn English and become Christians. They cut off our braided hair, they beat us if we spoke our Indian languages. We suffered much cruelty and abuse. (18)

Janice, another teacher candidate, selected Littlechild's book for her lesson plan because of the powerful visual aspect to his book:

> I chose *This Land Is My Land* initially because of the artwork, which really intrigued me. But reading the story, I thought it was really cool how George Littlechild took his own past and then his people's past and used that as the basis of all the artwork that he did. And, he talks about some really controversial topics, such as residential schools, and the prostitution of his people, and the assimilation of the native people in Canada.

One of the aspects of Littlechild's artwork that intrigued Janice was the way in which the book incorporated photographs of two types into his paintings. Referring to Littlechild's use of photographs of family members over several generations in conjunction with colonial photographs by Edward S. Curtis, Bradford (2007) notes that "such strategies effected a disassociation between the photographs and the material conditions of dispossessed Indigenous people, and Littlechild's insistence on the biographies of photographed individuals targets precisely this disassociation to demonstrate the persistence and durability of Indian cultures and the consequences of the past in the present" (21). As I read Littlechild's description of the far-reaching results of Indian residential schools, I cannot imagine a more profound and tragic example of "the consequences of the past in the present." "My mother and all her brothers and sisters went to these boarding schools, and so did my grandparents. They grew up without their families and never learned how to raise children of their own. Many boarding school survivors died on skid row of alcoholism, including my mother" (18).

Littlechild's book also speaks to the persistence and durability of Indian cultures. I will return to this topic, but first, I will turn my attention to an aspect related to one of the consequences of the past (in this case, residential school). Following the closure of residential schools, the mistreatment of native children continued with what became known as "the Sixties Scoop," a term used to describe the period where there was a sharp increase in the number of adoption of native children by Whites.[5]

Geneva, an Aboriginal student who participated in the research project, was taken away from her First Nations family as a baby. She mentions neither the Sixties Scoop nor why she was taken from her mother directly; however, her background fits the profile, as can be seen in this description of her childhood:

> I'm a First Nations student, I am going to be 34 this year, I have five children and I grew on a ranch in the Cariboo area. I lived with non–First Nations parents, since I was three weeks old, but they did not adopt me because they did not want me to lose my status … I did visit my mother and her family, back and forth until I started kindergarten. Then, my family told my mother that I could not go back and forth, that I had to be stable during the school year, but she was welcome to come visit me.

Although Geneva had contact with her mother's family during her childhood, she did not meet her father and his extended family until she was a teenager. Given her background, it is not surprising that Geneva chose the picture book *Two Pairs of Shoes* (Sanderson; *Beyer*, 1990), for her lesson plan assignment: "In the book, the little girl has to figure out how to live in the First Nations world and in the white world. She's looking at a pair of patent leather shoes in the store and she wanted those but her grandmother, her *Kokum*, which is Cree for grandma, gave her a pair of moccasins and Kokum tells her not to forget or leave her moccasin world behind." Geneva went on to describe her personal connection to *Two Pairs of Shoes*:

> I made that choice because that's what I feel like my life was. The way I grew up is I always had the patent leather shoes and everything I needed, since I was a baby. But, when I met my First Nations family when I was fourteen is when I started learning about moccasins and tanning and moose meat drying and smoking fish. And, that was very difficult for me because I didn't know how to do any of those things but by that time all my cousins and sisters had been doing that for many years, so I was made fun of a lot. I was called a red apple, white on the inside, red on the outside.

As with Maggie in *Two Pairs of Shoes*, Geneva's grandmother was instrumental in helping her to negotiate life in two different worlds:

> I went to my grandmother, and I was so sad. She just hugged me and said, "It's OK. I knew you'd come back to us." She told me, "You know the white man's world now and we'll show you the Indian world. And, one day our family will come to you for help and you'll know how to help us." And, she made all the frustration of not knowing my language or not knowing my people go away.

Curious, I asked Geneva if what her grandmother prophesied had already come to pass:

> It is already coming true. I actually feel it because several of my uncles and their sons have lived their lives as loggers and now with the pine beetle kill, there are no more logs. Now, they are coming to me and asking me what they need to do to get into trades, like firefighting, welding, and construction. And, I tell them they have to go to school.

Part of Geneva's journey has been learning when to wear which pair of shoes. By reading *This Land Is My Land*, I get the sense that George Littlechild has learned that as well. Janice alluded to the "consequences of the past in the present" with her comments about her lesson plan, but she also touched on the other aspect of Bradford's (2007) statement about "the persistence and durability of Indian cultures": "But, then Littlechild has a really optimistic ending, so that's something that I really liked because I think it would be easier to teach children with having that ending to those tough topics." Indeed he does. In Littlechild's last chapter, "This Warrior Goes Dancing," he describes the painting displayed in this section of the book: "This young traditional warrior is on his way to a powwow. He holds his head up proudly. He's off to go dancing. To dance is to celebrate life" (30). He goes on to explain the significance of the circle in traditional dances: "The circle is a very important symbol to all Indians because the circle represents strength and unity. When we say the circle has been broken, we mean that our culture has been tampered with. In Indian Country we are closing the circle by healing ourselves. We are reviving our culture and traditions. We are very hopeful and the future looks promising" (30).

Conclusion

In closing, I would like to revisit the notion of the "Last Best West" with which I began the chapter. In doing so, I return to the historical picture book *Josepha* and to Simpson's (2008) article. When Josepha plans to leave school to work bagging grain at threshing time, his teacher, Miss, begs Josepha to stay: "It is nineteen hundred. Nineteen hundred, Josepha. A fresh century in your chosen land. You are quick and bright and cunning. Oh, the wealth of knowing you could reap" (unpaginated). Her plea goes unheeded, as Josepha leaves school forever. More than a century later, in relation to the most recent "boom out west," Simpson remarks: "It can be fun being rich ... But the hardest thing in politics is to think ahead, way ahead. The No. 1 question every government should ask is: Can't we do better?" (A27). In my view, his question is easy to answer: of course we can do better. But, that reply is not good enough: we *must* do better. The preservice teachers currently enrolled in teacher education programs across the country will join the ranks of teachers who teach the contemporary Josephas. Although the setting has changed, from one-room prairie schools to, in most cases, urban classrooms, many immigrant students still struggle to adjust to a different language and culture in Canadian classrooms. The school completion rate for many of these students is grim (see, for example, Gunderson, 2007; Roessingh & Kover, 2003; Toohey & Derwing, 2008). However, given the location of Thompson Rivers University, the actual teacher candidates involved in my study will be most likely to teach students of Aboriginal ancestry. Sadly, the statistics for school completion rates for Aboriginal students are even worse (see, for example, Agbo, 2003; Schissel & Wotherspoon, 2003; Sterzuk, 2008).

In this chapter, I have focused on some of the historical picture books from the study; other books in the collection deal with contemporary issues of immigration. For example, *A New Home for Malik* (Steffen; *Stopper*, 2003) tells the story of a young boy who has just moved to Calgary from Sudan; written in four different languages, the book aims to help immigrant children adjust to their new country. Other books that deal with contemporary aspects of immigration include *Share the Sky* (Ye; *Langlois*, 1999), *From Far Away* (Munsch & Ascar; *Martchenko*, 1995) and *Courage to Fly* (Harrison; *Huang*, 2002). There are also books that look to Aboriginal language maintenance and revival, for example, Tomson Highway's *Songs of the North Wind* trilogy (*Deines*, 2001, 2002, 2003), written in both Cree and English, and *Someone Smaller than Me* (Cooper; *Padlo*, 1993), which was translated into Inuktitut. Hopefully, these books can play a role, however small, in repairing the damage to Aboriginal languages caused, in large part, by residential schooling.

As for the historical fiction books featured in this chapter, Galway (2008) draws attention to their significance:

> By choosing Canadian history as a subject and by claiming this past as their own, Canadian children's writers engage directly in the process of answering the questions, "Who are we?" "Where do we come from" and, by extension, "Where are we going?" By examining the past, by creating their own blend of historical fact and fiction, these writers engage in the process of envisioning Canada as a country with a unique history of which to be proud. What is more, they see the events of the past as part of a long journey of progress. (177)

This chapter has exposed much in our history of which Canadians should not be proud; at the same time, that there has been progress is clear. Whether that progress will continue will depend, increasingly, on the target readers for the picture books in our collection. Monica, who chose *Shi-shi-etko* to introduce the topic of residential schooling to students, clearly articulates how knowledge gained from the reading of such texts can be instrumental in the continuation of that long journey:

> With that knowledge, our students – the voices of tomorrow – will be more likely to ensure Aboriginal people receive that support into the future, even though residential schooling was not a direct part of their own social experience. This lesson gives students the opportunity to consider that, although they did not make the choices for the government and public of the time, social responsibility and social justice look to correct past wrongs, for Aboriginal communities and for others.

On that note, I will give the (almost) last word to Grant, an Aboriginal student in grade 4, *and* one of the voices of tomorrow. Along with his partner, Grant completed his Historica Fair project on Japanese internment; through their research, they linked Japanese internment camps and residential schools. I was able to pursue this in an interview with Grant: "Learning about the internment camp reminded me of when my great grandpa went to residential school in Kamloops when he was a kid. They [the Japanese] were taken away from their homes 'cause the government thought they were being a threat to them."

I asked Grant what difference students learning about the past could make to life today. His response: "If you bring stuff from the past to the future more people learn about it. And, in the future, they won't do the wrong things again." For Grant and the other students of his age, maybe *history will not repeat itself*. The phrase may be a cliché to some, but for the youth to whom this is a new, fresh, and not yet overused phrase, it can bring hope.

NOTES

1 In contrast to some of the other programs involved in our study, the selection criteria for applicants to TRU's BEd program were comprehensive: GPA, a written application, volunteer or paid work with children, reference letters, an interview with a panel, and a spontaneous writing task.
2 While there are legal and other differences associated with these terms, for the purpose of this chapter, the terms Aboriginal, First Nations, and native are used interchangeably. I will use the term that is most appropriate for the particular context that I am addressing.
3 Historica (or Heritage) Fair is a multimedia educational program developed to increase awareness and interest in Canadian history, unique community events, and family culture.
4 As part of a SSHRC-funded study, "Creating Third Spaces for Minority Language Learners in a School-University-Community Research Collaboration," teacher candidates from the TRU language and literacy course were paired with Aboriginal students in the band-operated school on the local reserve in a mentorship role to support students as they worked on their Historica Fair projects.
5 In actuality, "The Sixties Scoop" lasted for a period of twenty years.

4 Prairie Spaces Recreated: Aboriginal Education and Canadian Picture Books

ANGELA WARD

Communities are shaped in predictable ways by their natural environment. A river first connects and then, despite bridges and canoes, divides again. In the small prairie city that was one site for our national research study, the river marks boundaries between east and west, separates the university from "downtown," and becomes difficult for some to cross. In this city, schools with high proportions of Aboriginal students are on the "west side," but many of their teachers live on the "east side."

Beside the small town in British Columbia where I first taught, the river ran deep in its canyon, fast-flowing and clear, and Salish people still fished for salmon in its waters. It was here, forty years ago, that I encountered First Nations people, whose lives in school were difficult academically and socially, but who successfully maintained connections to the land through gathering local greens and berries, through fishing and hunting. Many of the children I taught knew how to prepare food from the land, but struggled with the world of school. I struggled, too, to find ways to support their learning and to understand community resistances to school. As I learned about residential school experiences, and looked at the school's basal readers (Mr Mugs and his suburban family) with critical eyes, I began a long journey in search of ways to bridge community and school for First Nations students. One of my initial tasks was to find materials where at the very least First Nations children could see themselves represented. I found a reading series that included First Nations legends and more current stories with photographs of children who looked like my students. I remember the day when those new books came to my grade 2 classroom – the students were enthralled to see themselves and their families reflected in the pictures: "He looks like Louie who lives by the railroad!" We had extended conversations about how the books were made, and the children reluctantly came to the conclusion that the photograph was not of Louie. It would be naive to believe that the materials themselves made a significant difference to the academic achievement of those children in British Columbia, but the books did open up conversations and engage my young students in ways I had not seen before.

"Aboriginal Education at the Heart of the College"

I came to the prairie university where I currently teach because the College of Education has a long-standing commitment to Aboriginal education. I did not realize at the time, however, that programs for First Nations and Métis teacher candidates run parallel to other programs, so chances to work together were limited, especially for non-Aboriginal faculty. The college has a strong commitment to "Aboriginal Education at the Heart of the College," but the separation of Aboriginal teacher candidates from those in other programs makes the fulfilment of this ideal a challenge. Program requirements for all teacher candidates are the same, but most Aboriginal teacher candidates are in a direct-entry program, meaning that they will spend two or three years in arts and sciences completing academic requirements, before fully entering the education program. They receive strong support from the Aboriginal-teacher education program staff as they take their academic coursework.

All teacher candidates at the college are required to come into the education program with at least two courses in native studies and then to take a cross-cultural, anti-oppression course as well. A significant number of non-Aboriginal teacher candidates have native studies as a major or minor area of study. Teacher candidates in the Aboriginal-teacher education program come with these formal requirements, but of course they have a wide range of personal and cultural experiences themselves. Some Cree, Dene, and Inuvialuit teacher candidates speak fluently in their mother tongues, while other First Nations and Métis teacher candidates have grown up in urban environments where they have been alienated from their cultural heritages. For them, the teacher education program is a chance to revitalize cultural knowledges and practices.

In addition, faculty and instructors in all programs are expected to "infuse" First Nation, Métis, and Inuit knowledges, perspectives, and world views into their courses. Given the wide range of faculty backgrounds, this does not always translate into a consistent focus on

Aboriginal education. Field experiences are also likely to challenge the emphasis on "Aboriginal education at the heart of the college." Westside city schools often enrol many Aboriginal students (close to 100 per cent in some instances), but many teacher candidates have rural placements where there are no Aboriginal students at all. In addition, some teachers who take on our interns resist the infusion of Aboriginal knowledges and perspectives into their teaching, despite curriculum guides that explicitly require it.

Many teacher candidates who participated in the study described in this book demonstrated a strong desire to develop school approaches that encouraged their students to respect diversity and become knowledgeable about First Nations history and traditions. As I talked with teacher candidates I came to recognize the range of knowledge and commitment to Aboriginal education that was evident in both First Nations and non-Aboriginal teacher candidates. It was a good reminder to avoid dualism, however difficult that may be in the context of a political and social system that divides us along cultural lines. There was a continuum of experiences, knowledge, and attitudes towards Aboriginal content and perspectives that blurred boundaries between teacher candidates, whatever their background. There are potential dangers in "hybridity" as a concept explaining this range of experiences (Bradford, 2007); the idea of an interspace between worlds can still keep those worlds separated and distinct and "susceptible to collapsing back into the binaries of colonial discourse" (64). There are questions, too, as to whether schools can do the work of decolonization, since most school experiences are representational rather than contextualized in an environment where Aboriginal ways of knowing are evident. To wrestle with understanding what decolonized schools might look like is to take on difficult knowledge and challenging practice.

The Study

In the prairie context of this study, there were five groups who participated in the workshop and filled out the survey. Since I was not teaching any of these teacher candidates, I was not able to have them implement an explicit lesson planning activity, and so did not know them well as individuals. However, I did carry out focus group and individual interviews with a number of teacher candidates after their internship (sixteen weeks of practice teaching). I had asked all the workshop groups to indicate on their surveys whether they would be interested in participating in follow-up interviews after their practical experiences in schools. Only about twenty-five indicated interest, and of those, eighteen teacher candidates participated in focus groups and twelve in individual interviews. The "conversation starter" questions can be found at the end of this chapter. Several participants were so engaged in what became, in some instances, a "debriefing" process, that we had two one-hour conversations. The interviews provided particularly rich data on teacher candidates' experiences with infusing diverse literature and Aboriginal perspectives and content into their teaching practice, as well as their developing insights into their own identities as teachers for social justice.

Workshop and Survey

I gave the workshop on using diverse picture books and the subsequent survey to two groups of secondary teacher candidates (thirty in each group) who were taking a required "literacy across the curriculum course." These participants were from all subject areas, including practical and applied arts and fine arts. The other workshop groups included one elementary education group (taking a required language arts class), one First Nations group, and one group from the urban Aboriginal program (mainly Métis teacher candidates). I will provide a short summary of the survey findings, highlighting interesting contrasts between the groups.

Despite having taken a children's literature course, very few teacher candidates seemed familiar with Canadian authors other than Robert Munsch. The participants were aware of critical approaches to looking at illustrations and text, and the majority noted stereotyping of First Nations in dress and activity, as well as omission or lack of representation. Many of the participants' "favourite" authors seemed to come from early experiences (Lucy Maud Montgomery, Gordon Korman) rather than from more formal introductions in the teacher education program. All participants understood the value of using Canadian picture books in their teaching (although, to be honest, those planning on teaching woodwork and other practical and applied arts had more difficulty in seeing the relevance of picture books). In general, teacher candidates thought the books were more relevant to their students' lives, offered diverse perspectives, and *might* represent Canadian First Nations peoples more accurately. Teacher candidates expressed the desire that students should be exposed to books from other countries as well, and suggested that teachers need to be alert to the possibilities of stereotyping that might occur.

The survey responses were most revealing on questions of Canadian identity. The non-Aboriginal teacher candidates were more likely than their First Nation peers to respond to "What does Canadian identity mean to you" with familiar words and phrases:

Multiculturalism, diversity
Pride in being Canadian
Respect, acceptance, tolerance, freedom

However, some non-Aboriginal respondents indicated that being "Canadian" meant something beyond the platitudes. A number of non-Aboriginal teacher candidates recognized that Canadian identities are developed in a country where "First Nations people face harassment and discrimination" and that "Canada is a country of inequality."

There were thoughtful personal comments such as: "Sometimes I have mixed feelings about my Canadian identity. It isn't an identity that followed its own course. It is an identity forced onto Aboriginal people." Or "Canadian identity is who I am. It means being proud to be from this wonderfully diverse country. However, I think that despite our pride in being diverse, 'Canadian identity' is largely decided upon by mainstream, white, Canada."

There was also some agreement that immigrants might appreciate Canada more than those born here, and be more passionate and patriotic.

Responses from the Métis teacher candidates indicated more of their own struggles for identity, perhaps depending on their degree of direct ancestry from First Nations peoples. One telling comment was, "People with Aboriginal ancestry are considered Canadian 'citizens plus.'" It was impossible to tell from the written comment whether it was meant in a positive or negative way. This group also noted that in the picture books we presented, ethnic and cultural groups, especially First Nations, were most often portrayed as living lives separate from other groups. This would, of course, directly contradict the experiences of many Métis teacher candidates, whose families (like those of First Nations peoples as well) wove together traditions across many boundaries. I had not been particularly struck by this until I read the survey comment, and then realized that many books I've been using do paint a picture of parallel worlds. In addition, authors (both Aboriginal and non-Aboriginal) are forced into "using the language of the colonizers to construct Indigenous narratives and meanings" (Bradford, 2007, 69); this co-opts writers into continuing the anomalies and discontinuities between the "two worlds."

The Indian Teacher Education Program began in response to the beginnings of "Indian control of Indian education" in the early 1970s. Although its radical roots are now deep, and perhaps less evident in some ways, the program still has a strong political agenda, and works hard to redress the social and educational fallout from colonization and in particular the damage to families caused by residential schools. Many graduates from the program teach in First Nations schools, and hopefully take their revitalized sense of pride in culture and language with them into the classroom. It is not surprising, then, that teacher candidates from this group were very aware of the political aspects of Canadian identity. The First Nations respondents to the survey were quite direct:

> The First Nations were the first to walk on this land and they know it more deeply.

> All our political powers are white and I've learned more and more about the under-representation of minority groups.

> My sense is that Canada believes that we are all in search of certain justices, but only as long as it is not too uncomfortable.

A number of First Nations teacher candidates considered that Canadian identity included only white middle-class people, an identity imposed by the government. However, there was some powerful evidence that First Nations participants had pride in being "original Canadians," having treaty rights, and inhabiting the place where their ancestors had lived and hunted. Several also noted that their own idea of identity was dynamic and still developing.

Troubling Canadian Identities

The structures imposed by colonization and settlement in Canada support racial, ethnic, and cultural identities as an important factor in deciding on funding for education, health, housing and other essential services for First Nations, Métis, and Inuit people. Rules about who is "Indian" or not have caused immense suffering and family division that continue for First Nations and Métis peoples today. A cumbersome bureaucracy still takes responsibility for many decisions about First Nations, Métis, and Inuit peoples before funding is devolved to provincial and community levels. The political structures in Canada support the idea of Aboriginal identity as fixed and easily recognizable. It is little wonder, then, that teacher candidates from all backgrounds in Saskatchewan found it difficult to think about "Canadian identities" without some discomfort. These tensions are reflected in the work of both Aboriginal and non-Aboriginal scholars reflecting on identity issues.

Eigenbrod (2005) draws on other scholars' metaphors of identity as hybrid, and always in transition, and uses Richard Wagamese's narrative voice (from *Keeper'n Me*, 2006 [1994]) to illustrate this: "The truth is that most of us are movin' between Indyuns. Movin' between our jobs and the sweat lodge. Movin' between school and pow wow. Movin' between English and Anishnabe. Movin' between both worlds. Movin' between 1990 and 1490. Most of us are the kinda Indyun" (137).

Identity in this view is always performative for all of us (Bhabha, 1994); situated in different contexts, we enact and understand our identities as they relate to the people and the environment in which we find ourselves. I construct myself differently as a university teacher than as a family member, and as well my identity as a member of the university has changed over the nineteen years I've worked as an academic. Age, experience, and confidence account for some of the ways in which identity shifts, but the perceptions of others are especially powerful in how we construct our own identities. A postmodern perspective theorizes multiple identities constructed through multiple contexts and reinforced through multiple stories (Sfard & Prusak, 2005). The stories may be told by the participant, to the participant, or about the participant in such a way that identity as "a good student" becomes a co-construction of parents, teachers, peers, and self. In this view, there may be a core identity, but "all people have multiple identities connected not to their 'internal states' but to their performance in society" (Gee, 2001, 99). A dialogical view of the self (Bakhtin, 1981) argues that the self is not separate from social relationships; hence, there is no single life story, but rather a landscape occupied by sometimes conflicting narratives (Raggatt, 2006). The First Nations, Métis, and non-Aboriginal participants in this study understood Canadian identity as a contested term, but could not easily articulate their own involvement in boundary making and boundary crossing. In practice, though, many of the non-Aboriginal teacher candidates worked actively in their field-experience internships to support students' understandings of First Nations content, perspectives, and ways of knowing. Their stories will be explored later in the chapter.

Diversity Education in Theory

In Canada, First Nations peoples have resisted inclusion in a multiculturalism implied by the "mosaic" metaphor. First Nations are moving towards "the recognition of our inherent right of self-government" (Fontaine, 1999, ix), through treaty rights and new agreements with federal and provincial governments. The special status of First Nations peoples in Canada has resulted in educational research literature that focuses specifically on "Aboriginal education." In my teaching career of over thirty years there have been evolving perspectives on teaching Aboriginal students, all of which were well intentioned and assumed to support students' academic achievements. During the 1970s, the deficit discourse about Aboriginal students was still prevalent, with teachers being urged to use more structured materials to support core skills in language and mathematics (for example, DISTAR – Direct Instruction System in Arithmetic and Reading), whereby students were expected to repeat sentence constructions and respond rapidly to teachers' questions. The materials were used for any students considered "at risk," which usually meant children from minority groups.

In response to this draconian and limiting approach, a number of ethnographic researchers in the 1980s spent extensive periods of time observing and participating in Aboriginal community life. Aboriginal students' interaction patterns were described as "culturally different" language use. In her landmark study, Philips (1983) carried out research into discourse patterns of Warm Springs children at home and at school, and found that school-talk conventions constrained Aboriginal students from participating in classroom discourse. At home and in the community, however, the children were lively and communicative. My own work on teacher-led discussions between Aboriginal and non-Aboriginal children in a kindergarten classroom (Ward, 1989) showed that the rules (spoken and unspoken) of typical classroom participant structures reduced Aboriginal children's capacity to contribute to discussion. Similarly, findings from the Kamehameha project in Hawaii (Au & Kawakami, 1994) suggested that changing classroom discourse structures (more exploratory, small-group discussions) would increase Indigenous students' participation and learning. Concurrently with this approach, many teachers of Aboriginal children sought out, as I did, books and other materials that represented Aboriginal peoples in the late twentieth century.

The last decade of the twentieth century muted the discussion of "difference" located within First Nations, Métis, and Inuit students, and took a broader sociological view of the effects of colonization on Aboriginal peoples. Aboriginal scholars (Cajete, 1994) wrote about their own explorations of Aboriginal content, perspectives, and ways of knowing; traditional knowledge, as embodied in elders, was sought by educational institutions. Non-Aboriginal teachers, and those Aboriginal teachers whose experience of traditional world views was limited, expressed concerns when asked to infuse Aboriginal material into their programs. Fears about stepping into spiritual areas sensitive for First Nations peoples were well grounded, and teachers heard (and still hear) contradictory messages about their role in Aboriginal education.

These concerns were real for all the participants in this study. Issues of authenticity, even for Aboriginal teacher candidates, can be a source of conflict and self-doubt. Verna St Denis, an Aboriginal scholar, has come to the somewhat controversial conclusion that "some of the efforts Aboriginal people have made towards cultural revitalization may not always be as liberating and healing as they were intended to be" (2007, 1075). Some Aboriginal people may come to be regarded as "more authentic" than others, with a resulting double marginalization of Aboriginal people who do not possess traditional knowledge. St Denis notes that, although some individuals and communities have benefited from the cultural revitalization movement, many Aboriginal people still experience poverty and marginalization. The movement to cultural revitalization has had some unintended side-effects – "it has both a positive and negative potential – it can create a positive sense of identity and common cause, but it also applauds some and discounts others" (2007, 1079). St Denis suggests that cultural revitalization is not enough to address the racism experienced daily by Aboriginal people, and puts too much pressure on some Aboriginal people to change yet again. She believes, based on her experience teaching preservice teachers, that anti-racist education is a crucial and powerful strategy for societal change.

Aboriginal content, perspectives, and ways of knowing are currently emphasized in the prairie education system (in both schools and the University of Saskatchewan College of Education) from which these study participants came. Teachers at all levels are expected to include units of study that focus on First Nations, Métis, and Inuit history and experiences, as well as to use Aboriginal resources, including picture books, wherever possible. The reality is that such implementation is sporadic and often confined to schools with significant populations of Aboriginal students. So teacher candidates going out into schools were frequently disappointed to find that their enthusiasm for Aboriginal education initiatives was not shared by cooperating teachers.

As Claire Bradford (2007) describes, non-Aboriginal people mostly learn about Aboriginal people through representations (for example, books and materials), not through relationships (10). This was certainly the case for the non-Aboriginal teachers in this study, who were part of parallel, rarely intersecting, programs of preservice education. So, despite worthy intentions, the interning teachers continued to carry "representations" of Aboriginal histories and cultures into their teaching activities, with occasional visits from elders or Aboriginal consultants if they were especially fortunate. Perhaps more optimistically, these school experiences could be considered a site for "transculturation" (Pratt, 1992) or the "contact zone" for developing at least some cultural knowledge.

Diversity Education in Practice

Many of the twelve non-Aboriginal preservice teachers who participated in focus groups and interviews following their sixteen-week internship were committed to the ideals of social justice and the decolonization of Canadian education. They would have known me in a general way as someone in the College of Education who was committed to Aboriginal education and anti-racist pedagogies. Clearly the teacher candidates who volunteered for the focus groups and interviews wished to share with me their hopes and disappointments in implementing the ideals fostered in their college coursework and our study workshop. The participants' background in native studies, and the course they had all taken in cross-cultural, anti-racist education, prepared them to examine their field experiences with a critical eye. Theories of situated learning (Wenger, 1998b) suggest that classroom contexts would have a powerful effect on preservice teachers as they attempt to put into practice what they believe about teaching and learning. The volunteers for the study came into it with positive intentions to disrupt racist thinking and to provide their students with more information about First Nations history and current experiences. A strong feature of the interviews and group discussion was the participants' critical reflection on negative experiences in their own lives, imagining their future students having more open and respectful relationships with Aboriginal peoples.

Probably because of the anti-racism course, discussion of their own white privilege and lack of experience with First Nations communities was evident in their early discussions:

> I grew up in a white society, and didn't realize about white privilege.

> It's difficult to face these things because as white people we come from the dominant culture … Your first reaction is to think, well no, I'm worth something and this power that I have hasn't just been handed over to me, I've had to earn it.

It was common for the participants to have grown up in small rural communities or in the suburbs of the university town. Some reflected on the attitudes prevalent when they were growing up.

> But as far as diversity [goes], I don't remember anybody who wasn't white in my classes ever. I remember there was an apartment building at the end of our block and there was a native family in there and it was just "That's the native family, leave them alone."

> I could see there was a great deal of segregation among the students.

> I grew up in an extremely diversified area, but along with that came a lot of clashes. We clashed with the Aboriginals, we clashed with this other group – there was a lot of clashing going on. So now I have a sort of defence mechanism that goes up.

Their own school experiences didn't reflect the social consciousness they had come to espouse:

> I come from a place where there is a high percentage of First Nations people and I don't remember in high school any kind of ceremony or activity or anything put on by the school to highlight First Nations culture or beliefs. I do remember taking some First Nations history out of a textbook, but it was fairly stereotypical.

One teacher candidate had a more memorable experience:

> I do remember in grade 4 learning about First Nations culture and history in Social Studies. We went out to a buffalo jump, tipi rings, we went to a

buffalo farm. We were learning about First Nations people and it was kind of interesting. I remember asking my dad, "Why did we just come here and take the land?" and my dad's answer was probably like anybody's answer who was born in the 50s and raised in the 60s ... "Well because they weren't doing anything with the land."

Once they arrived at university, non-Aboriginal teacher candidates valued courses that gave them historical information from a different perspective: "I came to university and took a native studies class – I had never heard of a residential school." Although the cross-cultural anti-racism course was challenging for many non-Aboriginal teacher candidates, those in this study found it transformative.

The whole class we talked about identity, construction of power, whiteness and the construction of whiteness. I still couldn't give you a definition of Canadian identity ... I don't know if anybody can. What I have come to the realization of in the last 8 months is how much of our Canadian identity is based on a constructed truth that isn't necessarily real.

Participants took a critical view of schools' implementation of Aboriginal education before they went out to do their final internship:

It seems like we only talk about the fun stuff: the powwows, and the ceremonies. We don't talk about the discriminatory laws, we don't talk about the residential schools. The white society is culpable for what happened to First Nations, and we don't talk about it because somehow, that would be bad.

This level of thoughtful critique was quite evident in the focus group with secondary teacher candidates:

So in terms of multiculturalism, I think we sometimes skirt the idea of racism and talk about culture. So I think there are some incidences of hidden curriculum and what I am conveying to my students when I think I'm being diverse and inclusive, but I may actually be overstepping something. So I think I would have never thought of that before coming to the College. There are only 15% of students who go to university and 85% of those who don't go may not be aware of this type of thinking.

Participants in the study went out to their assigned schools with a critical understanding of social-justice issues, some knowledge of multicultural and Aboriginal knowledges, and appropriate pedagogical approaches and materials, and also some apprehensions about what they would find. Perhaps one of the most difficult challenges for me and for the idealistic teacher candidates was to maintain a professional attitude towards some of the challenges they had faced in working with teachers in their schools who were sceptical about infusing Aboriginal content, perspectives, and ways of knowing into curricula. In all our conversations we tried hard to not "blame" individuals, and to think more broadly about systemic constraints and issues in the schools.

Field Experiences

Social attitudes in local communities intensified concerns about some of the schools where teacher candidates were placed for internship. This was commented on quite directly by participants in the study:

> My student teaching was at N——. It was a great experience. Everyone was scared that I was going there. They were telling me that I should ask for a different placement. I've heard other people talk about classroom management … our only problem was kids not coming to class. When they were there, they were participating and they did well.

There were initial concerns from two or three teacher candidates about being placed in "west side" schools, but in all cases, the participants were surprised that the schools were orderly and the students respectful and open. The secondary participants were quite creative in the ways they incorporated First Nations resources, including picture books, into their teaching. One used Robert Munsch and Michael Kusugak's *A Promise Is a Promise* (*Krykorka*, 1988) as the basis for a dance drama with grade 9 students in a physical education class. An intern in the visual arts area took George Littlechild's illustrations for *A Man Called Raven* (Van Camp, 1997) as the starting point for a stencil-making activity. She connected this activity with First Nations legends on finding a "helping spirit" and had students design and stencil their own guiding animal. For this beginning art teacher, "All of my art projects were about identity and social consciousness." She took her students to exhibitions of local First Nations artists, and explored art through books and other visual resources. As one might expect, her understanding of visual literacy was profound. "One thing I like about First Nations art is that the orientation of the page isn't necessarily significant and that images seem to continue right off the page. That's something that maybe we could learn from." We spent some time in her interview looking at illustrations in books from the project. Here is part of our conversation about *Shi-shi Etko* (Campbell; *La Fave*, 2005):

ANGELA: I wonder about the particular issues we've talked about, those very
   romanticized sorts of images. Part of me doesn't know how to feel about that.
ELAINE: It's actually the story of a young girl who's saying good-bye to her parents as she is going to a residential school but we don't know really until the
   end of the story that that is what is happening to her. What she's doing is going around and collecting memories to help her remember her world, so the
   pictures are quite beautiful, it's quite romanticized, as is the story, but it looks
   to me like that is the truth. This is a remembrance. In some of these images it
   looks like there's somebody higher up looking down to see what's happening. Almost kind of disconnected from it. But there's some sort of ownership
   of it. It's lovingly done. But I see the glow gives it that romantic style.

Elaine's heightened awareness of the visual world, along with her social consciousness, made her exceptional in this group of interns. She demonstrated her commitment to support students in thinking deeply about First Nations issues, using art as a "way in." Many study partici-pants were creative in how they fulfilled their responsibility to incor-porate multicultural and First Nations perspectives into the classroom.

In general, interns in elementary school settings had more freedom to incorporate First Nations and multicultural materials and approaches in their internship classrooms than those in secondary schools. They were often disappointed that there were few existing Aboriginal mate-rials in the schools, and sometimes felt that cooperating teachers were relying on them to do the "Aboriginal unit." Julie believed that her cooperating teacher expected her to do this, but felt that, although this was not an ideal way to deal with First Nations content, a complete unit allowed her to build her students' background understanding of Cree people. She worked with her class on treaty rights and responsibilities, and attempted to create a space where First Nations ways of knowing were respected: "I gathered First Nation artefacts from the university here and we passed them around. I didn't do it as a talking circle just because I found that Grade 1 weren't talking a lot. So I brought in arte-facts so students could look at them and say anything that they wanted to about them." Julie also used books from our project as artefacts in her sharing circle.

This sense of creating a space for First Nations cultural knowledge within the classroom was carried out more completely by Karen, who was an intern in a grade 4 classroom. Karen's international travel experiences had given her an openness to others' beliefs. "We started the morning with circles and just giving thanks. Not really being or doing anything that would be religiously compromised, but just that we all are part of the circle, no one's above, no one's below, we all have a place and if somebody's missing the circle is not complete." In a sense, Karen attempted a "mini-immersion" experience for her students. She wanted to share what she had come to understand as a non–First Nations person. "Because I feel enlightened by my university experience and I feel that I need to communicate that education to the kids so that they can take it home."

She also took very seriously the idea of infusing First Nations content into her teaching, and so incorporated traditional uses of plants into her biology unit (talking about the origin of aspirin, for example). Karen actually brought birch logs into the classroom so she and her students could sit around the "fire" and have conversations! In those conversations the class discussed Cree history and what happened when settlers came. They also shared *Caribou Song* (Highway; *Dienes*, 2001) and *Fox on the Ice* (Highway; *Dienes*, 2003) and retold these stories around the "fire." Karen used these books for further discussion:

> They'd read them and we would talk about the morals and why the story was written. We would talk about the purpose of storytelling in cultures, especially in First Nations cultures, and that it would be done during the winter because First Nations people would be busy in the summer preparing for winter and doing other things. I also had them draw a picture of where the story might be taking place.

Karen also used First Nations content when she read aloud to her grade 4 students. In a semi-humorous way she commented: "If I'd had another four months ... we would have gotten to the 1885 rebellion. But we talked about the Métis sash and we used books called *The Red Sash* [Pendziwol; *Debon*, 2005] and *Thomas and the Metis Sash* [Murray; *Dawson*, 2004], and we talked about them and the meanings and the various uses of the belt. The kids all really got into that."

For the beginning teachers in this project, the books we had used in the workshop became a starting point for more ambitious explorations of Aboriginal knowledge and perspectives. Some participants certainly used a wide range of the diverse books I had introduced, but the program emphasis on infusing First Nations content, and the provincial context, was most evident in the instructional choices they made.

Re-envisioning Places and Spaces

Vistas of the Canadian prairies suffuse the identities of those who live here, both Aboriginal and settler peoples. Rocks and grasslands, coulees and rivers, all permeate the imaginations of the Canadian preservice teachers in this study. But these are treaty lands, places lost to some groups and claimed by others, so identity is intricately bound with contested space and with guilt about its occupation. In responding to the study questions about Canadian identity, Aboriginal preservice teachers clearly saw themselves as different, original Canadians, while Métis participants had a more complex understanding of living together with family members from both Aboriginal and settler backgrounds. Non-Aboriginal survey respondents were most likely to take the official Canadian view of multiculturalism as an unalloyed good, but those who later volunteered to participate in focus groups and interviews were clearly conscious of their ancestors' colonizing role, and of their own complicity in sustaining it. Many tried valiantly in their field experiences to reconstruct spaces in their classrooms where students from all backgrounds could learn more about First Nations histories, and come to value art and stories from Cree, Dene, and Métis artists.

A troubling sense of "home" is interrogated by Wolf and DePasquale (2008), who describe the idyllic and historical focus of some Aboriginal picture books. *Shi-shi Etko* (Campbell; *LaFave*, 2005) is one example of a romantic portrayal of memory that was especially appealing to the non-Aboriginal teachers in this study. The concept of "home," according to Wolf and DePasquale, is constructed differently in Aboriginal cultures, not as a building owned and buttressed against the world, but as multilayered connections between the land, animals, and extended kinship networks. Wolf and DePasquale (2008) believe that Aboriginal picture books for children should evoke the difficult history of colonization, along with "challenges to the idea of the bourgeois family" (104). This overt politicization was somewhat evident in the practices of the interns in this study.

In fact, despite their own justified concerns about appropriation of First Nation, Métis, and Inuit knowledges, the non-Aboriginal teacher candidates in this group were attempting to decolonize education.

They were certainly using picture books to initiate activities in some decolonizing approaches suggested by Iseke-Barnes (2008): decolonizing history, reconnecting to land, and "looking to Indigenous artists, activists, and scholars" to honour cultural knowledges. Clearly these efforts were not "authentic" in drawing directly on deep First Nations traditional and spiritual knowledge. But the creative ways in which interns drew on their knowledge of Aboriginal history, and the sharing of books and stories written by First Nations, Métis, and Inuit authors, enabled them to at least begin to act on their consciousness of social injustice. Although the classroom experiences were a pale representation of cultural activities experienced on the land in authentic settings, they provided a glimpse into a world that many non-Aboriginal teachers have not yet dared to explore. The books and materials from the workshops gave the preservice teachers a "safe" place to begin this exploration. In the best of decolonized educational worlds, these beginning teachers would be teaching an anti-racist curriculum alongside Aboriginal colleagues and experiencing the natural world together with their students, while exploring different perspectives and world views. Until that world evolves, we must make sure that our preservice teachers, in Elaine's words, understand that "it's not just posters on the wall, or books on the shelf, but the need to demonstrate wisdom and respect" for peoples who share the land and cross the river together.

Initial Questions for Post-Practicum Interviews

1 Tell me about your own background – where you grew up.
2 Please describe the diversity of the classrooms where you were educated.
3 What drew you into teaching?
4 What grade level(s)/classes were you teaching in your student teaching?
5 In your student teaching experience, what was the composition of your class in terms of multicultural diversity?
6 What materials did you use? Did you use any picture books or see them used? In what contexts?
7 What teaching strategies and opportunities for learning did you implement?
8 How did the students respond?
9 Describe their understandings of "Canadian identity"?

10 How did your cooperating teacher incorporate multicultural material in his/her literacy program or other content areas?
11 Did s/he use picture books? In what ways did s/he use them?
12 What emphasis did s/he place on critical literacy? Give me an example.
13 How has your understanding of "Canadian identity" changed since you entered the teacher education program? What brought about the changes?
14 How has your understanding of "multiculturalism" and "diversity" changed since you came into the program?
15 How might the following be strengthened/revised to better prepare you for addressing diversity through the use of multicultural/diverse children's picture books: workshop? lesson plan assignment? the course?
16 Which courses in your BEd program have prepared you for teaching in diverse classroom environments? In what ways?
17 Would you deliberately set out to choose to teach in a school with a diverse population of students? Why or why not?
18 What links do you see between the theory and activities presented in the college and your experience in the school?
19 What disconnects do you see?
20 What is needed to help schools become more responsive to diversity?

5 Imagining the Possibilities: The Pedagogical Potential of Diverse Canadian Picture Books

MARY CLARE COURTLAND AND ISMEL GONZÁLEZ

Assembled on a table adorned with a Hudson Bay blanket were picture books authored by Jean Pendziwol as well as artefacts related to *The Red Sash*, a picture book that celebrates the rendezvous of voyageurs and gentlemen in Fort William. Jean invited volunteers to handle or wear artefacts as she explained their roles in the fur trade – a gentleman's top hat, a beaver pelt, a tin cup, and a red sash. As Jean explained the history of the North West Company, she pointed to a map of the trade routes. History came alive as our visiting author read *The Red Sash* to teacher candidates and faculty.

The Red Sash (Pendziwol; *Debon*, 2005) and *Dawn Watch* (Pendziwol; *Debon*, 2004) are works of art. They are especially poignant to those of us who live in Thunder Bay, the home of historical Fort William, and to those who have witnessed the majesty of Lake Superior, the body of water in *Dawn Watch* over which a little girl and her father sail through the night, into the faint dawn.

Canadian children, youth, and teens need to see themselves in the literature they read and to have opportunities to learn about and come to value and respect all Canadians. Picture books are a powerful resource for introducing students of all ages to concepts and issues related to Canadian identity, multiculturalism, diversity, and social justice. The intricate relations between text and illustrations speak to the essence of a theme. Picture books offer readers many experiences and touch them in different ways. Seeing themselves in books validates children's identities. Picture books may inspire, amuse, inform, and evoke deep interpersonal and intertextual connections; they may disrupt our beliefs or problematize an issue.

Figure 4. Author Jean Pendziwol reading aloud *The Red Sash* (Pendziwol and Debon, 2004)

This chapter describes the findings at one site through an analysis of the lesson plans developed by teacher candidates. Below we review related literature on teacher education. We then describe the site-specific context for the study. Next we present the two themes that emerged from the data analysis: "conceptualizing multiculturalism and diversity," and "pedagogical understandings." The discussion addresses the implications of the findings for literacy teacher educators.

Teacher Education

Professional development occurs over time and may be conceptualized as a continuum beginning with preservice preparation and continuing through the early and later years of teaching (Darling-Hammond, 2006; Feiman-Nemser, 2001; Liston, Whitcomb, & Borko, 2006). Teacher candidates bring with them to their preservice experiences personal and cultural assumptions and beliefs they have formed through their own experiences, particularly their experiences with schooling (Darling-Hammond, 2006; Grossman et al., 2000; Harste et al., 2004; Kosnik & Beck, 2009). Phillips and Larson (2009) note that family dispositions to literacy also influence teacher candidates' views of literacy teaching and learning. Beliefs also include teacher candidates' and practising teachers' understandings about multiculturalism and diversity (Brindley & Laframboise, 2002; Ndura, 2004),

There is a general agreement among scholars of teacher education (Darling-Hammond, 2006; Feiman-Nemser, 2001; Liston, Whitcomb, & Borko, 2006) that the preservice program should enable students to analyse their existing beliefs in particular, and construct new visions; develop subject-matter knowledge; develop a beginning repertoire of approaches and strategies; develop the tools to study teaching and learning; and apply appropriate strategies to resolve problems. Kosnik and Beck (2009) have developed a set of seven priorities for teacher education: "program planning; pupil assessment; classroom organization and community; inclusive education; subject content and pedagogy; professional identity; and a vision for teaching" (ix). While Kosnik and Beck do not elaborate on teacher beliefs, their priorities emphasize inclusive education broadly defined to address "a large set of concepts: equity, social justice, respect for difference, multiculturalism, anti-racism, academic mainstreaming, and so on" (87). Their emphases on inclusion as well as recognition of the need to go beyond the skills of classroom management to classroom organization and community represent a major step forward for conceptualizing the foci of preservice preparation.

A number of researchers argue that teachers need to explore and understand their own cultural identities in order to develop an understanding and an appreciation of their students' diverse cultural backgrounds (Bérci, 2007; Davis et al., 2008; Lee & Dallman, 2008; Ndura, 2004; Santoro, 2009). For example, Santoro (2009) conducted a qualitative study on eight preservice teachers' classroom interactions with culturally diverse students. She was interested in exploring how preservice teachers understood their own and their students' identities as constituted through and by ethnicity and socio-economic class. She found that participants possessed limited knowledge about their students' ethnic identities. This limitation was based on the preservice teachers' static assumptions about culture. The participants believed that students from particular ethnic backgrounds had predetermined dispositions towards schooling and, as such, would conform to certain cultural expectations. Santoro notes that such a perception of students' dispositions "constructs the students ... and the way they've been brought up as *the* problem and places the blame on the students and their families" (37). Santoro suggests that this perception has contributed to preservice teachers' lack of reflection on their own practices and conceptions of the "other," thus contributing to the marginalization of students of diverse ethnic backgrounds in the schools. She maintains that teacher education programs should provide preservice teachers with opportunities to develop knowledge about themselves at the same time as they develop knowledge about the "other": "Teachers need to come to know themselves as ethnic and encultured if they are to understand their students and engage with the complexities of teaching for diversity. This means understanding how their own ethnic identities shape teaching identities, their classroom practices and their relationships with students" (41).

Research conducted over the past twenty years suggests that teachers' knowledge and skill in working with culturally and linguistically diverse students may impact student success positively or negatively. Ladson-Billings (1995a, 1995b) and Gay (2000) note that when teachers understand students' cultural backgrounds and their own, and use these characteristics as strengths to build upon, then the students' own identities are validated and they are more likely to succeed. Further, they suggest that teachers who understand their students' cultural backgrounds and their own, are better able to design instruction that best meets their students' needs.

One approach that has been developed in response to the needs of children and youth of varying racial or ethnic backgrounds is *culturally relevant pedagogy*, a term coined by Ladson-Billings (1997), who defines it as "an approach to teaching and learning that empowers students intellectually, socially, emotionally, and politically by using cultural referents to impart/knowledge, skills and attitudes" (62). A related approach is *culturally responsive curriculum*, defined as one that "benefits all children to make learning more meaningful" (Bergeron, 2008, 7). This approach respects and responds to students' home cultures and strives to promote each child's achievement. A culturally relevant pedagogy adopts a social justice stance; a culturally responsive pedagogy might be compared to differentiated instruction, wherein each student's instruction is responsive to his/her needs. A concern which the authors of this chapter hold about current definitions about culturally relevant and culturally responsive approaches is that, while they are critical to the nurturing and development of students' identities and success, all Canadian children should have opportunities to learn about and consider Canadian multiculturalism, diversity, and social justice. Thus, we endorse the concept of a culturally relevant pedagogy that is inclusive of Canadian diversity and social justice.

Recently literacy scholars have investigated the potential of children's literature to promote teacher candidates' and practising teachers' understandings of multiculturalism, diversity, and social justice. Brindley and Laframboise (2002), instructors of children's literature, investigated how the use of diverse children's and juvenile literature challenged their students to "experience the cognitive dissonance necessary to re-examine their cultural beliefs" (405–406). Drama was the medium for engagement and response. The researchers note that the use of diverse texts provided a vehicle that allowed teacher candidates to explore their personal beliefs from a safe distance. They found that the issues raised in the books promoted participants' discomfort, and their enactment of these themes and issues through drama increased participants' sensitivity and capacity for self-analysis and reflection.

Dong (2005) notes that teachers are often resistant to incorporating diverse literature into their teaching because of their perceived inadequacies:

> They fear that their unfamiliarity with the literature about or by people from other cultures may reinforce stereotypes. They wonder whether their students can handle racial and cultural issues with maturity and respect. They are afraid that the racial tension imbued in these works may divide rather than unite a class whose students are increasingly culturally and linguistically diverse. (368)

Dong contends that introducing multicultural literature to preservice and inservice teachers "involves transforming their attitudes or orientations, as well as their methods of exploring the issues of culture, race, and diverse voices in multicultural literature and moving these issues and voices to the centre of discussions and reflections" (368). She designed a study grounded in reader response and cultural response approaches in which her participants were secondary English teachers enrolled in a multicultural literature course.

Dong initially asked the teachers to explain how their own cultural perspectives influenced their reading of two novels. While she found that many were aware of the impact of their points of view on their interpretations, she was surprised by some teachers' "denial of the cultural impact" (371). Students then participated in book club discussions about their selected novels. She explains that when students did research about the author and the cultural perspectives raised in the book, some students experienced a self-transformation: "They moved from avoiding a discussion on cultural differences to openly accepting their own ignorance and recognizing a need to learn more about other cultures" (375). In the third phase of her study, Dong asked each student to implement one multicultural text with his/her own class. She found the strategy successful with most of the students in promoting their cross-cultural understandings. She notes that in contrast to the role of "expert" that teachers may hold when teaching canonical literature, the use of more diverse literature changes this dynamic in that the students may be the cultural insiders where the teachers may be outsiders.

Dion (2007) notes that teachers deny knowledge of Aboriginals, thus positioning themselves in the role of "perfect stranger" (330). She has developed a strategy entitled "critical pedagogy of remembrance" (330) based upon her research with practising teacher candidates. The strategy, which she has used with graduate students involves juxtaposing artists, authors, filmmakers, and others with the texts of students' lived experiences. The assignment, a "File of un(certainties)" (339), "allows students a forum for investigating the biography of their relationship with Aboriginal people [and] provides a means of investigating their own investments in dominant discourses and supports the possibility of affecting a change in their ways of knowing and their ways of teaching" (339–40).

Like Dong, Howrey, and Whelan-Kim (2009) conducted a study to investigate how a multicultural children's literature project supported early childhood teacher candidates' understanding of culturally responsive teaching. The thirty-eight participants read ten picture books and novels representative of cultural groups located in the vicinity of the university. Participants were asked to prepare a poster presentation and book talk, as well as an individual two-page reflection paper, and to respond to an anonymous survey. The researchers found that teaching multicultural children's literature enabled participants to identify more closely with people of cultures other than their own. While there were differences in participants' individual reflections of what they had learned, overall they developed the following understandings: "awareness of teaching materials and culturally specific learning differences, an increase in their own personal cultural knowledge, and a commitment to foster cultural competence in children, build a classroom community and teach for social justice" (123).

As noted in chapter 1, Lewison, Flint, and Van Sluys (2002) promoted a critical literacy curriculum through social issues books. They identified four interrelated dimensions of critical literacy: "(1) disrupting the common place, (2) interrogating multiple viewpoints, (3) focusing on socio-political issues, and (4) taking action and promoting social justice" (382). The researchers studied elementary teachers' understandings and implementation of critical literacy. Based upon the respondents' answers to a questionnaire, the teachers were divided into three groups: "*newcomers* to critical practices, *novices*, and those *experienced* in critical pedagogy" (384). The researchers described the six newcomers as interested in critical thinking, but with vague understandings. The five novices "had read more than the newcomers and understood critical literacy to be reading texts with a critical eye; considering multiple viewpoints; and having class discussions or projects related to race, class, power, gender, language, and social justice" (385). The respondents received professional support through two full-day workshops, five study group meetings, and a national conference. They also read professional materials and received collections of books for their classrooms. The study illuminates the nature of professional development over time and the challenges educators encounter as they incorporate diverse literature into their literacy programs and try to promote social justice.

The literacy studies we reviewed above are significant in two ways. First, they demonstrate the potential of diverse children's literature in challenging the beliefs that teacher candidates and practising teachers hold about multiculturalism, diversity, and social justice. While only Lewison et al. (2002) focused specifically on critical literacy approaches, all of the studies involved critical literacy skills on the part of respondents. Second, each described a creative and practicable approach and/or literacy strategies that children's literature and literacy instructors may introduce in their courses.

Context

The Faculty of Education at Lakehead University has a concurrent program in which education and arts/science degree courses are taken simultaneously as well as a consecutive one-year professional program in which the education degree is taken after the arts/science degree is completed. Most of the education courses for concurrent education students take place in their fourth year and the students take courses with the consecutive year students. There are three divisions for certification: primary/junior (junior kindergarten–grade 6); junior/intermediate (grades 4–8); and intermediate/senior (grades 7–12).

Five classes participated in the study. Two were on Canadian multicultural children's literature. Mary Clare was the instructor for both classes. Students in these courses were in the junior, intermediate, and senior divisions. They were assigned a number of readings on diverse Canadian children's literature, read and responded to picture books, and kept a reflective journal. They were introduced through teacher modelling to such strategies as reading aloud, predicting, and developing questions that invite thinking beyond a literal level. The other three courses were junior/intermediate language arts methods courses. Mary Clare taught two of the courses, while a contract lecturer taught the third.

All respondents participated in the workshops and read a minimum of three articles on diverse Canadian children's literature. All completed a lesson plan that they were encouraged to implement during the field experience. In all classes, time was allocated to guided instruction and teacher-student conferences to provide scaffolding for lesson planning. One limitation is that most teacher candidates did not know their practicum placements until late in the semester.

There is little formal emphasis on multiculturalism and diversity in the BEd program. All participants in the study took a compulsory course (.25 FCE) on Aboriginal education. An elective course on multicultural education was also available.

Themes

Data analysis involved reading and rereading the preservice teachers' lesson plans to identify codes, categories and themes (Bogdan & Biklen, 2007; Patton, 2002). There were eighty-eight usable lesson plans for analysis; some plans were excluded because they were either unclear or were based on books not listed on the bibliography of diverse Canadian picture books supplied to all participants in the course syllabus. Most of the plans were prepared for grades 4, 5, and 6. Two themes emerged from the analysis: conceptualizing multiculturalism and diversity; and pedagogical understandings. It should be noted that some lesson plans based on Canadian picture books that raise issues of diversity omitted any reference to multiculturalism, diversity, or social justice. Instead, most of these lesson plans focused on subject areas. Alphabet books, in particular, were used to plan lessons around topics such as physical geography in various regions of Canada.

Conceptualizing Multiculturalism and Diversity

Participants selected over forty different picture books from the bibliography as the basis for their lesson plans. The themes they selected for the plans included: Aboriginal life; culture, immigration, citizenship, and Canadian identity; and social, political, and economic issues. The box below presents the topics addressed within each theme. Descriptions of the lesson plans highlight teacher candidates' perspectives on a theme or issue.

THEMES ADDRESSED IN THE LESSON PLANS
Aboriginal life. Four respondents developed lessons around *The Red Sash*. One respondent, Ellen, explained her description of the unit intended for a grade 6 class and her rationale for selecting this picture book:

> The picture book *The Red Sash* highlights the importance of fur trade marriages and the strengthened ties between the traders and native bands. This book is a fictional account of the life of a young Métis ("mixed blood") boy who lives with his mother in the native encampment across from Fort William in the early 1800's, during the height of the North West Company trade. The book is set in Thunder Bay and is relevant to our history and is told from a Métis perspective. I chose this book with the intent of illustrating the important role the First Nations women and their Métis children had in the fur trade as guides, interpreters and workers.
>
> Students should explore this topic specifically at the grade six level because this book can be integrated into the Social Studies, History and Geography curriculums which, in grade six, focus on Canada's Links to the World with an emphasis on trade. Students will gain understanding of the Métis perspective in Canada and will learn about the relevance of historical trade connections that Canada shares with the rest of the world which historically is based in the Fur trade from Canada to Europe. The beauty of this book is that it is relevant to the city's history because it is based right here.
>
> ... I chose this particular topic because it offers students an opportunity to understand a number of roles and perspectives by introducing characters

Aboriginal life

- Aboriginal and Métis culture and the fur trade at Old Fort William
- Aboriginal writers
- colonization/residential schools (historical analysis)
- early contact/discovery of the new world
- Role of Métis women and children at Old Fort William

Culture, immigration, citizenship, and Canadian identity

- becoming a Canadian citizen
- cultures and customs
- exploring one's heritage
- identity and self-esteem
- immigration
- lifestyles in the nineteenth century

Social, political, and economic issues

- ageism
- bullying
- fear of something or someone unknown
- homelessness
- homosexuality
- Japanese internment in the Second World War
- poverty
- teamwork/inclusion
- treatment of Chinese workers during construction of the CPR

that could be further analyzed. Not only is it an ideal introduction to daily life for a young Métis boy in the 1800s, it also touches upon the roles of the First Nation's mother and grandmother including their lifestyles and work; it touches upon the underlying romantic relationship between the sister Isabelle (also Métis) and John (son of a Caucasian according to his picture on the 3rd last page).

Culture, immigration, citizenship, and Canadian identity. Many of the plans suggested a conceptualization of multiculturalism, diversity, and social justice as broad and inclusive. For example, Carol developed a lesson plan for a grade 12 academic history course on the topic of Eastern European immigration to Canada:

> Students will read *Josepha: A Prairie Boy's Story*, and be asked to reflect on the story. This lesson is meant to be an introduction to the issues that were faced by immigrants to Canada's western provinces, during the early 1900s. It is meant to provide the students with a basic understanding of what it was like to be a stranger to the country, and show briefly the hardships that were faced. It is hoped that students will feel some compassion for the character of Josepha, and therefore be able to better identify with the plight that was experienced by thousands of immigrants as they tried to make a living in Canada.

While most of the plans focused on encouraging students to gain insight into the lives of "others" and to enhance their own understandings of diversity, there were other plans that were more sophisticated in their approaches to personal issues of identity evoked by the picture books. For example, Eric developed a comprehensive plan, which he intended to implement over seven days. The topic, "Our necessary journeys," involved students' engagement with and response to the journeys taken by protagonists in *Dawn Watch* (Pendziwol; *Debon*, 2004) and *Josepha: A Prairie Boy's Story* (McGugan; *Kimber*, 1994) as they created personal identity stories of their own journeys. Eric was an established writer who held a graduate degree and had taught writing at both secondary and postsecondary levels of education. His plan was creative, theoretically based, and pedagogically sophisticated. His conceptualization of diversity meant being culturally responsive to the "population diversity of the centre where I work":

> My "Necessary Journeys" theme in a broad sense means journeys of getting to know ourselves, discovering our identities and deriving meaning from them. These journeys take place both within and without us and affect our spiritual and emotional self-knowledge as well as our physical selves often due to the sensory imprint that accompanies travelling, experiencing or moving somewhere or something new.
>
> The two books I chose complement one another. Both are stories of experiencing "otherness." Meaning in both stories seems to unravel with time for contemplation. The lesson plans work in concert along with the theme. Both books are age-appropriate.

The theme and plans serve a learner-centred environment, one where my focus remains on my students' journeys and identities and local knowledge remains valued. The books and lessons enable my focus to root. My approach to multiculturalism in the classroom is, as much as possible, to teach to my students' background and to [the] local knowledge, history and population diversity of the centre where I work. Asking students to reveal themselves will, in all cases, provide thumbnails of the mosaic of their identity. Even if some do not zero in on "ethnic" journeys they've taken, I aim to focus students so that all should reflect their "known culture" meeting with an "other."

A strength of Eric's plan is that it would begin with students' cultural identities as a springboard to appreciating other cultures and ways of being. A caution is that if we are encouraging future teachers to incorporate diverse literature in their language arts programs, it is important to enable them to understand that the books they use must be culturally relevant and responsive. However, the program should also be inclusive of all Canadian multiculturalism and diversity.

Georgina planned a sixty-hour comprehensive unit for a grade 5 class entitled *A Gift for Gita: Feelings of Immigration*. Disappointingly, with the exception of the picture book selected and a drama activity, the activities included in the lesson plan were taken almost in their entirety from a unit on immigration available on the Internet. One of the activities articulated is problematic:

> Mosaic Activity: For this center you will need the introductory sheet: Canada – A Cultural Mosaic (BLM 1.1), some magazines to cut from and/or drawing paper and pencil crayons or felts. Students should first read the introductory sheet. Then they can complete the following activities:
>
> (A) Flip through the magazines and cut out pictures of people from different cultures and glue them on the Canadian Mosaic sheet (BLM1.1b)
>
> (B) Look through magazines again and cut out pictures of cultural influences and glue them on the Cultural Contributions sheet (food, clothing, music, sports, traditions). (BLM 1.1c)
>
> A paragraph discussing what was created should accompany the collages. This assignment can be taken home if additional time is needed.

Activity (A) asks students to select photographs based on visible differences among Canadians. We wonder whether an activity which highlights race and ethnicity, the "other," would not fuel the Canadian stereotype that members of visible minorities are from "somewhere else" (as several non-white participants in our study noted). Further, although the activity may have been done to "celebrate" visible differences, it may perpetuate racial profiling.

Social, political, and economic issues. The cluster of concepts categorized under the theme of social, political, and economic issues included ageism and homelessness. Several respondents extended their in-class study to social action. Shelley designed a lesson on ageism for a grade 5 class. Her description, rationale, and ideas for ongoing pen pal activity indicate her understanding of how social justice involves action:

> This lesson will take 60 minutes and will focus on age differences and the similarities and differences in culture associated with people at different stages in their lives (children and the elderly). The lesson will use a picture book to open up discussion about experiences with and possible fears related to people much older than the students. The story, *Red Parka Mary*, will give way to discussion about changing attitudes. Students will brainstorm reasons why stereotypes and prejudices may exist and how they may better understand elderly people. Pen pals will be set up between people at a senior citizens retirement home or a long-term care facility.

Lee-Ann explained the purpose of her lesson on homelessness intended for a grade 6 class: "It is important for students to know about world issues at a young age so as they mature, they know how to address these problems. Reading *Bagels from Benny* will not only demonstrate a religious (Jewish) aspect to the class, it will also give them a look at homelessness. This lesson is based around informing students about homelessness and letting them help."

One of the ideas for scaffolding in Lee-Ann's plan was having children individually list their ideas about homelessness to activate prior knowledge. This activity would be followed by small group discussion and synthesis of ideas, with groups then sharing their ideas with the whole class. She then planned to have the whole class discuss a fact sheet on homelessness. The facts are phrased in the following format:

> Fact: Over 742 million people in the world are now judged by the United Nations as hungry or starving.
>
> Do all people in our community have plenty of different kinds of food to eat?
>
> Yes___ No___ [Source not given]

The whole class discussion would be followed by discussion of the stereotypes articulated by children in the earlier brainstorming activity on homelessness.

Lee-Ann also planned an extension to the lesson in the form of a food drive: "Have students organize a food drive for the winter holidays. They will be responsible for setting up bins in the school (one in the office and one in their classroom), sending out letters to parents and contributing food, gently used toys and clothing. When the students collect the items, they will organize everything into Holiday Hampers to be sent out to homes in the community."

Shelley's and Lee-Ann's lesson plans illuminate their understanding of social justice and their sense of agency in action to promote social justice. Although their culminating plans would need to be refined, the ideas are practicable in elementary classrooms and schools.

Pedagogical Understandings

The curricular focus of lesson plans varied from those that addressed literacy learning within the language arts program to literacy learning in content areas. Most respondents envisioned the plan as an introductory or culminating set of activities in art, geography, history, or social studies. Several respondents planned units. Awareness of the potential of diverse picture books and the creative ways in which the teacher candidates imagined implementing them suggests a *creative envisioning* of the possibilities. Most lesson plans demonstrated understandings of the following concepts/strategies: social constructivist learning and reader response theories; concept and content knowledge; curriculum planning and development; flexibility of grouping configurations; and literacy approaches and strategies.

Ellen's unit plan on *The Red Sash*, intended for a grade 6 class, integrated literacy and social studies (history and geography) into a conceptual unit (Smagorinsky, 2002) that engaged students in an exploration of the role of Métis women and children in the fur trade and the economic import of the fur trade. Carol's lesson plan was intended for a grade 12 academic course as an introduction to a history unit on Eastern European immigration to Canada in the early 1900s. Both plans embody *creative envisioning* of the potential of picture books. Both offer evidence of the participants' understanding of a social constructivist framework that is also cultural and political. Both actively engage students in reading texts from critical and visual literacies perspectives. The use of picture books in both cases scaffolded the teaching/learning of concepts and historical content.

Ellen's and Carol's plans are well conceptualized and developed. Both built in several modes of presentation (Eisner, 2002) such as an emphasis on the visual components of picture books. For example, Carol's integrated digital and visual literacies through an interpretive activity in which students would analyse posters circulated widely in the early 1900s to attract immigrants. Both use literacy strategies such as reading aloud, predicting, questioning, and small group and whole class discussion.

The plans also suggest pedagogical challenges Ellen and Carol experienced in the development of their lessons. Ellen, in particular, had problems designing an appropriate assessment rubric. Carol experienced difficulty with phrasing some of her questions. Many other participants also encountered challenges in phrasing good questions. For example, one of Carol's questions is dichotomous, inviting a "yes" or "no" response: "Do you think that Josepha's experiences were different from other people's at the time?" Carol might have rephrased it to ask: "How might Josepha's experiences have compared with those of other immigrants who arrived in Canada at that time?" In another question to students, Carol imposed her own interpretation of the meaning of colour in an illustration: "The illustration on this page seems to have grown darker in colour. It is no longer filled with the vibrant oranges, browns, reds, and blues of the other illustrations. There seems to be a sense of foreboding in the colours used, especially over Josepha's home. What do you think this means? The language also changes. Which words stood out to you?" Had she withheld her own interpretation, she might have discovered what her students understood about how colour conveys mood, and how their understanding of mood informed students' interpretations.

Most plans demonstrated participants' implicit understanding of theory through the choices they made in the Canadian picture books, the resources they selected, and their *creative envisioning* of how the plans might unfold. Because of the variation across plans, plans provided different types of evidence of participants' understanding of the comprehension processes (pre-, during, and post-reading), which invited readers' engagement, interpretation, and reinterpretation. Depending on the purpose of the plan, some plans included opportunities for transmediation and representation through multimodalities (Siegel, 2006). Approaches and strategies mentioned in the plans included: reading aloud (all plans); tapping into prior knowledge through brainstorming; predicting, questioning, and discussing;

literature circles; guided writing; and response journals. Some plans emphasized visual and critical literacies; some included strategies for scaffolding.

Few plans integrated process writing. Where writing was incorporated, it took the form of "creative writing" that, if not completed in class, was assigned as homework to be then submitted for grading. Several plans also assigned unfinished tasks as homework. As noted above, assessment was one area where many respondents had difficulty.

Discussion

In interpreting the data the authors recognize that professional development in a preservice program is a complex, iterative and dynamic process; and this process continues into teaching. The lesson plans represent a snapshot of teacher candidates' understandings of multiculturalism, diversity, social justice, and pedagogy at the end of the first semester of their professional year and prior to the first field experience. At the same time, as literacy teacher educators, the data provide us with insights into the effectiveness of particular priorities (Kosnik & Beck, 2009), approaches and components for our literacy courses, and suggestions as to how we might begin to prioritize or highlight other concepts, strategies, and skills related to learning. For example, all the respondents participated regularly in picture book read-alouds. The instructors also modelled a variety of strategies to promote comprehension; participants experimented with the strategies and completed activities in class. Participants' plans affirm the power of modelling and experiential learning to influence visions of literacy teaching and learning.

The workshop was an effective springboard to introduce the participants to diverse Canadian picture books. The PowerPoint presentation enabled them to consider the artistic elements in illustrations, how illustrators convey meaning, and the connections between text and image. The time to read independently and share their discoveries with peers was effective in that they learned not only about new resources, but had the opportunity to discover the maturity levels of many of the books and to reflect on Canadian identity and how this is portrayed in a multiplicity of ways.

Participants demonstrated their understanding of multiculturalism, diversity, and social justice as broad and inclusive through the selection of a broad range of picture books and their focus on the themes

Aboriginal life; culture, immigration, citizenship and Canadian identity; and social, political, and economic issues.

Most teacher candidates recognized the potential of picture books as a resource for promoting multiculturalism, diversity, and social justice. Two respondents demonstrated agency in promoting social justice in the community; one promoted cultural responsiveness in relation to his students and the diversity in the community. Several plans included activities that were inappropriate and potentially damaging to students' understanding of Canadian multiculturalism, diversity, and social justice. As literacy instructors, it is important that we teach our students to be critical and reflect on their practices. Some plans did not address diversity. We do not have an explanation for the omission. It is possible that some students misinterpreted the assignment or some may have felt discomfort with the focus of the assignment. Further research is needed to explore this phenomenon. Failure to address the issue of diversity also suggests, however, a need for teacher educators to model effective uses of picture books to address social issues, such as residential schools, racism, and poverty, that emerge as themes in texts through class discussions, multimodal activities, and projects.

Many participants in the study demonstrated a *creative envisioning* of the potential of picture books. Many had an understanding of the theoretical underpinnings as well as concept and content knowledge. The plans overall were thoughtfully developed. They included a range of grouping configurations and literacy approaches and strategies which teacher candidates had seen modelled or had actively experienced. This affirms the power of experiential learning, the practical grounded in a theoretical context. The respondents would benefit by learning more about formulating "excellent" questions, process writing, and assessment. As well, some but not all plans incorporated critical and visual literacies and scaffolding. These concepts support the development of comprehension and expression of ideas, and should also be prioritized.

The literature suggests that teacher candidates would benefit from reflecting on their own cultural identities as well as coming to understand and address their perceptions of diversity (Davis et al., 2008; Santoro, 2009). Every professional program has or should have articulated a set of priorities (Kosnik & Beck, 2009) that highlights multiculturalism, diversity, and social justice. In our cross-Canada study several university programs were committed to diversity education; others were not.

As literacy teacher educators we need to ask ourselves what priorities we should identify for our literacy courses in relation to subject-area knowledge and what Santoro (2009) refers to as "multicultural pedagogies" (33). We see diverse Canadian children's and young adult literature as a portal through which teacher candidates enter and within which they begin to negotiate the spaces around identity in relation to others, develop subject-area knowledge, build understandings of diversity, and develop "multicultural pedagogies" and the capacity for reflection.

6 Very Far Away:
Traversing the Distance between
Imagination and Actualization

TERESA STRONG-WILSON AND HEATHER PHIPPS

Ivana read *Two Pairs of Shoes* (Sanderson; *Bayer*, 1990) to her kindergarten class. It had been her favourite book from the picture book study. The research was designed to probe preservice teachers' ideological understandings of Canadian diversity through contemporary Canadian picture books; it also encouraged teachers to adopt the books for use in teaching situations. *Two Pairs of Shoes* tells of a little girl who received two pairs of shoes as gifts. Her mother gave her a pair of shiny black patent shoes, which she proudly showed her grandmother. Her *Kokum* [grandmother] then told her to find the special box under her bed. Inside she found a beautiful pair of hand-sewn moccasins. The pictures in the book are spare – large-scale illustrations of the girl, her mother, her grandmother, the shoes – but the story, written by an Indigenous author, converges on a complex message about identity. Her grandmother advises her granddaughter: know when to wear each pair of shoes.[1]

Ivana was drawn to the story's moving portrayal of the passing on of culture from grandmother to granddaughter. In her classroom discussion, she captured the following exchange:

IVANA: Is it possible to have a little girl like her ... in your class?
KINDERGARTEN STUDENT: Maybe, but I don't think so. I haven't seen one yet.
They don't go to the same schools as us. They live far away.

"Very far away" is where Martin, a five-year-old, wants to go in Maurice Sendak's (1957) picture book of the same name. He goes looking for a place where all questions will be answered. "Where is very far away?" he asks each animal he meets, "Because that is where I want to go." For the student in Ivana's kindergarten class, "far away" marked the furthest boundary of her imagination. If she were to travel there, she would find people that she conceptualized as not yet having seen. For the students in an undergraduate children's literature class, "very far away" likewise signified an imagined place to which they had to travel in order to find people they did not know, except through books and movies conceived within a white imagination.

Data for the study (which is described in the introduction to this book) were gathered through surveys, interviews, and focus groups with teacher candidates. At the Quebec site, the data were gathered from March 2008 to April 2009 in an anglophone university. Participants were from four large sections (70–100 students) of two undergraduate courses (one section of Children's Literature; three sections of the Kindergarten Classroom). Ivana was in one of the Kindergarten Classroom sections. Teacher candidates in the teacher education program are primarily anglophone (from Quebec or Ontario), a minority are francophones from Quebec and a quarter identified as allophone, which is not surprising given Quebec's policy of encouraging immigration. Across the four sections, 218 students completed the surveys. The surveys revealed that of the total number of students surveyed: 115 (52.7%) were anglophone, 37 (16.9%) were francophone, and 56 (25.6%) were allophone students who identified as speaking a first language other than English or French (such as Italian, Russian, Spanish, Arabic, and Lebanese).[2]

In this chapter, we report on results from the fall 2008 children's literature course, in which the students worked collaboratively in groups to produce a literature-based culturally conscious lesson plan based on a picture book written by an Indigenous author. One hundred students were registered in the course; a total of 45 students completed the survey. The 45 students who completed the survey included 33 (73.3%) anglophone students, 3 (6.7%) francophone students, 1 (2.2%) student who spoke both English and French as first languages, 3 (6.7%) students with a language other than English or French as a first language (Cree, Giurati), and 5 (11.1%) students who did not respond to the language question on the survey. A total of 20 lesson plans were submitted to the researchers, and (as we describe later) 11 students participated in two focus groups while preparing their lesson plan.

In this chapter, we examine the challenges experienced by the students in creating their culturally conscious lesson plans. Their struggles involved traversing the distance between imagination and actualization:

how do predominantly white middle-class students travel from here to there in addressing a story written or illustrated by an Indigenous author? What evidence do the lesson plans provide of a learning process? Which lesson plans were more effective in traversing that distance and why? What can our own reflections on this experience tell us about what more needs to be done or could be done differently?

Travelling from Here to There ... and Back Again

The plane ride from Endurant to Ravenwing was short, just over half an hour, but in that brief time, I [Teresa] crossed into another world. There wasn't anything familiar to hang onto, beyond that fragile thread of a new friendship begun in the Endurant airport with a native man wearing a Ravenwing sweatshirt. He sat behind me in the plane. The planes are small; they carry twelve passengers, six on one side, six on the other. He would prod me from time to time, point things out, share important bits of information, but all of his efforts were lost. The sound of the engines eventually drowned out his voice. Even so, I don't think I would have heard, so deeply was I absorbed by the archipelago of islands amidst the most striking shade of blue: deep, iridescent, lapis lazuli. Soon we started to circle the boundaries of a forested island with a strip of streets and houses snaking along one side of its coast. In the descent, a familiar sensation in my stomach began to mix with a growing consciousness of the weight and enormity of this proposed sea-change and, momentarily alarmed, I wondered: what have I done? (Wilson, 2000, 7)

This is an excerpt from a teacher narrative that one of the co-authors (Teresa) wrote after having taught and lived in an Indigenous community ("very far away") for several years. (The name of the community is a pseudonym.) What is striking about the account, in the context of this book chapter, is the dawning consciousness on the part of the white teacher narrator/writer of what it might mean to cross a border from one world into another and how imagination failed her: she is unable to conceive of what that crossing entails until it is experienced, and even then, as the story suggests, the interpretation of her experience would require a local who could help her perceive aright. I (Teresa) taught in Ravenwing for six years, not without difficulty in the first year, but soon accompanied by deep learning and great joy.

However, it was not until my fifth year that I began to look critically at the kinds of storied texts that I was using in the classroom. This was when I first became aware of Seale and Slapin's (1992) *Through Indian Eyes*, in which the Indigenous authors provided often scathing reviews of "Indigenous" literature. I began to scrutinize more closely the kinds of books being made available to teachers and which teachers like myself sought out. Even if my pedagogical leanings were towards listening to Indigenous voices (for example, I regularly invited community members into the classroom to speak), it took many years before I could begin to understand how my own storied imagination influenced my perceptions and curricular choices. I find it interesting that critical examination of these texts (viz., stories) constituted the last frontier. I have since wondered why that was the case and what is entailed in moving from one imaginative world to another, assuming that such movement is possible.

The Borders of Imagination

"Why is it," Michael Doxtater [Mohawk] (2004) asks, "that when a white man draws a circle in the sand, he draws it around the circle representing what the Indigenous person knows and claims the larger circle as the boundary of all human knowledge?" (p. 619, cited in Strong-Wilson, 2008, 54). Many have examined the relationship between imagination and power, including Indigenous scholars and writers such as Elizabeth Cook-Lynn (1996), Gerald Vizenor (1994), Thomas King (2003), Scott Momaday (1966), Emma LaRocque (1996), and Lee Maracle (1990); Lee Maracle declared to non-Indigenous writers, "Move over," in a 1990 *Globe and Mail* editorial. Non-Indigenous scholars have also critically examined power issues; authors such as Hoy (2001) in *How Should I Read These?* (on how non-Indigenous readers can or should read Indigenous texts), Laura Groening (2004) in *Listening to Old Women Speak* (on what "moving over" involves in a Canadian imaginative context) and, within the realm of children's literature, Ingrid Johnston's *Remapping Literary Worlds* (2003) and Clare Bradford's *Reading Race* (2001) and *Unsettling Narratives* (2007).

Within a Canadian context, Chamberlin's (2003) *If This Is Your Land, Where Are Your Stories?* and John Ralston Saul's (2008) *A Fair Country: Telling Truths about Canada* have taken up issues popularized through Margaret Atwood's *Survival* (1972), on how Canada imagines Indigenous peoples as well as themselves. Atwood's text in turn drew on Northrop Frye, one of Canada's key public intellectuals, who wrote a series of essays on the Canadian imagination. It is in Frye's *Bush Garden*

(1995) that we find the suggestion that the Canadian settler imagination creates borders that become inscribed on the land as well as within literature; these borders influence how we are able to imagine the world: what we perceive and do not perceive. Frye was arguably short-sighted when it came to envisioning Indigenous peoples, this despite the extensive boundaries of his literary knowledge (Strong-Wilson, 2008). Returning to Doxtater's observation, this is not surprising; a circumference is a boundary, *no matter how large it is imagined to be*: "Colonial-power-knowledge communicates particular cultural presuppositions that elevate Western knowledge as real knowledge while ignoring other knowledge" (Doxtater, 2004, 619). That "other" knowledge has traditionally been represented as existing at the margins of socially accepted boundaries, yet becomes encompassed (viz., imagined) within the dominant paradigm. A good example of this occurs early in Western literature in travel accounts. Williams (1996) writes that having conquered the known world, Alexander the Great turned "his eyes … toward the wasteland that lies beyond it": there he found "the Plantings, slender giants with long, swan-like necks" and "Oxoli … red giants whose hair flows out in a fan shape" as well as "fleas as big as turtles, hairy, barking men, invisible monsters and disappearing trees, fire breathing fowl – one prodigy after another"; however, no matter how many he killed, they "elude[d] the control of the world-conqueror" (Williams, 1996, 236; cited in Strong-Wilson, 2008, 54).

While this account of Alexander the Great's adventures may seem far-fetched and remote, it connects back in interesting ways to Maurice Sendak's evocation of "very far away" and the frank remark of a kindergarten student who, having never seen "one of those," assumed they must exist "far away." It also connects in complex ways to childhood as an imagined space and especially to the formal and informal spaces for "playing Indian" that have typically occurred in a North American childhood, whether it is putting a feather in a band around one's head and whooping, playing Cowboys and Indians, making "Indian crafts" in school, or participating in wilderness activities through Guides and Scouts. "Much of what we learn about Indians we learn as children," says Francis (1992, 144), where "Indian" is conceived entirely within a white imagination. Deloria (1998) sees what we might call the childhood practice of "playing Indian" as extending into adulthood, strategically linked to seminal moments of constructing new national identities.

"I stood on the border, stood on the edge, and claimed it as central and let the rest of the world come over to where I was," says Toni Morrison,

African-American novelist and literary critic (cited in Fultz, 2003, 101). How did the students, by way of their lesson plans, negotiate the border of their white imaginations with that being claimed by Indigenous authors, who seemed to be inviting them to come where they were? The teacher candidates were invited to a place where "very far away" could meet the Indigenous person of here and now, the person who was, in fact, always here; who, as Emma Laroque (1996) says, has survived, and "we stand here to say, we have endured and we are not 'the Other' of White invention" (118). How did student teachers travel from imagination to actualization and begin to apprehend (if they did) a different circle, a different paradigm?

Description of the Research

Mary Ann began her children's literature class by reading the powerful words of the poem *I Lost My Talk* by Rita Joe (1998), a Micmaq poet. Bringing an extensive background in Indigenous education, the instructor was committed to using fiction and poetry to make students aware of the experiences of Indigenous peoples. We conducted two research workshops. In the first, we elicited the students' general conceptions of Canadian identity and diversity while in the second, in keeping with the emphasis of the course, we focused exclusively on Indigenous Canadian picture books. The focus, tailored to this particular course, likely differed from practices in other sites in the same research project. The following is a brief description of the second workshop. First, we read from *What's the Most Beautiful Thing You Know about Horses?* by Dogrib author Richard Van Camp (*Littlechild*, 1998) and linked this text with *The Important Book* by non-Canadian mainstream author Margaret Wise Brown (1977) (author of the often fondly remembered *Goodnight Moon*). We showed how Indigenous literature is both continuous with the kind of literature with which students were likely already familiar (viz., pattern stories), but also discontinuous with it, in that it broached a cultural landscape different from the students' own. Turning to the powerful visual imagery in *Shi-shi-etko* (Campbell; *La Fave*, 2005), one of the study's picture books, as well as *As Long as the Rivers Flow* (Loyie; *Holmlund*, 2002), another post-1990 Canadian picture book by an Indigenous author, the workshop serendipitously built on Mary Ann's introductory poem to engage students in trying to imagine, from a child's perspective, the rude transition from living in a world rooted in Indigenous culture and language to being taken away to residential school. We also provided examples of typical stereotypical representation of Indigenous cultures and showed how such representations have tended to characterize children's literature written by non-Indigenous authors. We emphasized the importance of Indigenous voices being heard. We also provided some examples of culturally conscious pedagogy in the classroom.

One of our main purposes was to first engage the students with the texts. Louise Rosenblatt suggests that story reading is above all an aesthetic experience. She writes that "only from emotional and intellectual participation" can an aesthetic reading become "a rich source of insight and truth" (Rosenblatt, 1982, 277). Truth in what sense? Aoki (Aoki, Pinar, & Irwin, 2005) states that when we consider the curriculum as "situational praxis," "what is equally important for teachers and students as they engage in interpretive acts is to be critically reflective not only of the transformative reality that is theirs to create, but also of their own selves" (121). How did constructing the lesson plans become a way for the teachers to reflect upon their subjectivity vis-à-vis Indigenous peoples?

The Lesson Plan Assignment

Mary Ann asked the students to construct a culturally conscious lesson plan that made central a picture book by an Indigenous Canadian author. That book needed to be drawn from the Diverse Canadian Picture Books collection and other books fitting the criteria for inclusion.[3] Students worked in small groups. The objective was to create a lesson "from a perspective that would be culturally sensitive or critical: sensitive of Aboriginal culture or critical of a dominant cultural paradigm based on the "imaginary Indian'" (excerpt from lesson plan assignment, Fall 2008 Children's Literature Syllabus). By choosing a picture book written by an Indigenous author, the preservice teachers were encouraged to have a "lived experience" with stories they may not have been familiar with prior to the course. Books by Indigenous authors were made readily accessible to the students by being placed on library reserve. In a subsequent class, eleven participants also joined a two-part focus group discussion. The teacher candidates had the opportunity to engage with the texts, and discuss the books to which they were most drawn; they then began to articulate their preliminary ideas for constructing their lessons. Feedback was provided, which we continued to offer via email. Teacher candidates who had not elected to be part of the focus group were free to email us or could meet with us; one did.

Insight into the teacher candidates' thinking processes was afforded by the focus group, but also by the lesson plans themselves, which acted like maps, indicating which pathways teacher candidates had followed. Important hints were also afforded in the reflective paragraphs at the end of the lesson, in which the teacher candidates explained how they had designed the lesson to actively foster an inclusive classroom respectful of Indigenous culture.[4]

Charting a Continuum

From Critical Emotional Engagement to a Refusal to Engage

Of the twenty lesson plans shared with the researchers, some were more effective than others in accomplishing a movement from imagination to actualization. Key to this process, we found, was active emotional and critical engagement. The lesson plans furthest from that goal often underwent a series of paroxysms to avoid directly engaging the text or addressing issues raised by the text. Consistent with a grounded-theory approach to data analysis, we read and reread the lesson plans, generating a five-point continuum that ranged from emotional critical engagement to avoidance and a refusal to engage. We reread the lessons several times to examine similarities and differences, and through discussion substantiated our categorizations. Each of the five points is briefly described below, and is followed by examples from the lesson plans and study of the teachers' "moves."

We need to bear in mind that while the learning process of one of the co-authors extended over six years in an Indigenous community and remains far from complete, the students only had six weeks in which to complete the assignment. We therefore read the lesson plans for the insights they can offer into a process of moving from one "circle" to another (within Doxtater's conceptualization). In particular, what can the lesson plans tell us of specific places where the students experienced difficulty and strayed from the task, thus reinstating Doxtater's "white man's" circle?

Critical Emotional Engagement: Story of Confrontation

"A story of confrontation … brings us back to where we began" (Greene, 1965, 423). When teachers reflect on their own ideologies and critically examine their own values and assumptions, they are engaging in situational praxis and producing a "story of confrontation" (423). Essential to the production of a story of confrontation is responding "aesthetically" rather than "efferently" (Rosenblatt, 1978). An efferent reading approaches a story as instrumental towards an external goal. This move typically involved the re-appropriation of Indigenous peoples within a colonialist, anthropological framework. Responding aesthetically means that we allow ourselves to experience emotions: the nostalgic ones characteristic of favourite "touchstone" stories (Strong-Wilson, 2006) as well as difficult emotions, like sadness, anger, confusion, and fear: "representations that cut too deep cause us to wake up, or to remember what we would prefer to forget" (Robertson, 1997, 461). A story of confrontation combines emotional awareness with criticality to generate self-awareness along with empathy so as to be likely to lead to social action or curricular change. The five possible points on the continuum are described next.

CRITICAL REFLECTION ALONE

A lesson plan may have been critical on a discursive level and successfully engaged students in examination of Indigenous issues but without evidence of deep engagement with the book's story or imagery. In other words, the text itself became instrumental to an argument that preceded the text. There was little or no awareness of the need to engage students in a lived experience with the text or the ideas embodied within it. Some texts by Indigenous authors lent themselves more to this discursive usage. *This Land Is My Land* (Littlechild, 1993) directly addresses a reader (who is positioned as white) so that a reader cannot avoid confronting political issues that have affected Indigenous peoples in Canada; the text guides the teacher's use, allowing little room for misinterpretation. However, even here, critical reflection alone would miss Littlechild's striking illustrations. In the context of the teachers' lesson plans, we found that engagement with the story became secondary when criticality was emphasized; what becomes primary in such a situation is the teacher's interpretation of the text. This can become problematic, resulting in an occluding of the Indigenous voice (as represented by the text) and of the student voice (by not allowing them a lived pathway to arrive at their own critically informed responses).

EMOTIONAL ENGAGEMENT ALONE: CONSTRUCTING A BRIDGE

Teachers who lingered over students' personal experiences constructed bridging-type lessons; they used their prospective students' emotional engagement with the book's content as a way to generate greater empathy and understanding. It was clear that in order to construct such lessons, teachers first needed to imagine a scenario, which involved pulling on those experiences with which they themselves were familiar and that, pedagogically, they reasoned, would constitute effective bridges to understanding. Certain Indigenous stories lent themselves more to this use than others: books that were beautifully illustrated or told a story using elements familiar to teacher or students. Where this kind of lesson plan often fell short was in finding a way to consciously link this aesthetic or personal experience with an Indigenous or critical perspective such that re-assimilation of the Indigenous story into a familiar circle/paradigm would be interrupted.

AVOIDANCE
Certain students constructed lesson plans that avoided risking engagement with Indigenous texts altogether by using them instead as springboards to focus on a "safe" or already known topic lying outside of the text. This was different from "Critical Reflection" (see above) because students avoided Indigenous issues altogether. Alternatively, a lesson plan would combine pedagogical strategies modelled in the workshop but in a recipe-like fashion, thus avoiding deep engagement with the Indigenous text.

Refusal to Engage: Retelling of the Colonial Story

In a minority of the lesson plans, the students refused to engage with the Indigenous stories at all. In what we call a "retelling of the colonial story," students fell back on traditional and uncritical approaches of teaching "about" Indigenous peoples and instead selected their own texts that could be read "efferently." This refusal meant drawing on an anthropological framework to relegate Indigenous people to a distant past "very far away" (using such categories as hunting, shelter, food, clothing, transportation, etc.) or teaching about Indigenous culture through "arts and crafts" activities, thus replicating the notion that Indigenous peoples are childish, arrested in their development according to a Western conception of civilization. By retelling the colonial story, students demonstrated a refusal to engage with the contemporary Indigenous voice of the author (LaRocque's "we are here now").

Lessons Created by Teacher Candidates

We now examine illustrative examples of lesson plans, focusing on four of the five points on the continuum. We highlight those movements within the lesson that can provide valuable insight into the preservice teachers' thinking process: what is involved in traversing the distance from the imagination to actualization as well as where they faltered, veered, or found themselves at a loss.

Critical Emotional Engagement

COYOTE COLUMBUS (KING; MONKMAN, 1992)

Hello, says one of the men in silly clothes with red hair all over his head, I am Christopher Columbus. I am sailing the ocean blue looking for India. Have you seen it?

Forget India, says Coyote, let's play ball.

This excerpt from *A Coyote Columbus Story* demonstrates the playful "counter-discourse" (Bradford, 2007) characteristic of King's story. The story presents a retelling from an Indigenous point of view of the colonization of America. One group's stated objective was to encourage students to consider "the difference between what they knew about Columbus and how he is depicted in *A Coyote Columbus Story*." Their plan centred on having small group discussions about the story, as students compared *A Coyote Columbus Story* with a historical text. The historical text bore a close relationship to a story with which the children would have already been familiar as part of their storied formation, namely, the story of how Christopher Columbus sailed over the ocean blue, etc. We argue that this lesson plan approaches a "story of confrontation" for its juxtaposition of a new text (*A Coyote Columbus Story*) with one familiar to the students, and for its engagement of the children in actively comparing the two versions.

However, the lesson contained certain contradictions. As the students explained: "In the United States it is common for children to perform a retelling of the first Thanksgiving – a revised Columbus story could be a culturally sensitive alternative." By choosing to situate their imagined school and lesson in the United States, the students suggest that the story of colonization belongs elsewhere, namely, outside of Canada. The students further reflected in their postscript: "By retelling the Columbus story without consideration of how European contact adversely affected Aboriginal peoples, society is ignoring our part in the plight of Aboriginal peoples today. The first step in helping Aboriginals is taking responsibility for what was done to them."

"One of the finest things about being an Indian," Vine Deloria (1969) remarks, tongue-in-cheek, "is that people are always interested in you and your 'plight' … People can tell just by looking at us what we want, what should be done to help us, how we feel, and what a 'real' Indian is really like" (191). By using language of "helping," the teacher candidates performed a further distancing of the story from themselves. Critical reflection, we maintain, involves acknowledging the story as pertaining to one's own history. Through the textual juxtaposition, the lesson plan pedagogically performed this move, but then retracted from it theoretically and personally.

HIDE AND SNEAK (KUSUGAK; KRYKORKA, 1992)

Allusha is very connected with her natural surroundings. She pauses to look at plants and butterflies. She can't resist joining in the fun and games of playing with the Ijiraq despite her mother's warnings not to play with this creature. The Ijiraq is known to help Inuit children hide, but then they may never be found again, as it chants:

Hide-and-sneak, hide-and sneak
How I love to hide-and-sneak
I hide and you seek
You won't find me for a week

The landscape is a predominant presence in many stories by Indigenous authors (e.g., *Sky Sisters* by Waboose; *Deines*, 2000), as it is here in Kusugak's story. The teacher candidates capitalized on this, proceeding in a graduated sequence:

- The students play "I Spy" in the classroom.
- As a class, they create a map of the school playground on the blackboard, then describe the playground to the teacher, who draws a large map.
- Story mapping: in groups of 3–4 the students draw a map of the story, including the creatures and landmarks Allushua encounters.
- Each group shares what they have drawn.
- The class goes outside for a game of Hide and Seek.

The hide and seek game marks the culmination of the lesson, drawing the children's attention to their surroundings as a place in which to survive: "Our activity is centred on the environment. The lesson encourages students to take a second look at their own surroundings, and to take note of what they had originally missed (e.g., a small berry plant, the presence of seagulls, etc.)." They take a familiar activity and imbue it with new significance. In their reflections, the teacher candidates also pointed to the factuality of the setting: it is a place that, though far away geographically, is within our grasp, thus challenging the notion of Indigenous peoples as imaginary beings.

The teachers veer away from criticality when they relegate Aboriginal knowledge to "folklore": "For the extended activity, students not only have to be attentive, but also have to learn about Aboriginal folklore in order to describe the Ijiraq." It may presume too much to assume that this sole use was intended to be disparaging. However, combined with the students' observation on the "lack of toys" in Northern communities, it does suggest, as in the lesson on *A Coyote Columbus Story*, that there is an underlying discourse at work that constructs Indigenous peoples as "backward."

Emotional Engagement Alone

CARIBOU SONG: ATIHKO NIKAMON (HIGHWAY; DEINES, 2001)
Caribou Song: Atihko Nikamon (2001) written by Cree writer Tomson Highway, is the story of Joe and Cody; their parents are caribou hunters in Northern Manitoba. The story is written in both Cree and English, and many Cree words are interspersed in the English text, as we see in the following passage: "Joe played the accordion, the kitoochigan. From morning to night he played and sang, 'Ateek, ateek! Astum, astum! Yo-ah, ho-ho! Caribou, caribou! Come, come! Yo-ah, ho-ho!'"

One group created a lesson that combined two activities: first, by looking closely at the images of *Caribou Song* and imagining phrases to describe associated colours and feelings, and second, through the creation of a character sociogram. The sociogram invited the reader to understand the emotions and playfulness of the two brothers, as well as the close relationships that the two boys have with their parents. For the non-Indigenous reader, "*Caribou Song* renders meaningful modes of behaviour, interpersonal relations, and emotion located in Cree culture, and traditions[;] at the same time, the text maintains a sense of the apartness and specificity of the characters" (Bradford, 2007, 57). Having students examine the interpersonal relations was therefore a meaningful way for them to engage with the text.

While emphasizing emotional engagement, the lesson stops short of actively involving students in the story content. There is no awareness generated, for instance, of geographical and cultural context (here, "the bush"), whereas this was present in the previous lesson (*Hide and Sneak*). Nor is there any reflection on the story's language and how that might be part of the aesthetic experience of the story. Overall, the lesson aims for emotional engagement but without entirely knowing with what and why; it fails to integrate the two activities and to link them to a larger critical purpose.

SHI-SHI-ETKO (CAMPBELL; LA FAVE, 2005)

Shi-shi-etko tells the story of a little girl who is leaving for a residential school in the fall. Before she leaves, she tries to remember everything about her home. The strong relationship that she has with her family and her home evokes emotion in the reader. To help her remember her family, she is given a small bag from her grandmother, which she fills with her memories from the surrounding landscape that is her ancestral home.

This story subtly deals with the issue of residential schools in Canada. Teacher candidates found the illustrations and text to be evocative and emotional. One group created a lesson to help children appreciate the emotions that Shi-shi-etko is experiencing. The lesson plan included a discussion of the way that Shi-shi-etko is feeling as she is getting ready to leave for school. The class then made their own memory pouches, which they filled with five personal objects from home. Their reflection on the lesson plan indicated that they would like children to be able to compare their own feelings with those of Shi-shi-etko.

However, the lesson plan passes over the residential school system itself, perhaps out of sensitivity to the age of the students (five to eight years), but perhaps also because the teacher candidates themselves lacked key critical knowledge about the schools (on the importance of such knowledge, see Robertson, 1997). Again, what is missing is a sense of purpose and direction for the activity. Why do we need to remember our surroundings? The teachers suggested that the story can provide an "unbiased" perspective, which suggests an avoidance of critical perspectives through focusing on emotion:

> By focusing on feelings more so than on explicit details of the Residential school scheme, the book provides an unbiased perspective which creates an appropriate foundation for teaching about those schools ... Without imposing our own feelings and beliefs of the subject matter we give the children the opportunity to generate a basis for their understanding of Shi-shi-etko's situation as an Aboriginal child.

Avoidance

It was evident that some students found it difficult to traverse the borders of their imagination. Their lesson plans avoided engaging emotionally or critically with the Indigenous picture books. Here we present examples of such lessons, in which the picture books primarily served as springboards to talk about something else.

One lesson is based on the story *Sky Sisters* by Indigenous author Jan Waboose (*Reczuch*, 2000). In the lesson's introduction, the teacher candidates explained that after reading the story and juxtaposing it with *Millicent and the Wind* (Munsch, 1984; *Duranceau*, 1984), they would focus on an "environmental theme." Activities include having students think about sustainability practices and create journals about daily activities, including calculating ecological footprints. These do not directly relate to *Sky Sisters*; we may even wonder whether the teacher candidates read the story. The teachers pass over the text to arrive at a more familiar story and author (Robert Munsch) and a familiar destination (the environment theme). Indigenous people remain imagined and very far away indeed.

This was not the case with another group of teachers, who had clearly read *Hide and Sneak* (Kusugak; *Krykorka*, 1992). The group did not begin with the story but with a poem about an Inuksuk. The students found the poem on the Internet. Authorship is anonymous and presumably not by an Indigenous person, yet the poem emits signals that suggest it is written "as if" from an Indigenous perspective.

I am Inuksuk

I am made of the rocks that surround me.
Like you, I come in many shapes and sizes.
I stand alone on hilltops worn smooth by glaciers of a forgotten time.
Small animals seek shelter in my shadow from the bitter relentless winds of winter.
I have spoken to the Inuit for thousands of years without uttering a single word.
When you find me, keep me at your back.
I point to sacred places and ancient hunting grounds used by your ancestors.
I mark a trail of dangers, tragedies, and happiness.
Walk, paddle, sail. Use your sled and dogs.
Use your strength and knowledge of the land and sea to reach the destination you desire.

Follow me, I will allow you the way.
I am Inuksuk.

– Author anonymous (emphasis added)

While reading a poem can be a creative way of engaging students to think and feel about the inuksuk, the poem is then left behind. The poem strategy signals the beginning of a succession of moves that, though ostensibly intended to promote emotional engagement and understanding (as per the teacher candidate reflection), are truncated. Accumulated, they take the teacher candidates farther away from, rather than deeper inside, the story, and so back to the "far away" of the white man's Indian. The "your" (rather than "our") in the poem performs the first distancing. It is worth examining how this distancing proceeds.

In Kusugak's narrative, Allushua is guided by the Inuksuk to find her way home. Following the reading of the story, an Indigenous speaker visits their classroom to talk about legends and inuksuks. This is an important acknowledgment on the part of the teacher candidates of the importance of including Indigenous culture and knowledge in the curriculum, in keeping with *Shared Learnings* (BC Ministry of Education 1998), one of the curricular sources created by Indigenous educators that was suggested as a resource in the focus group; these teacher candidates were participants in that group. It also represented an encouraging change from their original lesson plan, which was to move right away to what they referred to as an "arts and craft" activity of building a miniature inuksuk. Following the visit, students instead research the "uses of rocks and their usefulness to human beings." This activity, though more closely connected to the story, still represents an efferent reading – a desire to treat Indigenous culture as object. Although the lesson plan focuses on the significance of the Inuksuk as an important aspect of the story, the students unduly fixate on this object, to the neglect of Allushua, whom Kusgak made the focalized character (Bradford, 2007): we experience her pleasure and excitement as she runs and plays outside; we connect with her feelings of being afraid and sad when she realizes that she is lost in the dark cave; we recognize her courage and strength when she realizes that she is able to find her way home by following the landmarks. The plan falls short of allowing the students an opportunity to connect on an emotional level with the character when she is lost, and engage critical knowledge in order to find a way home, as the other lesson had done.

Refusal to Engage

Here Indigenous peoples are completely subsumed within the circle of "we (as white people) know you because we know all about you." The lesson completely avoids an aesthetic engagement and goes straight to an efferent reading, one that is in keeping with how Indigenous peoples have been constructed within a once dominant anthropologically centred discourse (Deloria, 1997).

The lesson has students "gather information about the clothing, food, housing, family life, rituals, etc. of a specific indigenous group." There is no inclusion of the Indigenous authors' picture books introduced in the course. Rather, the lesson plan focuses only on materials written *about* various Indigenous groups in Canada. The teachers' resistance to engaging with the literature is evident in their reflection:

> Our lesson actively fosters an inclusive classroom that is respectful of Aboriginal culture by teaching the students to explore the facts, before jumping to conclusions. Our lesson does this through a multifaceted approach. Firstly, the students explore the true facts of their group's assigned Indigenous tribe ... The students use non-fiction sources, therefore gaining non-biased and factual knowledge.

Discussion of Lesson Plan Moves

Certain moves enabled the teachers to engage emotionally and critically with the texts. First of all, if the lesson centred on the Indigenous author's story, it showed that the teacher candidates had engaged with it themselves. Further evidence was provided by concretely engaging children with the story as a whole, rather than with only one part of it. If the new story was then juxtaposed with a lived engagement with a familiar story or with a lived experience that was intimately familiar to the children – as familiar to them as a script (like the game of hide and seek), this allowed for emotional engagement but also provided a lever for critical analysis and comparison: How is this story like/unlike your own? In certain cases, such lessons even created an opening for children's re-envisioning of their familiar storied landscape from the perspective of the Indigenous story. The most successful lessons accomplished these movements gradually, through a succession of carefully thought through activities that had as their goal a critical awakening or re-envisioning. Those lessons that relied only on the personal connection, without engaging the critical, lacked direction. Those lessons that veered away from the texts to Indigenous and non-Indigenous things outside of the texts tended to be "activity"- or "recipe"-based or grounded in a theme peripheral to the story but of interest to the teachers, for instance, ecology.

Where most lessons fell down, at one point or another, was in re-invoking discourses that positioned Indigenous peoples as backward, which suggests that one of the most pervasive and deep-rooted of myths is that of the "imaginary Indian" (Francis, 1992) and, along with it, the assumption of Western hegemony and the superiority of White/European civilization. Numerous critical, engaged encounters with Indigenous literature, along with a commitment to using it meaningfully in the classroom, combined with critical reading on the subject (Robertson, 1997), may eventually counter that myth.

Entering the Contact Zone: From Imagination to Actualization

Bradford (2007) suggests that "Indigenous texts offer a path toward cultural understanding for the youngest citizens of postcolonial societies" (69). But in light of the study's findings, how should we understand this invitation? At face value, the statement invokes Rosenblatt's hope: "For years I have extolled the potentialities of literature for aiding us to understand ourselves and others, for widening our horizons to include temperaments and cultures different from our own, for helping us to clarify our conflicts in values, for illuminating our world" (1982, 276). This hope arguably still underlies current practices in schools, evident across teachers' choices of texts, library offerings, textbook selections and curricula, and book reviews and recommended lesson offshoots in professional development magazines and journals. At issue is the relevance of empathy: "Rosenblatt's proposal ... will strike feminist educators as a naïve and paternalist conception of the transformative force of empathy," Taylor (2007, 300) argues, because it is predicated on a notion of Otherness disguised as, and thus reduced to, sameness. It is the case of Narcissus all over again; we fall in love with our beloved touchstone stories and remain within the imagined categories created through that storied formation (Strong-Wilson, 2008).

Bradford's argument is that certain texts resist identification; *A Coyote Columbus Story* (King; *Monkman*, 1992), for instance, positions the non-Indigenous/White reader in a way that is already unsettling. A similar argument has been made for consciously crafted narratives like those of

African-American children's author Julius Lester (e.g., his picture book *From Slave Ship to Freedom Road* [1998]). Certain texts resist identification but by first pulling the White reader in; this is Cynthia Lewis's (2000) argument for Christopher Paul Curtis's novel (1995), *The Watsons Go to Birmingham – 1963*. Lewis re-interprets Rosenblatt's notion of "aesthetic" as critical as well as engaging, arguing that the "lived through experience" and identification with characters becomes a vehicle for being forced to think about racial hegemony and its implications, including questioning one's experiences of identification as a White reader. Others likewise say that the "structure of feeling" within the text needs to find an echo within the reader, such that "something *snaps*" (Robertson, 1997, 460; emphasis in the original). But not all Indigenous children's literature is of this kind. In most cases, as we have seen above, it finds an echo in teachers because it reminds them of a story they can incline towards.

The process of thinking through and writing the lesson plan needs to become an occasion for re-entering what we call the "contact zone," this for the purpose of composing a different kind of story. The "contact zone" is temporally and spatially located in the colonial encounter between Europeans and Indigenous peoples (Pratt, 1991, 1992). A "story of confrontation" is a narrative that a teacher creates through examining the interstices produced between storied sources: "It brings us back to our beginnings in story (in home, family and community); to the beginnings of story, which need to be sought in the places we first heard and imbibed stories (in early childhood); to the topos, or touchstones, from which our own stories began to be told; in short, to formation in and through story" (Strong-Wilson, 2007, 124–5). Desmond Manderson (2003), coming to children's literature from a legal perspective – "once upon a time, law was myth" (1) – locates the re-enactment of law's mythic origins in the primal scene of children's literature: "Childhood is the scene of the mythic emergence of sociability in each and every life, repeated and constantly renewed. Children's literature, then, is not *like* myth. It is myth. Children's literature is not a source of information *about* social structures of subjectivity in our society. It is the very site of their emergence" (9; emphasis in the original).

Arguably, the "contact zone" constitutes one such primal scene. As Toni Morrison (2002) suggests, stories about subduing threats to the social order, at least within the Western canon, owe their imaginative origins to the Anglo-Saxon epic of Beowulf and Grendel: Grendel is the fiendish monster devouring Hrothgar's people, while Beowulf is the hero who comes to destroy him and his mother. This colonial encounter is continually being re-inscribed by way of what Manderson calls the sociability story, in which the "savages" are tamed, as in Sendak's *Where the Wild Things Are* (Manderson's prime text). However, this story is also capable of being rewritten and seen from an Other's perspective, not unlike John Gardner's (1971) rewriting of Beowulf from the point of view of Grendel.

Children's literature has in fact become a site for "contested pasts" (Hodgkin & Radstone, 2003). The question of whose story is being told (i.e., from whose perspective) is now endemic to the contact zone. However, it is also a question for children's literature as a whole, in terms of which and whose stories are being published as well as taken up in libraries, schools, and, by extension, at bedsides as well as on Internet sites. It is a question that Nancy Larrick first posed in 1965 with her seminal article in *Saturday Review*, (then) provocatively entitled "The All-White World of Children's Books."

In the context of the present chapter, then, the question becomes one of how to carry oneself as teacher in a zone of contested pasts and contested stories. "Very far away" articulates a certain construction of Indigenous peoples as belonging to an imagined and a distant past. This "very far away" can be traced in a straight line from the teacher candidate to the five-year-old child in Ivana's lesson who articulated a profoundly insightful yet misconceived social understanding. If one applies Manderson's argument, the lesson plan becomes a critical site for being re-confronted with the colonial encounter, except that, as we have also seen, it now also marks a fork in the road. Choices need to be made about which kind of teacher story (viz., lesson) to tell. As teachers, we need to "distinguish the world we received as children from the one we are responsible to create as adults" (Grumet, 1991, 79–80). Central to a good telling, and to good pedagogy, is the kind of emotional and personal engagement with children's stories by Indigenous authors that can also lead to a deepened critical understanding. Only in this way can teachers hope to grasp the significance of Doxtater's circles and chart a different way forward.

NOTES

1 The use of "Indigenous" in this chapter is grounded in Alfred and Corntassel's (2005) argument that this term (more than Aboriginal or First Nations) emphasizes solidarity among Indigenous peoples and resistance

to colonialism. Within a Canadian context, "First Nations" would risk excluding Inuit and Métis peoples while "Aboriginal," though used in official government documents, has been criticized for that very reason: as a "political and cultural discourse designed to serve an agenda of silent surrender to an inherently unjust relation at the root of the colonial state itself" (Alfred & Corntassel, 598).

2 Nine (4.1%) students did not reply to the question concerning language, and 1 (0.4%) student claimed both English and French as first languages.

3 Criteria for inclusion are set out in the book's Introduction. *Coyote Sings to the Moon* (King; Wales, 1998) and *Coyote's New Suit* (King; Wales, 2004) were added. The author is featured in the study's annotated bibliography, and the two books offer examples of contemporary Indigenous literature.

4 Unlike with most other sites within this research project, opportunities to follow the teacher candidates into their practica were lacking. This was due to various factors: large class sizes, the timing of practica, and constraints within practica. Ivana (whose account opens this chapter) was one of the few who used or was able to use one of the study's books in her teaching. She voluntarily emailed us about it several months after we had conducted the workshop in the Kindergarten Classroom course.

7 Connecting Visual Literacy and Cultural Awareness through Picture Book Illustrations

ANNE BURKE

Visual images take many different forms as they characterize the ways in which we interpret our world. It's important, therefore, for young readers to learn how to read and create meaning from visual images: in the mental construction of a child's developing literacy, visual images are often the connectors that consolidate and reinforce important concepts in their reading worlds. Furthermore, it's important that children learn to critically analyse different kinds of images. Using picture books in students' foundational educational experiences creates opportunities for them to gain a critical understanding of others' lived worlds as presented through the artistic elements found in the designs and media used by illustrators. Picture books invite readers to return again and again to images, allowing exploration and reflection, and the opportunity to consider the illustrator's purpose in choosing different types of media to represent different images. Being able to readily construct meaning and critically analyse such visual texts depends upon the reader's ability to see the interdependent relationship of text and illustration – how they work together to convey meaning. As learners read and interpret the written text and illustrations in picture books, they build on learned literacy skills. Rebecca Lukens (2002) argues: "Pictures make the verbal visible and extend the textual meaning; they permit the artist to add personal interpretation while staying within the story, but do not overwhelm the text" (40).

As Rosenblatt (1983) reminds us, the act of reading literature requires readers to consider themselves in relation to the text. This in turn leads to considerations about our connections to others, a necessary process as we become more globally connected. Books that incorporate issues of diversity can be used to build a child's self-concept in connection to their community, their country, and the world (Loh, 2009). These picture books convey multilayered meanings through their use of visual grammar, wherein the story is a seamless blend of text and illustrations. They offer the reader opportunities for exploration, discussion, confrontation, and the celebration of cultural heritage and the beliefs of a particular group (Arizpe & Styles, 2003; Galda & Short, 1993; Gangi, 2004; Keene & Zimmerman, 1997; Kiefer, 1995; Stewig, 1995). Living in a visually oriented world, children need to understand the importance of the image, and to engage actively in reading images. While developing an aesthetic appreciation for the art in picture books, it is possible for children to gain greater understanding, empathy, and appreciation for others living in other life spaces (Burke & Peterson, 2007; Kiefer, 2010; Hughes, 1998). Teachers can enhance children's reading experiences through encouraging them to read and interpret illustrations in diverse picture books, pointing to the key role visual literacy can play as a building block towards students' greater global and cultural awareness.

During a children's literature course I taught, preservice teachers responded to a selection of diverse Canadian picture books. Making strong connections to the artistic elements of design created by the illustrator and the text offered by the author, these preservice teachers discussed the importance of the visual in creating spaces for readers' greater understanding of our global society. This chapter also chronicles preservice teachers' experiences during their practicum placements in attempting to raise their students' cultural awareness, their sense of diversity, and development of an understanding of how history and culture contribute to the making of the Canadian cultural mosaic. In doing so, I present the voices of preservice teachers describing how their efforts ultimately led to the building of global connections for the children in their classrooms.

Connecting the Global to the Local

Diversity is now very much part of our teaching lexicon. Our world has become smaller as the Internet creates broad and instant access to others' ways of being – with "ways of being" referring to how others live and carry out their everyday existences in various communities (Wenger, 1998a). While discussion of themes relating to social responsibility, tolerance, respect, and acceptance of others are common in our classrooms, the terms themselves can vary according to cultural practice. Teachers may use many different resources to provide positive and negative examples of these types of character traits. Suzanne Langer (1995) argues that the use of literature can offer opportunities for self-study, reflection, and understanding of others. Becoming self-aware through social responsibility and cultural awareness connects children to their own identity within a global society. If they are to ensure inclusive practices in their classrooms, pre-service teachers require a close understanding of themselves and others. Vicarious experiences are offered to readers through the characters in picture books. Chin Loh (2009) terms these experiences "textual mediation – the ways they are read contribute to the imaginings of individual subjectivities by providing visions of different worlds, and influencing the perception of self in relation to others in the world" (Loh, 2009, 288).

One step to broadening such perceptions and global understanding is through the use of children's literature, especially books that reflect the diversity of Canadian students' lives. Books that raise issues of diversity may be used in a number of ways to increase understandings of cultural perspectives among populations with little diversity and cultural growth. The research site in Newfoundland qualifies as a historically isolated population. Located in the North Atlantic, far from the economic centres of Canada, Newfoundland received few immigrants over the last number of generations. In the past decade, however, an oil boom has made the capital city of St John's an attractive destination for new arrivals from all over the world. This immigration, combined with a sudden influx of local transients from rural areas, has changed the Caucasian English-Irish make-up of the local culture and, more importantly for this chapter, its classrooms. Newfoundland is still largely an island of small homogeneous communities, and the expense of travel has meant that many children do not have an opportunity to directly experience cultures other than their own. Instead, the art and text of picture books can help build tolerance, respect, and a greater curiosity about others who live in our world. Lawrence Sipes (2007) advocates: "As children embrace or resist texts through language and a variety of artistic modes they are forging links between literature and their own lives. Such links have the potential to be both informative and transformative for their developing sense of themselves as individuals and members of society" (34).

The shifting demographics of schools in urban Newfoundland create an opportunity for educators to use diversity literature as a way to welcome newcomers to the province and celebrate their cultural heritage.

Providing students with culturally authentic texts allows them to see themselves in their school reading, and is helpful in promoting positive self-constructs and understanding of the beliefs and practices of others. The experiences of the preservice teachers in this study speak to the pedagogies they used to demonstrate how diversity literature could be used to make global connections for children.

Diversity literature exposes children to a broad view of the world. Narrative voices from characters within the plots of picture books can open doors to other cultures, and provide cultural insights that may not have been possible in the past (Burke, 2009; Burke & Peterson, 2007). According to Au (1993) and Heath (1983), culture includes our interactions with the world around us, our ways of knowing, beliefs, values, and thinking. Fact-based books are often ineffective in helping children to connect their own stories of identities to those pictured or discussed in the books. In informational texts, discussions about people from unfamiliar cultures may pertain to clothing, the foods they eat, holidays, and how they live, building an informational understanding for the child. In contrast, diverse literary texts can convey a deeper understanding of a particular group, and create respect and understanding of how a group thinks about the world. These new understandings can be beneficial for students, yet also very complex (Norton, 2009). One advantage of imaginative literature is that children can find common ground with narrative characters, an experience they are not likely to have when reading an informational text (Winters & Schmidt, 2001).

In the next section, I discuss aspects of visual literacy and show how the preservice teachers in our study connected with the narratives and characters within the Canadian picture books. The focus here is on the artistic elements of illustrations that are relevant to the preservice teachers' insights and experiences of reading and teaching picture books during this study.

Visual Literacy

Perry Nodelman (1988) discusses how neither the text nor the visual image can be considered separate entities: "The words and the pictures in picture books both define and amplify each other, neither is open ended as it would be on its own" (8). The understanding of picture books, and how the sum of their parts work together, is not a natural process of understanding that comes easily to children. Nodelman and Reimer (2003) maintain that "pictures are no more 'concrete' and no less abstract than words are. They are what practitioners of semiotics call signs – representations whose meaning depends on a repertoire of learned strategies" (275).

Visual literacy may be defined as "the skills to understand and critically interpret the function and meanings of different visual representations and orders" (Seppänen, 2006, 4). Winch, Johnston, Holliday, Ljungdahl, and March (2001) argue that "visual literacy is more than the ability to decode images. It is the ability to analyse the power of the image ... in a particular context" (407). In this study, preservice teachers came to understand how images can create meaning and can be used for teaching in varying contexts.

Expanding Our Visual Interpretation of Picture Books through Multimodality

Picture books come with their own visual language, or grammar, created through the interaction of various images and text on the page to evoke meaning. Multimodality refers to the multiple modes of representation used in a text to communicate a message. Modes are essentially the parts of a communicative message, interpreted according to their form, but also via the cultural associations the reader evokes as a part of their response (Jewitt, 2008; Kress, 2003). Multimodality is essentially the mixing and melding of modes such as the written and visual, through different fonts and the use of photographs and modes with movement through animation (Bearne, 2004; Kress, 2003). Children learn to read the artistic elements in picture book illustrations while building early literacy skills. Reading pictures is one of the first literate skills shown by children, and reveals their understanding of how the elements of design and written text interconnect with each other. As opposed to simply decoding the written word, children's interactions with the visuals of picture books show a sophisticated ability to identify the meaning of the text, as it is carried in modes that are visual, spatial, with texture and colour, and so forth. An example of multimodality in a picture book would be the combination of words, the colours used by the illustrator, and the illustrated gestural actions of the character. The multimodality of the picture book illustration constitutes a complex understanding of how the construction, design, and meaning making work in concert. Serafini (2009) suggests that the artistic elements in picture books enhance the intended meaning of the text, and an understanding of these visual cues and nuances enables the reader to comprehend the interaction of characters and their surroundings. Burke and Peterson (2007) argue that children might become more connected and empathetic towards prior social conditions and historical periods when they learn to read picture book images with more insight.

A multimodal reading of text may motivate children to move their understandings beyond the plot of a book, ultimately encouraging them to think more critically about a given situation.

The Aesthetics of Visual Literacy

McKenzie (2003) says that visual literacy can be used to project power relations and social values in line with, or in contrast to, the written text. She suggests that this literacy is adaptable to the classroom, where children and adults can learn how power and social values can be incorporated into and displayed by visual images. In the article *Picturebooks and Metaliteracy: How Children Describe the Processes of Creation and Reception*, Arizpe and Styles (2003) consider how children analyse visual texts, including how they perceive the processes behind the creation of illustrations. Overall, the children they studied felt that pictures are vital to a book, and not mere adjuncts to the words present in the text. In many cases, children can perceive that the illustrator may be telling a story that differs from what is expressed in the written text. When we consider that children's first engagements with literacy are often through wordless books, with guidance from parents asking, "What is happening in the picture?" we can see how children would associate these early engagements with visual aspects of a text being of primary importance. This perspective can be vital when looking at the illustrations in picture books that raise issues of diversity, where the images can give significant and important understandings into the culture and beliefs of a particular group. Grigg (2003) conducted a study of children's observations of works of art in a gallery setting. His study suggests that young children are better able to access sensory language, and as a result, children's interpretation of artwork can seem more focused and expressive than that of an adult. Because they are not yet tied to the text, children depend more upon the visuals in picture books to extract meaning.

Lewis's (2004) article "A Word about Pictures" examines the features in a visual image, and provides insight into how the illustration contributes to the meaning conveyed by the image as a whole. Line, colour, action and movement, size, location, and symbolism all influence the image in different ways. In addition, a number of conventions are employed in picture book illustrations that are widely known to children, conventions which readily contribute to the understanding of an image. Consequently, misinterpretations of pictures can occur if an illustration is ambiguous, or if the artist does not adhere to established conventions. Lewis also reviews the concept of visual grammar, indicating how the structural organization of an image can be considered. However, he states that an illustration should not be broken down into its component parts. Instead, the visual grammar should be taken into account in relationship to the other aspects of the image. His work speaks to the importance of educators understanding and broadening their perspectives, and finding ways to bridge to children's visual understandings and perceptions.

The Language of Picture Book Design

The interplay of text and illustration in picture books demand different forms of reading and understanding of how different texts share different meanings with a reader. The visual elements of design communicate important messages to the reader about the text; the illustrator chooses to emphasize and utilize art elements to communicate the narrative. The use of such media should complement and expand the plot developments and characterizations, intensifying the reader's involvement in the setting of the action. For example, particular objects or characters will often be placed to the centre of the page to draw the eye to a central focus. The use of lines in an illustration may convey emotions: sharp and angular lines show strength and ruggedness, while soft and curved lines communicate warmth and softness. Vertical lines share a feeling of sense and aspiration, while diagonal lines project a sense of movement, and horizontal lines a sense of peace and comfort. The use of shape can project a sense of openness or closeness, and may be received through a character's actions and gestures. Colour may be interpreted through its cultural context and use, and interpretation of colour should be through the cultural representation of the book itself. When engaging with North American picture books, the interpretation of colour comes quite naturally to children as seen in expressions of emotions such as "blue" for sadness, "red" for excitement or anger, "yellow" for calmness, or "green" for growth (Burke, 2002). Essentially, the use of lighter colours can evoke less restriction, more freedom, and a light airiness, whereas darker or bold colours can be more dramatic in creating mood, indicating space for personal reflection. The composition and design of picture books, through the illustrator's communicative use of artistic elements, expand children's understandings of the picture book text. Importantly, there should be a sense of unity in how these forms work together. The composition and design should motivate a reader's aesthetic appreciation and response. As McNair and Colabucci (2007) explain: "These elements (color, brush stroke, perspective, size and placement of figures) when carefully chosen convey feelings and moods, elaborate on themes and provide important information not presented in the text" (39).

Artistic elements of design are expressed through various media such as acrylics that create an opaque effect, which dries and allows the artist to rework the paint, creating depth, dimension, and texture. Gouache is water-based powder that is mixed with chalk. It can give illustrations a bright look and softer tones. The use of techniques like "scratchboard," wherein the paint effects and illustrations are scratched using a sharp tool, create a vivid sense of texture and mood. The use of collage combines material such as cloth and paper on a flat surface. Other illustrative forms, such as charcoal and pencil drawing, can help define the lines and space of the character. The range of styles of illustrations can be used to share the artist's vision. Illustrators become known for the forms in which they represent their art. Most children's literature uses representational art. Children can easily interpret and respond to the illustrations based on what is represented in the pictures. Realistic imagery in a text can create greater understanding of the world in which we live and provide a basis for discovery for readers.

Preservice Teachers' Responses to the Visual in Diverse Picture Books

The preservice teachers who participated in this study were students in a course I taught with a colleague on the use of children's literature in the primary and elementary grades. This thirty-six credit-hour course looks in depth at the vitality and use of children's literature as a resource and as core material in primary and elementary classrooms. Areas of focus include the interconnection of text and illustrations, design and composition elements, genres of literature, and literature that raises issues of diversity. Among the students who were completing a bachelor of education as a first degree, there were mature students who were seeking a second degree and had decided the sixteen-month intensive degree program would be more in keeping with their needs and desire to enter into the teaching field more directly. Many of the preservice teacher participants in this study had experienced other careers in nursing, Information Communications Technology, social work, media and advertising. One participant had a master's degree in theology and had served in a youth ministry. The varied experiences and understandings this group of preservice teachers brought to the course provided for rich discussions and understandings of the varying aspects of picture books. The following section presents discussion of their perspectives on visual literacy related to the picture books, and of their pedagogical experiences of teaching the texts. Themes of diversity, cultural heritage, and the presence of powerful cultural and historical disruptions emerged from preservice teachers' engagement with the visual and textual elements of the diversity literature.

Diversity

Jordan, a preservice teacher in the study, discussed *If You're Not from the Prairie* (Bouchard; *Ripplinger*, 1993). This book largely consists of idyllic scenes of nature and agriculture, snapshots of life on the Canadian prairies. The reader enters into many pastoral experiences through both the poetic text and the vivid oil paintings that present aspects of prairie life such as skipping stones across a pond, chasing the relentless wind, and watching the vast and endless sky. The illustrator's portrayal of a sunset using colours such as orange, red, and yellow create a warm feeling of freedom and endless hope in the above example.

The interplay of illustration and text evoke a sense of freedom for both the land and the human spirit. Jordan commented:

> We read it and talked about the meaning. So you get to the end and there's the twist that changes it from being a book about excluding people to including people. So we went through to make sure they understood the change and we talked a bit about the culture, like what are the interesting characteristics of the prairies? And did we share any of them? And then we added a list of what makes Newfoundland distinctive and at the end we made our own book. So each student wrote a page and illustrated it.

Her comments show the natural way in which illustrations and text can build critical awareness of diversity in the reader, especially when the text and illustrations work in concert to create meaning.

Figure 5. Illustration from *Red Parka Mary* (Eyvindson and Brynjolson, 1996, unpaginated)

Jordan's responses were generated while she was teaching a lesson on cultural awareness and diversity as part of a multicultural unit for a class of grade 2 students. Jordan's discussion captured the important role of the visual in conveying meaning to the reader.

Vera, a qualified teaching assistant who had worked for a period of time in Western Canada, shared her understanding of how definitions of diversity had widened beyond ethnicity, race, and sexual orientation to include learning disabled and socially disadvantaged individuals, and that diversity involves just a "range of differences." As a New-foundlander from a small rural town, she readily admitted that she was afraid of how she used terms, afraid that she might mistakenly "label" inappropriately. Her use of illustrations from *Red Parka Mary* (Eyvindson; *Brynjolson*, 1996) in the example below shows her growth in understanding that diversity includes those who are homeless and disadvantaged. Her comments suggest that the illustrations in the picture book fostered greater understanding and reflection on the human condition on her part as a reader.

> My picture book, it's a lot about age diversity, now I mean there's a lot of cultural diversity because it talks about native American. But I just could relate because my book deals with ... You always find one person in your community that you always remember and this happens to be an older lady and she dresses funny and so much more. I'm sure everyone can look back in their own community and say, "oh I knew a person like that" and everybody always says stuff about that person without even knowing them.

Vera's comments also suggest that diversity comes with a preconceived judgment about a person and their actions. Focusing on the main character in *Red Parka Mary*, she helped the children in her classroom learn another person's story through an exploration of the actions of a little boy who learns not to judge people by their appearances.

Barbara, another teacher candidate, discussed the illustrations in *The Missing Sun* (Eyvindson; *Brynjolson*, 1993). Upon first looking at the book she was captured by the illustrator's use of colour and light, which resembled her memories of Inuvik. The illustrator's use of rich texture, colour, and light creates shadows on the snow which contrast with the soft colours the characters are pictured wearing. In the exchange below she explained how she impressed upon her students the concept of diversity through comparing her personal vacation pictures with the illustrations in the book. She made a comparison chart to assist students in understanding the commonalities and differences between their Newfoundland culture and that of Inuvik.

> Yes, and I had pictures from Inuvik because I had been there before and I showed them my personal pictures and we looked at the pictures. I had the pictures that were similar to the ones that were illustrated in the book so we talked about that. Then we talked about what St John's is like and based on what we had just read about Inuvik and what Inuvik is like. So they were able to pick out the differences.

Figure 6. Illustration from *The Missing Sun* (Eyvindson and Brynjolson, 1993, unpaginated)

Dietrich and Ralph (1995) say that "one of the values of seeing commonalities across cultures is the avenue it creates for students to establish lines of communication with people of diverse cultures" (3). Having children see differences, yet at the same time commonalities, builds a deeper respect and understanding of the identities of others.

Cultural Heritage

> Then if it is a picture book, I look at the pictures first ... so I am looking for them just to be imaginative. So is there somewhere that they can go ... they can make their own connections to the book.

In the above focus group discussion, Emma explained why she saw the illustrations as a way for students to make personal connections to the tender story of a grandfather and grandson experiencing nature together during a canoe paddle in *Morning on the Lake* (Waboose; *Reczuch*, 1997). What struck her was the illustrator's artistic detailing of the loons in the early morning pictured amidst cool colours and mist, adding to the crispness of the morning air and sense of renewal of another day. Many of the visual representations in the picture books from which the preservice teachers selected helped them to explore cultural heritage. Howells (2003) argues that becoming visually literate is necessary in today's world, as it helps children to think critically about the messages being conveyed, such as the illustrator's choices in extending plot lines within a book. Artistic techniques can help us to think and connect more visually to what is being presented to the reader. Perry Nodelman (1988) explains that in looking at the visuals and the ways in which they help children, "the texts and illustrations of a book have an ironic relationship to each other: the words tell us what the pictures do not show, and the pictures show us what the words do not tell" (222).

Through teaching *The Mummer's Song* (Davidge & Wallace, 1993), an illustrated ballad that tells of the famous Newfoundland Christmas tradition of mummering, Jennie created a classroom connection to students and their cultural background.

> I introduced them to *The Mummer's Song*, which being in rural Newfoundland the majority or all of them actually were familiar with it. So then I brought in the picture book and let them look at the book and then seeing the pictures with the words helped them relate more to things that

have happened and they could actually then bring back stories about how mummers had showed up at their house and things like that and how they were dressed. They really enjoyed the pictures because they'd seen the pictures of how mummers dress up in Newfoundland. So, of course, they related it back to, you know, just seeing that themselves and how a book could be, how someone could write a book and illustrate and just use the words of the song and draw pictures and they were really fascinated by that. So I definitely think that helped visual learners for sure.

Jennie's comments on how the children responded to the book speaks of the building of the students' critical understandings of how particular texts such as a traditional song may be represented in other forms – in this case, a picture book. In this classroom moment, we see how this book, which presented a traditional local cultural practice, was particularly meaningful to the students. It confirmed for them the value of a tradition and cultural practice that may seem odd to those who live outside the province. The book related to their cultural heritage and evoked their grandparents' recollections of past holiday times in a storytelling class assignment. This was a special connection for Jennie's students. Revisiting a familiar text in a different form builds the children's critical literacy for the appreciation of different texts.

Historical and Cultural Disruptions

Well what better way to introduce ideas or to address these situations than through a picture book where students can relate to the pictures or may have a lot of questions ... I'd think that they would be more open to talking about those things if they came from a book.

Preservice teachers such as Elizabeth, quoted above, saw the use of the Canadian picture books offered in the study as a way to bridge to new understandings for their students. In Newfoundland, many of the children live in what we would call encapsulated communities. Interesting comments were raised by several preservice teachers, who said diversity was difficult to explain in smaller communities because "many of our children just do not see it" (i.e., people from different cultures). Although this may be the reality for many children in smaller communities, children need to see how their ideas, beliefs, actions, and decisions affect others. Many of the picture books in the study had the potential to make such connections. In some ways the use of illustrations in the picture books opened the door for children to contend with weighty issues such as the Japanese internment, residential schooling, immigration, and same-sex marriage. Some of these issues created struggles for some of our preservice teachers, who had to disrupt their own personal and cultural beliefs to teach about diversity, an essential component of the Newfoundland curriculum.

During the interview, I asked participants to describe the types of challenges they faced in classrooms or with their own constructed identities as teachers. Some participants recalled the frustration of working in schools where little or no value was placed on diversity. Many of the schools were unchanged culturally from their previous existence as part of the established Catholic denominational schooling system that operated until the 1990s. Many school cultures were still deeply steeped in religious practices. Although this system was eventually abolished, these changes were more readily accepted in schools that did not have religious orders associated with them through either teaching staff or ownership of the building. Many of these schools also served the social needs of a community through school functions such as concerts and community gatherings. Some preservice teachers had begun to see the political and social implications of teaching in these particular schools with their narrow belief systems.

Others expressed concerns about the use of particular books that presented diverse perspectives on same-sex families. These books challenged the dominant cultural and gender beliefs within a school and encouraged one preservice teacher to choose another book that would move him "away from causing a fuss." Brian shared his conflicted religious and personal understandings of diversity. He commented:

> I saw the book that Carrie had selected, *Mom and Mum Are Getting Married!* by Ken Setterington, and I immediately thought I could basically ruin my internship by picking up that book and bringing it up in that school, and that caused this debate in my head, you know, those children, like you know it's the parent's choice to raise the children in the Catholic way which teaches many good things. But there also is Doctrine which would teach that it is not okay. It made me debate whether it's the parents right to not expose the child to that and it created a huge controversy in my head.

Brian's discussion echoes a common concern among students: that the controversial points of connection in certain picture books would be a challenge when a teacher took into account the social and political nature of the schools and personal understandings, even though many felt the visuals in the picture books could gently illustrate complex family situations.

Jennie used the book *Grandfather Counts* (Cheng; *Zhang*, 2000), which challenged students to think about their connections to China, in hopes of creating a more global understanding for her grade 2 classroom. She described in this interview what happened after she read the book to the class: "It was really neat. I brought in a few little Chinese New Year's calendars and a few things, like what was in the book, to introduce them to Chinese culture. I was showing them how different things in our home like a TV remote are 'made in China' just to give them an idea. They noticed a lot of their clothing was made in China."

Jennie had experienced a culturally disruptive moment, one which occurred when the children realized that their lives, and how they live, are connected to others and to their well-being and survival. She listened to the children asking about the origin of many of the possessions in their lives, making real-life connections.

One participant, Alanna, was raised in a family of five and grew up in a small rural Newfoundland village of 150 people, which she described as being insular and characterized by traditional understandings and values. Nonetheless, racial awareness and teaching pedagogies to support an acceptance of multiculturalism and social justice were important to Alanna. She felt that the attitudes in her small community could only change if children taught the older generations through their school experiences. She shared with her class Maxine Trottier's book *Flags* (Trottier; *Morin*, 1999).

This book is about the internment of Japanese Canadians during the Second World War. In her interview, Alanna described how the students were moved by the book's watercolour illustrations, which depict a Japanese garden left unattended when its caretaker was interned.

> They liked the picture. It was the colour. It was the texture in it as well. It was like sand and rocks and plants and things. And they liked how it looked real. That's how they described it to me. But one girl said to me, I think it was here the double page, the picture looks sad. I am assuming she was relating to the darker colors but not necessarily. "He looks very sad because he is going away and they are friends, and, like, my friend when she moved away was really sad the day before she left." So probably the colour might have, … with the sun setting, ending his time here. I think that is what she meant by that.

Figure 7. Illustration from *Flags* (Trottier and Morin, 1999, unpaginated)

Further to this experience, Alanna described how the picture book helped the children to relate to a period in Canadian history when identities and actions were disrupted. The students questioned the history and actions of Canadians during the Second World War:

> So they talked about [how] life is not fair and they didn't like how Mr Horoshi was treated as we were reading the book. They would shoot up their hand or just blurt out, you know, "Why did they do that? Didn't he live in Canada?" Questions like, "Miss, what's the point of that? What are they doing that for? Did they actually do that? Did that actually happen?"

For Alanna, this was a telling moment, when the children realized that history was not just a story but about the experiences of pain, hurt, and suffering of others. Their critical connection at this moment brought a restorative understanding to Alanna, to see how she could address racial attitudes about culture in small communities that had been steeped in traditional and small-town values.

A new cultural moment of understanding occurred for Sarah when she shared the picture book by Robert Munsch, *From Far Away* (Munsch & Ascar; *Martchenko*, 1995). This book tells the story of Susan, a new immigrant child to Canada, and how she found the cultural differences in Canadian society and school to be a frightening experience. In one illustration, Martchenko has pictured the teacher and the child in a comforting embrace, among the backdrop of artefacts such as skeletons, pumpkins, and bats representing Halloween, a Western cultural celebration. Working in a city-centre school with a growing immigrant population, Sarah commented that this particular book raised awareness and created empathy within the class for new children coming from far away. "Yes, I must say the children were pretty understanding and accepting. I asked for them to think about Susan from the book *From Far Away*, if she came to our classroom and we were the first classroom that she'd been into in Canada ... how they would feel and how they would treat her. They went around the class and they each shared because they were so anxious."

Overall, students felt that the interconnectivity offered through the text and images offered in the picture books could provide a wider access to other cultures and experiences for their students. Many of the historical disruptions discovered through the students' teaching experiences called upon them to revisit their own viewpoints about diversity and the Canadian mosaic. Life connections, and the ways we come to knowledge, can lead to a disruption of self and identity, as these beginning teachers came to realize. For many of them, their time in the classroom working with culturally sensitive picture books led to a greater understanding of how children could begin to see their place in the world around them. However, they also learned that they had more issues to grapple with as they began their teaching journeys.

Conclusions

This research study demonstrated that if preservice teachers develop critical understandings about their communities and their practices regarding diversity during their teacher education programs, it can lead to greater personal cultural awareness on their part, which in turn can be taken into their future classrooms. The preservice teachers in our study were sometimes challenged by the social responsibility of teaching cultural awareness, and as one said when discussing multi-cultural educational practice: "It is not as widely accepted as it should be, but I think it depends on the individuals that are out there teach-ing." Other participants felt that the program offered at the university needed rethinking and that teacher educators need to be more active in the teaching community: "If we were to have a program here where we could take social action courses, then you learn how to use all books and resources as you would in other courses, but you know you still need to have workshops for teachers out there." Another student pointed out that "my internship sponsoring teacher said that my program is the same as hers, and she graduated ten years ago." The last comment speaks to the need for change in programing to acknowledge a more diverse population including newcomers to the province.

Plainly, as seen in the data, the preservice teachers found many pos-itive ways to use picture books to further the awareness of cultural diversity in their classrooms, and to create an awareness of some of the social history behind the development of the Canadian mosaic. Their students easily grasped, through a combination of illustration and text, how children in other cultures live and see the world. Using mul-ticultural picture books as a place of departure for looking within and beyond, these preservice teachers saw their students make insightful connections between themselves and others. The multicultural picture books drew attention to universal themes and understandings, which is perhaps the first step in enhancing global connectedness for a new generation of students and preservice teachers. As we can see from the preservice teachers' comments in this chapter, however, issues of diversity were not a meaningful part of their teacher education program. In order to embrace the new cultures of immigrant Canadian students in our school classrooms, our programs will need to become more attentive to diversity if we are to address the needs of a changing population.

8 Generative Ways to Promote Political Activity and Social Change with Picture Books

ROBERTA HAMMETT[1]

Preservice teachers often begin their education programs with idealism, wanting to "make a difference" in their classrooms and the lives of children they will teach. Consider these statements as to why three preservice teachers want to teach:

> I want to make an influence in [children's] lives and make them the person they can be and try to make a difference in each one. – Karen

> I want to inspire the way teachers have inspired me. I want to make sure students have someone who wants to inspire them. – Tara

> Well, I like children and I'm really intent on just doing something for my career that has a significant impact on [others]. – Matthew

Such admirable ideals imply a concern for social justice and an intention to engage in "teaching as a political activity and embrace social change as part of the job" (Cochran-Smith, 1995, 494). In Newfoundland and Labrador, where these data were collected, such ideals are often accompanied by a lack of experience with cultural and ethnic diversity. For example, questioned about their lived knowledge of multiculturalism, these preservice teachers explained:

> I grew up in [community] until I was nineteen and all that time I've only known two non-white families. – Matthew

> I came from a really small community, everyone is from the same place, everyone is the same culture, and then I go somewhere else and there are people from different races and I was taken aback. – Tara

These examples are representative of most students' experiences and seem to limit expressed ideals when classroom realities meet a lack of experience with diverse cultures.

Knowing how to broaden experiences such as these is a challenge to teacher education and the goal of the action research described throughout this book. As teacher educators, we are well aware that we must "challenge each candidate to quickly acquire new skills and to readily incorporate new ways of 'thinking and being'" (Burns, 2009, 19). Teacher educators, members of this research team, are committed to such enacting theories as constructivism, poststructural concepts of identity, and critical responses to conservative and neo-liberal ideologies. We want to provide learning experiences that engage teachers as producers of "knowledge of teaching" (Cochran-Smith & Lytle, 1999, 254). We want to position teacher candidates as active inquirers into teaching, not consumers of best practices. Wilhelm (2009) describes this as "developing a critical literacy of teaching," and, paraphrasing others, notes that "the critical stance is described as conscious engagement, i.e., the willingness and capacity to try on alternate ways of thinking and being and practicing, the consciously taken responsibility for inquiry (open-minded exploration, data-driven decisions, disciplinary ways of thinking – both for students and teachers), and a wide-awake reflectivity and reflexivity" (36).

As teacher educators, we hope teacher candidates will explore their own beliefs, not just about teaching, but also about the society that they should help build and maintain as influential members of communities and as significant mentors of future citizens. In our education programs, and in this study, we have considered it important to expand our definitions of multiculturalism and diversity to include race, ethnicity, socio-economic status, sex/gender, geographic region, sexuality, religion, language, and ability/disability (Cushner, McClelland, & Safford, 2003).

This chapter, then, will draw on the data collected in Newfoundland and Labrador, primarily in 2006, 2007, and 2008, from preservice teachers in either a primary-elementary integrated education degree program or a post-degree bachelor of education program at Memorial University. The participants were taught by either Anne Burke, co-researcher in this study, or by another instructor who agreed to facilitate the study. The participants, like most students in the primary-elementary programs, are mostly Newfoundlanders and Labradorians. However, increasing numbers of our students come to Memorial from other Atlantic provinces as well as other parts of Canada. Most are in their early twenties, but increasingly older students are found in post-degree education programs.

These data were collected in surveys, focus group discussions, lesson plans, and post-practicum interviews. As a researcher in this project, I participated in all these data collection activities in some of the years; at other times I was absent from campus during data collection. I analysed the data that I collected and that was shared with me. I have a strong research and teaching interest in multicultural education, teacher education, literature, and multiliteracies; thus, all aspects of this picture books study – its diversity, identity, and visual literacy elements – appealed to me.

In this chapter, I will theoretically contextualize the discussion of the data, drawing on several relevant themes in published research on teacher education. I will conclude the chapter with reflections on the research and teaching process as experienced in Newfoundland and Labrador.

Research Literature

There has been considerable research related to multicultural and diversity education and reflections on courses designed to prepare preservice teachers to teach in classrooms different from the ones they experienced growing up (see, for example, Cochran-Smith, 1995; Ladson-Billings, 2001; Delpit, 1995). Engaging future teachers in experiences that increase their knowledge and understanding of how to teach in diverse and urban classrooms is a challenge (Wright, 1980; Fuller, 1994, Sleeter, 2001). Researchers have identified colour blindness (Cochran-Smith, 2000; Johnson, 2002; Lewis, 2001; Milner, 2005), lack of awareness and understanding of racism and discrimination (Gay, 2000; Banks et al., 2001), "subordinat[ing] any interest in multicultural education to demands of their cooperating teachers" (Sleeter, 2001, 95), and lack of preparedness for the overwhelming challenges of such teaching (Nieto, 2000) as some of the many issues in this struggle. We have experienced similar challenges; we've also noted paying lip service to "official multiculturalism" (Saldanha, 2000; Grant, 1992) instead of real commitment as a challenge. In our cross-Canada research, as well as here in Newfoundland and Labrador, we noted beliefs and understandings such as the following: multiculturalism and diversity are an "add-on" to curriculum planning and practice; diverse/multicultural material is controversial in teaching practices and in schools; and concern for social issues, social justice and equality can be turned off and on.

Our study was designed to incorporate several activities to encourage among our preservice teachers a multicultural awareness and preparedness for social action – as Cochran-Smith (1995) puts it, "generative ways ... to explore and reconsider their own assumptions, understand the values and practices of families and cultures that are different from their own, and construct pedagogy that takes these into account in locally appropriate and culturally sensitive ways" (495). As has been described elsewhere, instructors and researchers involved in the study made available some eighty different picture books selected to provoke discussion and foreground diversity themes and issues (see appendix B for our picture book list). The learning activities in the study were often the data collection devices: surveys that asked preservice teachers to articulate their thinking, classroom lectures and discussions, book talks they performed in class, focus groups, unit plans built around text sets, practicum activities (implementing unit plans and using our selected books, where possible), and post-practicum interviews. Our discussions and focus group questions played a role in shaping the preservice teachers' sense of ethnic identity, and they in turn attempted to similarly address identities in their classrooms.

Knowledge of Multicultural and Diversity Education: The Context

In the province of Newfoundland and Labrador "place" figures prominently in the identities of preservice teachers' understandings of multiculturalism and diversity. For example, Janet commented, "Personally, I have a better understanding of a 'Newfoundland/Labrador' identity than a Canadian one." Another of the preservice teachers said, "Canadian identity really talks to me about landscape ... I feel people in Canada have a really strong sense of place. And whether that's a city or whether they grew up in a rural area, or whatever province they're from, people seem to really strongly connect with where they grew up." In a province which is largely monocultural, populated mostly by descendents of immigrants from the British Isles, this leads to reflections like Sandra's when asked about her participation in the activities of our research:

> I think the study is really about more awareness to myself about multiculturalism, living in Newfoundland. There aren't very many people around that have a different race or a different religion, not too many, like you know, compared to ... other centres. So I think this really brought out more

awareness for myself about what we should do in our school systems and what we should teach and educate our students.

Sandra's use of the phase "awareness to myself" suggests that she is considering a need for new ways of thinking and being. Similarly, Alexandra said:

> Well, I feel more strongly now that something should be addressed in the classroom, like from my experience of multiculturalism of never really thinking about it, wasn't really something that was sort of talked about I guess, that I could remember. But … the way the world is going, I feel that before I sort of address any sort of other culture that maybe I would like to do more research on that culture because I don't want to be talking or teaching about something that I don't know much about myself. I think it's important for the teachers to have at least a basic understanding about culture.

Alexandra has recognized that she must become an inquirer into multiculturalism and diversity. The "way the world is going" has meant local changes in population demographics and economics demanding change in schools and education systems as well as communities. Newfoundland and Labrador (NL) is Canada's newest province, joining the confederation in 1949, almost fifty years after other provinces. The province also has Canada's oldest settlements, fishing stations established over five hundred years ago. The island part of the province consists of a number of small rural communities (outports), with a population of around 420,000 people spread over the approximately 110,000 square kilometres (with about 200,000 of the population in St John's). The Federation of Newfoundland Indians (FNI) represents approximately 10,500 non-status Mi'kmaq people, with about 800 living on the status reserve at Conne River (Higgins, 2008). Beothuks, Aboriginal inhabitants of earlier Newfoundland, became extinct in 1829. Labrador (295,000 square kilometres) is part of mainland Canada and was joined with Newfoundland during confederation with Canada; there had been well-established links throughout their common history. Labrador has approximately 30,000 inhabitants, 2200 of whom are Innu First Nations (Innu Nation, n.d.); around 2200 are Inuit, living in Nunatsiavut (Statistics Canada, 2008); and about 6000 are Métis First Nation (Labrador Métis Nation, 2007). The remaining two-thirds of Labradorians are of mixed descent, with most having a long family history in Labrador (Chui et al., 2004).

Recently, with the development of off-shore oil and other social and economic changes (such as the cod fishing moratorium), and increasing refugee arrivals, there are slight changes in cultural and ethnic demographics here in the province. In addition, in June 2008, Newfoundland and Labrador enacted its own multicultural policy to support the Canadian multicultural policy, again indicating changing or potentially changing demographics and proactivity in the politics of multiculturalism and diversity. School curriculum and Department of Education policies are responding gradually to the province's newly adopted policy. Our data illustrate the challenges of adjusting monocultural settings so they become more accepting and diverse environments (Hammett & Bainbridge, 2009). In schools our students witnessed problematic acts, all motivated by lack of knowledge and awareness – "ignorance" as one student, Cathy, in our study put it. Examples previously reported (Hammett & Bainbridge, 2009) included lack of understanding of Muslim food proscriptions such as not eating pepperoni on pizza and celebrating special days in the Christian calendar with traditional religious symbols and practices. Given that many schools in Newfoundland and Labrador were faith based until 1998, combined with the presence of many long-time teachers, such events are not surprising. Nonetheless schools, school districts, and the Department of Education are all working to make schools places in which all children are successful and respected (Eastern School District Newfoundland and Labrador, *Vision statement and goals*, n.d.)

In the classes associated with the study, preservice teachers embraced the opportunities to gain knowledge of diversity. As reported earlier (Hammett & Bainbridge, 2009), many participants felt their education program should have included more explicit attention to multiculturalism and diversity education; their comments include the following:

I wish I had more information. – Vera

I would probably love to do an elective course on diversity because it's becoming so popular and we're not getting enough. I read books on diversity but I'm not shown how to teach it. – Nancy

Nonetheless, many preservice teachers were enthusiastic about what they had learned and were keen to implement picture books in their teaching. Vera stated: "I'm going to use them for just about every subject ... I found that there is a picture book for everything." Jaclyn remarked, [I'll use] picture books [because] in classrooms where there are different types of learners, ... you've got visual and auditory and kinesthetic [possibilities in picture books]."

Many of the preservice teachers became enthusiastic about the pedagogical possibilities of the picture books, but they were also aware of the controversial nature of some of the themes and were expecting challenges. As Jaclyn and Samantha anticipated, constructing oneself as a teacher is a process:

> It's almost like an apprenticeship because you get the gist and understanding of how to go about being a teacher but once you actually get there you become a teacher of yourself. – Jaclyn

> It's something you feel and also you know if ... You need to be in a situation and experience it a little bit to really know how to handle things. – Samantha

Thus, with some knowledge and experience, with good intentions, and with some trepidation, our preservice teachers set out for an extended internship in provincial schools.

Constructing New Identities, Rethinking Ideologies

As noted above, many of the preservice teachers came to our education program and our research with limited knowledge of other cultures, a phenomenon that has been well documented in research literature (e.g., Sleeter, 2001; Banks, 2001; Grant, 1992). Others, though raised in monocultural settings, had lived experiences that had prepared them for teaching for diversity. For example, Vera had recent experience gaining knowledge of an Aboriginal culture and community. She joined her mother in a northern Saskatchewan Aboriginal community and explained her learning this way:

> I learned a lot when I went to Saskatchewan and opened my eyes because their culture is very different, they have different [customs]. Like some of those parents take their kids out for hunting; they leave and I'm just like, oh my goodness, like, and it wouldn't happen in Newfoundland, but they get so much of their own culture from doing it with their parents. Their value of education is a little bit different, like we tend to value it [formal schooling] more so but their culture is different. Like they have fishing camps, so my background there helped me to be more open to differences.

Vera speaks, perhaps, without consideration of Innu and Inuit communities in Labrador, the mainland portion of Newfoundland and Labrador, where education customs are similar to those she describes in the Dene community she visited. Even so, as I describe later in this chapter, Vera continued to build her knowledge of teaching in ways that incorporate diversity.

Not all preservice teachers find it easy to adopt new identities and ideologies. Rory declared himself against homosexuality, but did see himself as able to follow the demands of the curriculum. Asked if there were any books he would find it difficult to teach, he responded, "With my background the books that were on the same-sex marriage." He explained:

> I know that curriculum, now, it's changing and adapting that notion of same sex into the classroom. Personally, I have issues with that. Knowing that it's areas that may have to be covered … I might have to present that to the class saying, … "This is a book … recommended by the board that we have to teach; however, you know sometimes you see on TV [that] the views and opinions are not necessarily those of the [sponsor]."

Rory's position is interesting. His Salvation Army religious beliefs are strong, but he is able to understand that, as a teacher, a more open position is demanded of him. This is not to say that he is able or unable to articulate a sense of responsibility, as a teacher, to actively promote mutual religious respect and social justice, because the interview conversation did not turn in that direction. He shows "an awareness of [his] own beliefs and attitudes, as well as being willing and/or able to think critically about them" (Garmon, 2004, 205). Rory admits that he did not see critical literacy modelled by the mentoring teacher in his practicum classroom, although he had mentioned that she had challenged his use of the term "Newfie," considered derogatory by many Newfoundlanders, in front of the students.

Jordan also expressed some reluctance to use picture books like *Asha's Mums* (Elwin & Paulse; *Lee*, 1990) or *Mom and Mum Are Getting Married!* (Setterington; *Priestley*, 2004), noting: "I think sexual orientation … would be a challenge and I think that's because it has so much to do with the teacher's attitude and, you know, you don't want to pass judgements and you want kids to form their own opinions. So I think the teacher has to be comfortable with the topic to teach it."

Jordan is building her understanding of diversity gradually. She says that to prepare to teach in a diverse environment, "I think about just walking in every day with an open mind." Despite the potential contro-versy, the need to consider the mentor teacher's possible attitudes, and her own need to gain knowledge, Jordan is committed to influencing change.

The processes of rethinking ideologies and constructing new identi-ties are difficult ones; generally change occurs best within supportive settings where participation in established discourses is possible. In these cases, the needed discourse in diversity education seems not to be present, at least in the case of Rory and Jordan. In the next section, I focus more directly on school culture.

School and Classroom Cultures

In attempting to implement the research project's mandate and their own desire to "make a difference," the preservice teachers entered schools and classrooms with a wide variety of established cultures and populations. Some were placed in schools and classrooms much like the ones they had experienced growing up. For example, Tammy says of herself: "I was brought up in a fairly Catholic Irish home. My dad's side of the family was fairly Catholic. My middle name is actually – I'm named after a nun who is my great-aunt." Tammy noted with critique that activities and reading leading up to approaching Easter were all Christian in emphasis and included a version of the Crucifixion story. Tammy explained that she read *Bagels from Benny* (Davis; *Petricic*, 2003) with grade 2 students and noted that there was already a copy of this book in the classroom. Tammy does not explain how she approached the depictions of Jewish customs and religious symbols in the book. Perhaps she didn't realize Benny's family are Jewish. Tammy subverts the book to her own safe ends here, emphasizing a theme that will be non-controversial, even though she has noted the exclusive Christian culture of the school. In doing so she avoids the issues of religious dif-ference and how Jews have long been regarded by Christians, espe-cially at Easter time.

About the book, Tammy says:

> It's a book about a little boy who gives bagels and then he realizes that they're being given to a homeless man, and the children – I found in Grade Two really try to do positive things and try to help other people and in this book that's what the little boy did – and they could relate to it because it's from a little boy's perspective and they could really relate to helping other people, and it [brought out] conversations in giving old clothes to charities

and doing things like that. The children really feel, I found at that age, too, really try to give back to the community and they were so proud to say that, "Oh I gave my old clothes to, you know, so and so down the street or to the charities around town."

Tammy seems to be endorsing a neo-liberal perspective on social justice here. Perhaps because of their young age, sharing used clothing may be an acceptable sign of caring in grade 2. Learning how to engage in action for social change with school-age children is difficult, particularly because Canada pays lip service to ending child poverty but does not seem to work towards it.

Another intern, Jane, noted the discomfort of her cooperating teacher when lesbian parents came in to discuss their child's progress. Jane observed that the teacher directed her comments to the mother and ignored her partner's questions and comments even though it appeared to Jane that they were parenting equally and the mother's partner was very active in supervising homework. Jane also heard from other interns that the teacher had made homophobic comments in the staffroom, and she explained: "I'm glad that I didn't find out until my internship was practically over because I think that really would have strained the relationship because I would have confronted her on it." This incident illustrates that not all school cultures are accepting of diversity, and newcomers, especially interns, have dilemmas as to how to challenge the existing cultures and live their own politics in comfort. New teachers like Jane and Tammy who are committed to transformative education are embarking on a process of reflective and reflexive inquiry into their own practice, attitudes, and beliefs.

Other preservice teachers found themselves in schools with some cultural diversity and among teachers who encompassed diversity in their teaching. Charlene describes some examples:

One example: the other Grade One teacher had a little girl who was from China. They brought some books in during Chinese New Year and they did this whole reading unit on it for her so in that way she could explain. And, like I said, we had a lot of children in our class who were from different cultures and anytime we talked about something that kind of related to something they knew, they could come up and talk and explain what they knew about it. We had a little boy talk about sushi and how they use chopsticks and stuff like that in class.

This somewhat superficial celebration of difference may be a step towards understanding that Canada is ethnically, culturally, and linguistically diverse and that each citizen, irrespective of ethnicity, culture, or language, is Canadian. Charlene also described a wealth of book resources in the classroom, though they included few of the picture books used in our study. However, this could change, as in many cases teachers buy books for the class library with their own money.

During the practicum, some preservice teachers witnessed practices that caused tension. Alanna described witnessing homophobic slurs in the playground when "one of the little boys yelled at the other one, 'Get away from me, you faggot.'" She also noted that little girls "were like, 'You're so gay.'" Alanna does not say how she addressed the situation when she heard these comments, but later in this chapter I describe her successful lesson on discrimination and her reasons for not using the book *Tiger Flowers* (Quinlan; *Wilson*, 1994), which includes the story of a gay man who died from AIDS. Despite a desire to influence change, the challenges in actual experience seem overwhelming and commitment turns to lip service.

Charlene also felt unable to venture beyond her own comfort zone in teaching despite the supportive environment of the school. Asked if she had implemented her lesson plan, Charlene explained:

> No, I changed my book because I was going to do *Mom and Mum Are Getting Married!* and my unit was still based on family, but I ended up switching to *And Tango Makes Three*, which was about two male penguins in Central Park Zoo who raised a baby egg. So I went on with diversity within [the] family and how everybody's family is different but it is still special.

Asked by the interviewer to explain the switch, Charlene said: "It was my own personal – the school was fine with me doing it but I think I was a little nervous still, where I was just starting out and I wasn't sure if I was going to be confident enough to deal with questions if parents came in and weren't happy about it. So I figured it was safer to go with penguins, which actually tied into our penguin unit, too."

Charlene experienced conflict and tension, despite endorsement from "the school." She worries that she will have to face any controversy that is evoked, or at least will feel responsible for it. Her words convey her own unsettled knowledge; while supportive of same-sex parenting, Charlene conveys discomfort. It is safer that the parents are penguins and the baby is an egg. The relationship is different "*but* special" (emphasis mine). Charlene can go "on with diversity" without engaging in the hard challenges of critical literacy and social justice.

Jordan experienced teaching in a school that displayed diversity in ability but not ethnicity. She felt diversity education seemed more of an "add-on," and she didn't see it as part of everyday practice within curriculum. She described a special event, a talent show in which new students from Russia and countries in Africa demonstrated circus performances involving juggling and uni-cycling (Russian boy) and drumming (brothers from Africa). Jordan observed that other students "were amazed and just really impressed" and "instant friendships" developed then. However, at another point, she noted that the school has a "peace works program" with the "big component [being] respect and tolerance." She also explained that the program involved "this marble awards class" because "you would collect marbles throughout your school day for how well you got along with your classmates." Jordan observed that the school, located in the inner city, "was a community. I felt it was open and accepting and that every student in that school knew one another and there were never any issue with bullying." Jordan was noting different approaches to diversity and was grappling with a critical stance on equity. She recognized "add-on diversity," noting a deeper commitment to change in the peace program, but struggled with a language to describe it (i.e., "tolerance").

Allan also noted a climate of diversity and multiculturalism in the school in which he did his practicum in St John's: "Right off the bat in the foyer there was a sense of multiculturalism. There is a globe and the children around, this kind of concept. They had the Canadian flag in there right off the bat, too.– Canadian and Newfoundland flags."

However, Allan noted, "the curriculum is so loaded that multiculturalism almost gets pushed to the side a bit." Even though there's a school board policy on curricular outcomes, teachers have to "incorporate multiculturalism into them" and this takes time. What Allan seems to be saying is that diversity is an add-on or even a neglected theme, because there's no urgent need ("their multicultural population isn't that strong") and teachers don't have time for the reflection needed to incorporate multiculturalism and social justice issues across the curriculum. In a different classroom, Allan knew that "grade 5s did a unit on multiculturalism," but not the details of the unit. Allan, like Jordan, was grappling with understanding diversity as a way of thinking and being in the world on a day-to-day basis, rather than as curriculum content and displays of multicultural symbols. These are complex concepts to understand and integrate into one's identities in the post-structural sense, when structures, school cultures, subject positions, and practices can reflect and reproduce or contradict one another. New teachers' sense of agency may be challenged or difficult to conceptualize in a context where the institutional culture of "multiculturalism" contradicts the deeper understanding of diversity and social justice as always being embedded in pedagogy.

Constructing Knowledge with Students

During their practicum experiences, some of the preservice teachers had opportunities to implement their planned lessons and help children construct different perspectives on knowledge, self, and community, while the preservice teachers themselves developed understandings of diversity and education for social justice.

Vera had lived and taught in a northern Saskatchewan community, where she had experienced teaching Aboriginal children whose native language was a mix of Dene and English. In her classroom there, she had read *My Kokum Called Today* (Loewen; *Miller*, 1993) with her students, who understood references to *kokum* (grandmother), bannock, skinning rabbits, and making moccasins. During her practicum in St John's, when she read the same picture book with first graders, she found she had to scaffold their learning and help them construct knowledge around difference. She says: "Some of the kids couldn't get over the fact that they skinned rabbits ... I had to explain to the kids that it's part of their culture and they hunt for the rabbits, the same as we hunt for moose and we hunt for rabbits here, but we just discard their carcasses" (i.e., skins and non-edible parts).

As her unit continued, Vera read additional books, like *Red Parka Mary* (Eyvindson; *Brynjolson*, 1993), and engaged the Newfoundland students in correspondence with the Aboriginal students in Saskatchewan exchanging letters and pictures. The children also loaned the books to another St John's school, and accompanied them with class letters about the books and "little boxes of love," following the idea of the exchange in *Red Parka Mary* between the narrator and Mary.

Vera noted the children's learning, commenting on hearing them talk about the books, as well as reading from the pictures, using newly acquired vocabulary (chokecherries, bannock) and making connections within their own lives and experiences:

Like they went home and you could hear them talking about certain words and like actually I left my book on display and you could hear them reading it. They weren't actually reading because the book was too high levelled for some of them. But like they would go through the pictures and then they would be like, oh look they're eating bannock or that's choke berries and they use different words, like even in their journal writing that they did later. They talked about *Red Parka Mary* – how I taught them about this different book and how excited they were to wait for their letter to come back and it was just amazing, they actually understood and more than I thought they were going to get from it. And then they tied into the fact too that [*name*], which was the boy from Burma, he's from a different culture but they still love him just the same, I mean it was amazing, so.

Such experiences of success in implementing unit plans designed during the education course may motivate new teachers to continue diversity education and negotiate through controversies and challenges in teaching for equity and social justice. The children's excitement about learning and making textual connections to meaning support Vera's learning.

Elizabeth experienced similar satisfaction in teaching. Using the book *Shi-shi-etko* (Campbell; La Fave, 2005), which relates to a young Aboriginal girl's experiences before leaving home for residential school, Elizabeth explored meanings of identity with her third graders.

And they really didn't know what it [identity] meant to them, was really something that I found. I was quite shocked at that and when we talked about, we talked about the background of it as well. Like I kind of talked too because we were doing communities and Social Studies. So we talked about different communities and stuff like that and how our environment and our family and what kind of things are incorporated into our sense of identity and how your background, and where you come from and where your family comes from how that impacts to you, you feel that you are the person and how that all interplays.

Here "quite shocked" suggests an element of surprise and seems to speak to Elizabeth's own self-reflection about her identity. Thus, it appears that diverse Canadian picture books can serve as a catalyst to ignite questions that challenge taken-for-granted assumptions about identity, place, and family among preservice teachers; Elizabeth describes the book:

So she goes on a walk in nature and she creates the memory bag with her grandmother … I really liked that idea. When I first did up the lesson that was kind of what we were going to do, but I found I wasn't able to do that because I wanted to take them for a walk in nature in around their community, you know ... But where it was the middle of winter there wasn't a lot to do ... And the sidewalks weren't cleared and then there was all kinds of snow, so that was a little bit of an eye opening experience for me, like you planned [but could not carry out the plan].

Here her choice of words implies the importance of a sense of memory and its influence on one's identity, but Elizabeth struggles to make sense of this complex theme in relation to carrying on curriculum activities when winter intervenes.

We read the book and then we went back to the idea of identity and we talked about that again and then ... we just talked about nature and you know that was kind of nice to bring that into [it] because where they're an inner city school, a lot of them ... The only nature that they are exposed to is that which surrounds them, you know. So a lot of them had never been out of the city to experience that. So anyway we had a really interesting discussion on ... their identity and then what I had done was that I peeled birch bark from one of my neighbour's woodpiles. Because we talked about the different kinds of trees and stuff that we would find in our own surroundings and they then took their birch bark and they painted on it a few different things that they felt represented who they were. So the focus was mostly on identity.

Elizabeth works out a solution that let her carry out her lesson plan and allowed her to lead the children through the activity that Shi-shi-etko and her grandmother also accomplished.

I think I would have pursued that a little bit more and maybe talked, maybe kind of delve into it a little bit more taking up a few more classes, you know and just to understand even within Newfoundland how people would identify themselves differently and maybe make the connection because we were doing Fogo in Social Studies. So you know it would be really interesting, it could have been lots of different links that we could have made.

This exchange illustrates the process of knowledge construction during the practicum, when classroom structures and cooperating teachers' support creates a space for exploration and reflection. Elizabeth, through dialogue using the picture books, was able to conceive extensive activities so the children could reflect on their own identities within the context of the story and artefacts like birch bark that Shi-shi-etko collected, thus presenting students with an opportunity to experience and appreciate similarity and difference, which is an important concept in diversity education and the picture books we selected. In so doing, she also explored her own identity as a teacher and as an advocate of social justice.

Jordan assisted her cooperating teacher in reading aloud the novel *Stone Fox* (Gardiner; *Sewall*, 1983), which led to talk about "native rights and First Nations." Jessica said, "We did bring up that this also happened in Canada ... , but it was with, and I don't even know this correct pronunciation, but the Shoshone Tribe." The class did research on land claims and engaged in discussion. "[We] tried to get the kids to voice a lot of feeling questions, you know, just try, how would you feel in this situation or what could you do in this situation or what could you do to make it different."

Jordan didn't say how the children reacted to these reading and learning activities, but she seemed to feel everything contributed to the peaceful climate of the school. She wanted students to feel and express empathy for the characters depicted in the books. As both Jordan and Elizabeth experienced, books can be used as a springboard to challenge current practices, initiate dialogue, spark debate, question assumptions, and illuminate the complexities of teaching and learning in diverse sites when values collide. Still, much more research and work is needed to engage preservice teachers in exploring various aspects of diversity and the kinds of inclusive practices that make possible equitable learning for all children within socially just schooling.

Alanna also experienced and described the willingness of students to empathize with characters in the picture books. Reading *Flags* (Trottier; *Morin*, 1999), Alanna noted that "they talked about life is not fair and, if they didn't like how Mr Hiroshi was treated as we were reading the book, they would shoot up their hand or just blurt out, you know, 'Why did they do that? Didn't he live in Canada?' Questions like, 'Miss, what's the point of that [internment of Japanese Canadians]? What are they doing that for? Did they actually do that?'"

Having convinced the students that these injustices really did occur in Canada, Alanna observed that "they were just sitting there." She said, "I think they understood more about the repercussions of what people's actions are." Alanna also noted that the lessons extended into Internet research on immigration policies and practices currently and in the past, with students observing incidents of discrimination, restriction, and unfair treatment based on language, skin colour, and country of origin. Alanna said, "[Someone would say] look, and then they all crowd around one computer ... and they would be looking, look they did it to [interned and discriminated against] these people and they did it to these people and they just went down through it [the website] and they said, 'Miss, they did it to everybody.'" As a positive end to her unit, Alanna created a time-travel scenario within which her students could meet Mr Hiroshi and other interned Canadians. The students wrote letters, and as Alanna recounted, wrote things like, "Come into Canada now, it's a lot fairer." "You won't be treated that way." "You know it's more accepted." "I can't believe they did it to you." Like, they expressed their empathy. "Sir, I feel so bad for you." "I can't believe they did things like that. It only happened so many years ago. And, you know, I'm twelve now, this is really shocking."

As they worked with the picture books, Alanna, Jordan, Vera, and Elizabeth were able to explore and construct their own knowledge of pedagogy and diversity. Thus, even if these "preservice teachers ... enter these courses without any (or very limited) prior knowledge and understanding of diversity or of individuals quite different from themselves" (Liggett & Finley, 2009, 58), they are able to gradually build this knowledge and understanding.

Fear of Rocking the Boat

As previously noted, some preservice teachers are hesitant to engage in or suggest what they perceive as controversial activities that may challenge existing school cultures. As Liggett and Finley (2009) suggest, "We maintain that the teacher candidates' concern about engaging in practices that 'would rock the boat' within their school context was due to a disconnect between understanding the possibilities of enacting positive change on an individual level versus the daunting undertaking of striving to change school culture or educational institutions as new teachers" (33).

For example, Alanna, who was able to help the children empathize with Mr Hiroshi, was reluctant to read *Tiger Flowers* (Quinlan; *Wilson*, 1994), a picture book that depicts the sadness a family experiences when their uncle's same-sex partner dies of AIDS. Alanna said,

> I didn't feel comfortable using it. I would definitely love to use it ... but I
> was kind of held back from using it because ... I would prefer if I was in

[the school] for a longer period of time than just coming in for a couple of months and then being remembered as the intern that came in, in the students' language, that read the story about the gay man who had AIDS. Like, that's how the attitudes [are], just generally speaking of the children. [With] recess duty you're around [the school], you hear them talking and you know what they're doing and you can see the social cliques and attitudes right away.

As I noted previously, Rory and Jordan felt constrained in using particularly controversial books, especially those portraying homosexuality. During focus groups and interviews many of the students expressed this fear of rocking the boat and initiating controversy, particularly as presevice teachers whose grades and future employment were on the line. Because of these fears, as teacher educators we need to support our preservice teachers by constructing a discourse of diversity that facilitates exploration of cultural values, perspectives, and practices. As transformative educators, we may not see change unless we do rock the boat and educate ourselves and others about what it means to support equity, diversity, multiculturalism, and social justice.

Conclusion

Diversity education is generally understood to include awareness and understanding of difference and how to address and teach about it in classrooms; preparation for living amicably and respectfully in multi-cultural communities; and, as a teacher, recognizing and accommodating the needs of individual children (Ghosh & Tarrow, 1993). In our research and the accompanying classes, we used picture books to help preservice teachers understand these objectives and be prepared to address them in their classrooms. As the foregoing vignettes illustrate, sometimes we and they were successful, at other times not. Conducting our research, we noted weaknesses in our program and brought these to the attention of our colleagues in seminars and articles (see, for example, Hammett & Bainbridge, 2009). We hope that education students in our institution will continue to experience programs that "help [them] become aware of and understand the ethnic, racial, and cultural expressions of diverse students in their classrooms, understand and appreciate cultural differences and similarities, [and] apply ... the 'transformative' approach, weav[ing] a range of cultural perspectives throughout the curriculum" (Smith, 2009).

NOTE

1 I am indebted to my co-researcher Anne and her graduate assistant Teeba
   for interviews and focus group data and to my friend and colleague
   Deborah Toope for her very helpful critique of drafts of my chapter.

Afterword

INGRID JOHNSTON AND JOYCE BAINBRIDGE

In reflecting on the multi-site case studies that constitute this research study, we recognize that professional development in preservice teacher education programs is a complex and dynamic process, and that this process continues into teaching in the kindergarten to grade 12 school system. As literacy teacher educators we need to ask ourselves what priorities we can identify for our literacy courses in relation to subject-area knowledge and to what Santoro (2009) refers to as "multicultural pedagogies" (33). We see diverse Canadian picture books as a portal through which preservice teachers can enter and begin to negotiate the spaces around identity in relation to themselves and others, develop subject-area knowledge, understandings of diversity, "multicultural pedagogies," and the capacity for reflection.

In our research, we used picture books to help the preservice teachers move towards more complex understandings of diversity education, including a broadened awareness of multiculturalism and the possibilities for addressing diversity in the classroom. A majority of the preservice teachers across the country were enthusiastic about using Canadian picture books as classroom resources. Even secondary-route participants who were initially sceptical about the appropriateness of picture books for older students found books they deemed engaging and likely to be of value to students.

Our participants came to recognize that neither the text nor the visual image can be considered separate entities and that "the words and the pictures in picture books both define and amplify each other" (Nodelman, 1988, 8). They understood that "pictures are no more 'concrete' and no less abstract than words are" (Nodelman & Reimer, 2003, 275). Through our multi-site workshop, in which we closely examined the illustrations and text in the picture book *Josepha* (McGugan; *Kimber*, 1994), preservice teachers had an opportunity to see first-hand how to "read" these images in relation to the words in the book and how the illustrator used aspects of space, colour, dimension, and perspective to convey meaning. Participants were encouraged to see the power of visual literacy for gaining more complex perspectives on the potential of images to engage readers on multiple levels and to elicit strong emotional as well as cognitive responses to the content and themes of a text.

The ideologies and representations of difference in the picture books challenged participants to confront the experiences of marginalization represented in many of the books and to come face-to-face with their own preconceived values about race, indigeneity, culture, language, disability, gender, and sexuality. These concerns highlighted a conflict between their taken-for-granted notions of a "multicultural" Canada and what is actualized in classroom settings today. Providing opportunities for our participants to encounter difference through the mediation of picture books allowed us as researchers to gain new insights into "how the learner comes to identify and dis-identify with difficult knowledge" (Britzman, 1998, 119).

We have learned that asking our preservice teachers to engage with questions of difference and identity, even in seemingly simple picture books, is complex and often fraught with tensions for both teacher and learner. Some of the preservice teacher participants engaged deeply with the issues of diversity represented in the texts, while others resisted or remained indifferent. We were initially surprised at the strength of the resistance some of the preservice teachers expressed. The perceived controversial nature of the books, particularly those addressing Aboriginal histories and residential schooling, and those dealing with current issues of sexual orientation and same-sex marriage, presented a considerable challenge for many of our participants. Our data suggests that the preservice teachers' discomfort around bringing Indigenous issues into their classrooms resulted partly from a lack of knowledge of Canadian history in relation to residential schools, and partly from stereotypes about Aboriginal peoples still entrenched in Canadian society. Some of this resistance also stemmed from a concern about "political correctness" in discussing the books with school students. Books that addressed issues of sexuality, such as sexual orientation and same-sex marriage, also created discomfort for many participants because of concerns about the acceptability of these texts in particular school districts. As new teachers, they felt there was too much risk in addressing issues that might be frowned upon by the school principal, parents, or school board. These participants often supported the ideals associated with social justice, but were not yet ready or able to take action. They appeared to be more concerned, at this point in their careers, with parental/school district censorship of their choice of resources than they were with the responses and experiences of their students.

After listening to these participants' thoughts and concerns, we found ourselves able to see more clearly the supportive and facilitative role teacher educators can play in "airing" such issues and in raising the preservice teachers' dilemmas to consciousness. Further research might delve more deeply into ways beginning teachers can come to understand their important role in promoting social justice in schools through paying attention to the lived experiences of all their students, including those outside the mainstream, and offering their students resources that support diversity.

Some participants across the country felt the picture books were valuable classroom resources because they addressed the experiences of individual students whose lives, backgrounds, and experiences have traditionally been marginalized in mainstream classrooms. This was a perception strongly articulated in programs that had a large component of Aboriginal and Métis preservice teachers. These teachers began to think about the strategies they would use to incorporate the books into their classroom activities. Once again we could see the important role teacher educators play in providing space for discussions and for the development of planning and implementation strategies. We see future challenges as teacher educators in working on ways to help our non-Aboriginal student teachers to become more sensitized to historical and current issues of marginalization among Aboriginal peoples and to feel comfortable in sharing these insights with their own students.

The preservice teachers often selected as "favourites" those books that were embedded in local traditions or reminded them of childhood experiences. In general, many participants were more comfortable with the "white landscapes" of some of the books in the collection, perhaps perceiving then as being "culturally neutral," a perception challenged by Aboriginal participants. Occasionally, a biased and racist viewpoint was put forward regarding the ways in which the portrayal of diversity in the texts disturbed some of the preservice teachers' own sense of Canadian identity. And in some of our surveys and focus group discussions, white participants exhibited a somewhat superior attitude of tolerance towards diversity. Can we perhaps see these attitudes as a failure of our

Canadian multicultural policies to address underlying issues of racism still evident in the responses of these participants? As Dudek (2011) elaborates: "Nations – such as Canada, the United States, and Australia – progress from a racist ideology of assimilation to an ideology of tolerance embodied in a multicultural society … A rhetoric of tolerance often does not go far enough towards describing and enacting an ethical citizenry based on a deep respect for cultural difference" (156).

Despite these rather disturbing responses from some of our preservice teachers, we were encouraged to see that many participants did find positive ways to use the picture books to further the awareness of cultural diversity in their classrooms, and to create insights into the social history behind the development of the Canadian mosaic. Using diverse Canadian picture books as a place of departure for looking within and beyond, they saw the potential for their K–12 students to make insightful connections between themselves and others.

Our findings also showed that preservice teachers in various provinces had different experiences of what it means to be Canadian, and many found resonances with the particular landscapes and cultural contexts of the books. Their responses to the books were deeply embedded in their local contexts and histories, and in their sense of place or geographic location. Preservice teachers in Newfoundland and Labrador saw their province as predominantly "monocultural" and were concerned that they had had little experience with cultural difference. They acknowledged that recent shifts in their economy had created changes in demographics, and they understood the need for an exploration of multiculturalism and diversity in schools. The participants in Montreal, Quebec, struggled to position themselves in zones of "contested pasts and contested stories." Their lesson plans often fell into line with the myths of the supremacy of white/European civilizations and the marginalization of Aboriginal and immigrant cultures. At the same time, they acknowledged that the picture books were potential critical sites for colonial encounters with the past. At Lakehead University, Ontario, the preservice teachers had opportunities to put lesson plans into action in the schools in which they were student teaching. In the interviews for the study, their reflections suggest a *creative envisioning* of the possibilities for increasing understanding of Aboriginal cultural perspectives; immigration and citizenship; and social, political, and economic challenges.

In Saskatchewan, Aboriginal preservice teachers who responded to the study survey saw themselves as different, original Canadians, while Métis participants had a more complex understanding of living together with family members from both Aboriginal and settler back-grounds. In their responses to the survey, non-Aboriginal participants at this site were more likely to accept the official Canadian view of mul-ticulturalism as intrinsically good. However, during focus groups and interviews, some of these preservice teachers became more conscious of their ancestors' colonizing role and their own complicity in sustain-ing it. In Alberta, many preservice teachers expressed interest in books such as *Josepha* that were situated in a prairie landscape. They were more wary of books that dealt with aspects of diversity such as same-sex relationships and residential schools, fearing that these texts would not be accepted in small rural communities where there was little acknowledgment of diversity. In British Columbia, participants related particularly to their local history, to books portraying the Second World War internment of Japanese Canadians in camps close to where they grew up, and to the exploitation of Chinese labourers in building the railways.

Most lesson plans developed by participants in this study demon-strated an implicit understanding of theory through the preservice teachers' individual choices of diverse Canadian picture books, the resources they selected for their lessons, and their envisioning of how the plans might unfold. The process of thinking through and writing lesson plans became an occasion for an encounter between "self" and "other." Some participants developed simplistic plans that represented diversity at a superficial level without engaging with more complex ideological tensions. Others were able to work with their selected pic-ture books to come to a greater understanding of how they and their students could begin to see their place in the world around them and to challenge some of their taken-for-granted belief systems and ideolo-gies around diversity. A number of these preservice teachers who were able to implement their lesson plans saw their students make reward-ing and insightful connections between themselves and "others." We see further challenges for us as teacher educators in modelling a deeper engagement with issues of cultural sensitivity in books for young and adolescent readers that will help our beginning teachers in their resource development.

Our study points to the value of introducing preservice teachers to the potential of diverse picture books as an aspect of critical literacy in their classrooms, and to the crucial role of teacher educators in creating space and safety for preservice teachers to explore the issues raised by the books. It was apparent from our study findings that, in most teacher education programs across the country, there is a need for more explicit teaching about critical literacy and more opportunities for preservice teachers to understand and experience how to read and respond critically to a variety of texts through learning about narrative voice and point of view, addressing stereotypes, seeing gaps and absences in a text, and probing the discourses and ideologies underpinning the text. These insights could enable preservice teachers to develop criteria for assessing the value of diverse books for their classrooms and to become more aware of how a text is a social construct that is never neutral in its intents to inform or persuade its readers.

Although there were problematic issues that emerged from some participants' responses to the picture books used in the study, overall we were pleased to see the varied and generally enthusiastic responses of our preservice teachers to representations of "Canadianness" in the books. As a research team situated in five different provinces with variations in our teacher education programs and literacy curricula, we tried to be responsive to each other's locations and to appreciate that our findings would be context specific as well as offering valuable national data. In reflecting on the study, we see that in each site the research offered the potential for participants to reflect on their responses to the texts and to reconsider how they might address difference in their own lives and teaching. Many of the preservice teachers did begin to question their beliefs and assumptions about Canadian identity and diversity in the context of their university coursework, and to make more informed decisions about classroom-resource selection processes and the criteria they would apply.

In a number of research sites, participants who were able to develop lesson plans for specific picture books and take them into their student teaching encountered challenges when their practising mentor teachers did not share their interest in introducing diverse Canadian literature into their classrooms. In most cases, these experienced teachers had little familiarity with Canadian picture books and little background in selecting literature or seeing picture books as a resource for promoting cultural responsiveness and social justice in their classrooms. These findings have prompted the authors of this text to develop a new study in which we are working with inquiry groups of practising English language arts teachers from grades 4 to 12 in six Canadian provinces. In these collaborative settings, the teachers are considering the potential of Canadian literature from various genres to promote issues of social justice in their classrooms. Their conversations, together with the pedagogical decisions they make, should be enlightening in helping us to understand how practising teachers approach social justice issues and how they come to their decisions about resources and teaching approaches.

The research team continues to ask how we can more successfully support preservice and practising teachers in their explorations of potentially controversial books in their K–12 classrooms and in their engagement with issues of Indigeneity, race, culture, disability, gender, and sexuality. How can we most effectively demonstrate the teaching of critical literacy to preservice and practising teachers and demonstrate the use of critical literacy teaching strategies for K–12 classrooms? Perhaps most importantly, how can we most effectively and safely encourage preservice teachers to move beyond their own experiences to envision and implement new approaches and strategies, and to select resources that are inclusive of all Canadians and that will promote social justice for all students? We need teachers to enter the profession with knowledge, confidence, and sensitivity regarding diversity, difference, and the marginalization that can occur when different groups, cultures, languages, and histories come together in learning and teaching environments.

Appendix A
Course Data Sources

University	Course	Grade level
Thompson Rivers University (Kamloops)	*Language and Literacy*	Elementary, grades K to 7
	Children's Literature	Elementary, grades K to 7
University of Alberta (Edmonton)	*Introduction to Language Arts*	Elementary, grades K to 6
	Curriculum and Teaching for Secondary English Language Arts Minors	Secondary, grades 7 to 12
University of Saskatchewan (Saskatoon)	*Introduction to Oracy Education: Oracy and Literature in the Elementary School* (First Nations and Métis students)	Elementary, grades K to 6
	Introduction to Oracy Education: Oracy and Literature in the Elementary School (Non-Aboriginal students)	Elementary, grades K to 6
	Introduction to Literacy: Secondary	Secondary, grades 7 to 12
Lakehead University (Thunder Bay)	*Canadian Multicultural Children's Literature*	Junior, Intermediate and Senior, grades 4 to 12
	Language Arts Methods	Junior/Intermediate, grades 4 to 8
McGill University (Montreal)	*The Kindergarten Classroom*	Elementary, grades K to 6
	Children's Literature	Elementary, grades K to 6
Memorial University (St John's)	*An Introduction to Children's Literature for Primary and Elementary Educators*	Primary, grades K to 3, Elementary, grades 4 to 6

Appendix B
Canadian Picture Books Used in the Research Project

Badoe, A. 2002. *Nana's Cold Days*. (B. Junaid, illustr.). Toronto: Groundwood Books.

Nana is coming to visit from Africa, and her grandsons have been looking forward to her visit for months. However, it's icy cold when she arrives, and all she can do is drape herself in covers. No one can dream up a way to entice Nana from her nest.

Ballantyne, E. 2001. *The Aboriginal Alphabet for Children*. (J.M. Ross and N. Head, illustr.). Winnipeg: Pemmican Publications.

Using the illustrations from an alphabet book from the 1930s (*A Canadian Child's ABC*), this contemporary text in verse accompanies the illustrations along with a simple quatrain for each letter of the alphabet. There is also a set of slightly longer free-form poems, one for each letter, at the end of the book.

Bannatyne-Cugnet, J. 2000. *From Far and Wide: A Citizenship Scrapbook*. (S.N. Zhang, illustr.). Toronto: Tundra Books.

In her scrapbook, Xiao Ling captures memories of special moments in becoming a citizen of Canada, from the recitation of the Oath of Canadian Citizenship to the singing of the national anthem and the party afterwards.

Bear, G. 1991. *Two Little Girls Lost in the Bush*. (J. Whitehead, illustr.). Saskatoon: Fifth House.

Nêhiyaw/Glecia Bear tells about her experience as a little girl when she and her sister tried to watch over a cow that was about to have a calf. When the cow wandered into the forest, the girls became lost. Eventually, they followed an owl, who led them back to safety.

Bedard, M. 1999. *Clay Ladies*. (L. Tait, illustr.). Toronto: Tundra Books.

When a small girl finds a wounded bird she goes to the Church for help, a place where she knows she'll find the Clay Ladies. While nursing the wounded bird back to health, the Clay Ladies teach the little girl about the

magic of the sculptors' art. The story is based on the lives of artists Frances
Loring and Florence Wyle, both of whom sculpted with clay.

Bouchard, D. 1993. *If You're Not from the Prairie*. (H. Ripplinger, illustr.).
Vancouver: Raincoast Books & Summer Wild Productions.
Capturing nostalgic memories of the prairies, the book consists of images
from the past. It is a visual and poetic journey describing the allure of the
prairies: the wind, the sweep of the sky, and the experience of playing
hockey on the river, lying under the big sky in a field of long grass, and
wading in a spring pond.

Bouchard, D. 2006. *Nokum Is My Teacher*. (A. Sapp, illustr.). Red Deer, AB: Red
Deer Press.
This bilingual picture book explores the reasons why a young boy has to
leave the reservation to go to school and learn to read. The book shows
the bond between the boy and his beloved mentor as well as the richness
of Cree life, past and present. A Cree translation sits side by side with the
English poem.

Brouillet, C. 2001. *Un héros pour Hildegarde*. Quebec: Musée du Québec.
On Hildegarde's twelfth birthday, her cousin Julie decides to tell her all
the secrets of their grandfather Émile's adventurous life. After his fateful
love for Aurélie, Émile joins a convent in France and then enlists in the
Resistance during the Second World War. On the train trip to Dieppe, he
embarks on a final adventure that brings him home and seals his destiny.

Brownridge, W.R. 1995. *The Moccasin Goalie*. (P. Montpellier, illustr.). Victoria,
BC: Orca Books.
Danny spends the winters playing hockey with his three best friends.
Because of a crippled leg and foot, Danny cannot wear skates, but tends
goal in his moccasins. When a "real" uniformed hockey team is established
in the community, Danny and his friends are elated at the prospect of
becoming members, but their happiness is short lived, as the coach selects
only one of them for the team.

Butler, G. 1998. *The Hangashore*. Toronto: Tundra Books.
Set in a tiny fishing village in Newfoundland, the Second World War
has just ended and an important magistrate has arrived to represent the
government. The magistrate does not understand John, a boy with Down's
syndrome, and threatens to have him sent to an institution.

Campbell, N. 2005. *Shi-shi-etko*. (K. La Fave, illustr.). Toronto: Groundwood
Books.
As Shi-shi-etko counts down her last few days before leaving for residential
school, she tries to memorize everything about her home. She does all in
her power to remember the little things that are familiar to her, and after a

family party to say good-bye, her father takes her out on the lake in a canoe. Her grandmother then gives her a small bag made of deer hide in which to keep her memories.

Carrier, R. 2004. *The Flying Canoe*. (S. Cohen, illustr.; S. Fischman, trans.). Toronto: Tundra Books.

On New Year's Eve, 1847, eleven-year-old Baptiste finds himself far from his friends and family in the woods of the Ottawa Valley, where he is living and working among "the finest lumberjacks in Canada." Resolved to see their families again before the stroke of midnight, the crew board a magical canoe that lifts them into the air, across villages, and closer to home. This retelling of a Québécois folk tale is also available in French, entitled *La chasse-galerie*.

Cheng, A. 2000. *Grandfather Counts*. (A. Zhang, illustr.). New York: Lee & Low Books.

Grandfather, who speaks no English, has come from China to live with Helen and her family. One day, Helen and grandfather sit watching the train cars go by. Grandfather begins to count in Chinese and soon the two are teaching each other a new language. This is an intergenerational story that demonstrates how language barriers can be overcome.

Condon, P. 2000. *Changes*. Saskatoon: Gabriel Dumont Institute.

A young Métis child undergoes a personal journey by learning that the changing seasons closely interact with her emotions. She is guided along the way by the Gathering Spirit, who teaches her about accepting change and celebrating the richness of life's emotions.

Cooper, J. 1993. *Someone Smaller than Me*. (A. Padlo, illustr.). Iqaluit, Nunavut: Baffin Divisional Board of Education.

Peter wants to catch a lemming, but what does a lemming look like? After asking many creatures, all too big, Peter finally finds someone smaller – a lemming! Translated into Inuktitut to aid Inuit children in learning their native language, the book entertains with its patterned prose and illustrations of northern animals.

Cummings, P. 2004. *Out on the Ice in the Middle of the Bay*. (A. Priestley, illustr.). Toronto: Annick Press.

This reissue of a 1993 story describes how a little girl wanders away from her home, and her napping father, towards an iceberg in the bay. At the same time, a polar bear cub saunters away from his sleeping mother towards the same iceberg. Both the girl's father and the mother polar bear search frantically for their offspring. As the parents dramatically confront each other, the girl and the cub appear and are rescued.

Davidge, B., and I. Wallace. 1993. *The Mummer's Song*. Toronto: Douglas & McIntyre.

Written as a tribute to a centuries-old custom in danger of disappearing, the story tells of several outlandishly costumed mummers who appear at Granny's house on a cold, clear Newfoundland night shortly after Christmas. Erupting in a burst of joking, singing, and dancing, the family is caught up in merriment. When the evening's festivities come to a close, the mummers are bid a fond farewell until next year.

Davis, A. 2003. *Bagels from Benny*. (D. Petricic, illustr.). Toronto: Kids Can Press. Benny's Grandpa has a reputation for making wonderful bagels that his customers say are "made with love." A wise Grandpa explains to Benny that it is God who must be thanked. Benny wonders how he might also thank God. An inspiration leads him to the synagogue, where he leaves bagels for God inside the holy Ark.

Demers, D. 2003. *L'oiseau des sables*. (S. Poulin, illustr.). Saint-Lambert, Quebec: Dominique et Compagnie. A father tells his son about the wishes he was granted throughout his life by five sand birds that his own father gave to him when he was a boy. The book explores the power of the inner voice that guides the individual, the vital choices that shape our lives, and the unconditional love that binds parent to child. The dense, dark tones of the illustrations evoke the bygone days presented in the story.

Downie, M.A. 2005. *A Pioneer ABC*. (M.J. Gerber, illustr.). Toronto: Tundra Books. Zebediah makes his two sisters an alphabet book. B stands for bandalore, a forerunner of the yoyo; H for the hornbook that taught children to spell. This book, passing through the seasons on a pioneer farm, is full of historical information.

Elwin, R. & Paulse, M. 1990. *Asha's Mums*. (D. Lee, illustr.). Toronto: Women's Press. The story of Asha and her two mums promotes awareness of different kinds of families and different kinds of relationships. When Asha's mums both sign a field-trip permission slip for Asha, the teacher requests that the form be redone "correctly." The story highlights the difficulties children of gay and lesbian families can encounter when teachers are not aware of their family structure.

Eyvindson, P. 1993. *The Missing Sun*. (R. Brynjolson, illustr.). Winnipeg: Pemmican Publications. When Emily and her mother move to Inuvik, Emily has a hard time believing her mother's claim that the sun is going to disappear for many days. When they really do lose the sun, Emily has to wrestle with conflicting explanations. Her mother tells her that the earth is tilted, while her friend Josie says Raven has stolen the sun.

Eyvindson, P. 1996. *Red Parka Mary*. (R. Brynjolson, illustr.). Winnipeg: Pemmican Publications Inc.

The little boy in this intergenerational Christmas story is afraid of his elderly female neighbour. When his mother reassures him that she is a friendly and kind person, he grows to appreciate and cherish their friendship. Mary has much to teach him, and he has much to give to her.

Fitch, S. 2001. *No Two Snowflakes*. (J. Wilson, illustr.). Victoria, BC: Orca Book Publishers.

Lou and Araba are penpals; Lou in Canada and Araba in Africa. In a letter to her friend, Lou shares her knowledge of snow with Araba, who has never felt it squeak beneath her feet or melt on her tongue. Just as no two snowflakes are alike, no two people are alike.

Gay, M. 2000. *Stella reine des neiges*. Quebec: Dominique et Compagnie.

"Is the snow cold?" asks Sacha. "Is it hard?" he asks. It is Sacha's first snowstorm and he is full of wonder. He asks many questions of his big sister Stella, who seems to know all the answers. The two children go exploring in the snow to discover all the tastes, sights, and sounds of winter's first snowfall.

Gilmore, R. 1998. *A Gift for Gita*. (A. Priestley, illustr.). Toronto: Second Story Press.

In the third book in the series about Gita, her father receives a job offer back in India. What should the family do? Eventually, the family decides that, although they miss India, they belong in Canada now. This is a story about Indian cultures and traditions, job relocation, immigration experiences, family heritage, and the meaning of "home."

Gilmore, R. 1999. *A Screaming Kind of Day*. (G. Sauvé, illustr.). Markham, ON: Fitzhenry & Whiteside.

Scully, a young hearing-impaired girl, loves to play outside in the rain, away from her brother Leo and her busy mother. After escaping briefly to the wet green trees outside, she is grounded and not allowed to leave the house for a day. As evening approaches, Scully and her mother are able to reconnect as they share a special moment together watching the stars.

Gorman, L. 2005. *A Is for Algonquin: An Ontario Alphabet*. (M. Rose, illustr.). Chelsea, MI: Sleeping Bear Press.

The book introduces young readers to the beauty of Ontario. The story describes Ontario's inhabitants, history, flora, and fauna. The book answers a variety of questions such as: Is the longest street in the world really in Ontario? And the world's longest skating rink?

Gregory, N. 1995. *How Smudge Came*. (R. Lightburn, illustr.). Red Deer, AB: Red Deer College Press.

Cindy, who has Down's syndrome, lives in a group home and works as a cleaner in a hospice. One day she finds a puppy, which she hides in her room and then takes to work with her. Cindy's "secret" is discovered and the puppy is whisked away to the SPCA. A happy resolution is celebrated against the darker backdrop of early death (the hospice residents) and the lack of freedom that living with a cognitive impairment can entail.

Gutierrez, E. 2005. *Picturescape*. Vancouver: Simply Read Books Inc.

Triggered by his imagination, a young boy's visit to the art gallery sends him on a journey across the country through some of Canada's greatest twentieth-century paintings. In this wordless book, the boy travels from Vancouver Island to Newfoundland. Appealing to children of all ages, the book contains endnotes about each of the paintings featured in the book and information about each artist.

Hampton, M.J. 2001. *The Cat from Kosovo*. (T. Heikalo, illustr.). Halifax: Nimbus Publishing.

This is the true story of how a refugee cat found a haven and a home in Nova Scotia. When a young couple in Kosovo found a small brown-and-white-striped cat, they opened their hearts to it. But the happiness of their lives was threatened as the war grew closer. As they journeyed to Macedonia and then on to Canada, no one could have guessed that of the more than two thousand immigration cards issued for the Kosovo refugees, one would be for a cat.

Harrison, T. 2002. *Courage to Fly*. (Z. Huang, illustr.). Red Deer, AB: Red Deer Press.

Meg moves from her Caribbean home to a new city, where nothing seems familiar. She stays in her room rather than play outside with friends. One day, Meg finds and rescues a sick swallow. Although the swallow quickly recovers, it remains silent and still in the box Meg has provided. An elderly Chinese man, who has become Meg's friend, advises her to release the swallow. This allows both Meg and the bird to find the freedom they need.

Highway, T. 2001. *Caribou Song* (*Atihko Nikamon*). (B. Deines, illustr.). Toronto: HarperCollins Publishers.

The story, the first book in a trilogy entitled "Songs of the North Wind," is set in northern Manitoba. It is told in both English and Cree. Through the long winter, two brothers, Joe and Cody, dance and play the kitoochigan and, in the spring, become part of a family adventure following the *ateek* (caribou) with a sled pulled by huskies.

Highway, T. 2002. *Dragonfly Kites* (*Pimihakanisa*). (B. Deines, illustr.). Toronto: HarperCollins Publishers.

Joe and Cody stay in a tent near a different lake each summer. Summer means a chance to explore the world and make friends with an array of creatures. They catch dragonflies, gently tie a length of thread around the middle of each insect before letting it go, and then chase after their dragonfly kites through trees and meadows and down to the beach before watching them disappear into the night sky.

Highway, T. 2003. *Fox on the Ice* (*Mahkesis Miskwamihk E-cipatapit*). (B. Deines, illustr.). Toronto: HarperCollins Publishers.

In this, the third in Tomson Highway's "Songs of the North Wind" picture-book series, a fox distracts the family dog team from a winter ice-fishing expedition, and it is left to the family's pet dog to save the day – and the fishing net. The dog is part of the family unit, and family togetherness is a theme stressed directly and indirectly in this story.

Jennings, S. 2000. *Into My Mother's Arms*. (R. Ohi, illustr.). Markham, ON: Fitzhenry & Whiteside.

This is the story of a special relationship between a mother of Japanese descent and her daughter. Told from a little girl's point of view, a mother and daughter share their day-to-day experiences featuring breakfast together, grocery shopping, some time in the park en route home, and finally bath and bedtime.

King, T. 1992. *A Coyote Columbus Story*. (W.K. Monkman, illustr.). Toronto: A Groundwood Book, Douglas & McIntyre Ltd.

In this retelling of Columbus's "discovery" of America, King overturns numerous stereotypes about colonization. He tells the story from an Aboriginal perspective, and cleverly interweaves figures from popular culture with the figure of Coyote, the trickster, to elucidate new truths about history and about the ongoing forces of colonialism in North America.

Kusugak, M. 1992. *Hide and Sneak*. (V. Krykorka, illustr.). Toronto: Annick Press.

Allushua is not much good at playing hide and seek because she is distracted by the butterflies, fish, turtles, and birds near her home. One day an Ijiraq – a hide-and-seek creature – offers to help her hide. Allushua disregards her mother's warning, "If an Ijiraq hides you, no one will ever find you again," and sets off with the funny little creature. Allushua eventually outsmarts the Ijiraq and returns home.

Kusugak, M. 1993. *Northern Lights: The Soccer Trails*. (V. Krykorka, illustr.). Toronto: Annick Press.

Soccer is a traditional game of the Inuit and it is their belief that the northern lights are the souls of the dead, running all over the sky chasing a walrus head they use for a soccer ball. Kataujaq learns about her Arctic home from her mother, travelling with her across the sea ice, picking flowers during the summer, and gathering berries in the autumn. When tuberculosis strikes her mother, she is flown to a hospital in the south.

Kataujaq never sees her again, and is deeply saddened by her loss. Grandmother tells Kataujaq the story of the Northern Lights, and it helps Kataujaq to accept her mother's death.

Littlechild, G. 1993. *This Land Is My Land*. San Francisco: Children's Book Press.

This is an autobiographical account of the struggles George Littlechild's family endured through many generations. The author offers poignant stories of delight, humour, and healing as he tells of his family, his childhood, and his work as an artist. The book heightens awareness of the history and experiences of Aboriginal people in Canada.

Loewen, I. 1993. *My Kokum Called Today*. (G. Miller, illustr.). Winnipeg: Pemmican Publications Inc.

When her *kokum* (grandmother) phones from the reserve, a young Aboriginal girl living in the city knows she can expect a special experience. This time it's a dance on the Reserve. She learns that women, especially grandmothers, are the ties that hold together the many Aboriginal families dispersed in rural and urban communities.

Loyie, L. 2005. *The Gathering Tree*. (H.D. Holmlund, illustr.). Penticton, BC: Theytus Books.

This is the story of a rural First Nations family facing HIV. When Tyler and Shay-Lyn learn their cousin Robert has HIV, they become anxious about Robert's health and are afraid he will die. The story provides insights into ways of learning, the influence of elders in the community, and cultural activities such as traditional gatherings. Aspects of physical, spiritual, mental, and emotional health are addressed.

Major, K. 2000. *Eh? to Zed: A Canadian ABeCeDarium*. (A. Daniel, illustr.). Red Deer, AB: Red Deer Press.

From Arctic, Bonhomme, and Imax to Kayak, Ogopogo, and zed, this book takes readers on an alphabetic, fun-filled tour of Canada. In tightly linked rhyming verse, the words resonate with classic and contemporary images from every province and territory in the country.

McGugan, J. 1994. *Josepha: A Prairie Boy's Story*. (M. Kimber, illustr.). Red Deer, AB: Red Deer College Press.

The story, narrated by a young boy, tells of the difficulties encountered by his friend Josepha, an immigrant from Eastern Europe, in 1900. Josepha is adjusting to a new home and a new language. Because he doesn't speak English, Josepha is seated with the very young children in school. Eventually Josepha makes some precious friends among the primary-grade children, and when he has to leave school to work on the farm, the children are sad to see him go.

Moak, A. 2002. *A Big City ABC*. Toronto: Tundra Books.
Toronto, Canada's largest city, means different things to different people. For some, it is the business centre of the country, and for others, it is the arts capital. In this book, the author sees Toronto through children's eyes, presenting the places he feels make Toronto a wonderful city for children. (Originally published in 1984.)

Morck, I. 1996. *Tiger's New Cowboy Boots*. (G. Graham, illustr.). Red Deer, AB: Red Deer College Press.
Each summer, Tiger takes the long bus ride to his Uncle Roy's ranch to participate in the cattle drive. This summer, instead of wearing runners, Tyler has new cowboy boots. After a day of riding a horse in dusty conditions, crawling after an orphan calf in the bush, and sloshing through water and mud to move the cattle across a river, Tyler's cowboy boots are noticed by his friend Jessica, and Tyler knows he is now a real cowboy.

Munsch, R. 2001. *Up, Up, Down*. (M. Martchenko, illustr.). Markham, ON: Scholastic.
Anna loves to climb, and although she is told by her parents not to do so, she continues to climb anything in and outside the house. The results are unexpected for the whole family. The book introduces elements of magic realism into a familiar family story.

Munsch, R., and S. Ascar, 1995. *From Far Away*. (M. Martchenko, illustr.). Toronto: Annick Press.
Robert Munch co-authors the heartwarming story of Saoussan, who came to North America from Beirut when she was five years old. Saoussan tells her own story – one that grew out of a series of letters she wrote to Munsch, capturing the emotions and frustrations of being a newcomer to Canada.

Munsch, R., and M. Kusugak. 1988. *A Promise Is a Promise*. (V. Krykorka, illustr.). Toronto: Annick Press.
When Allusha goes fishing alone on the sea ice, in spite of her mother's warning about the Qallupilluit, she doubts their existence and calls them by name. The creatures finally appear and drag Allusha down beneath the sea. Allusha escapes by promising to bring her brothers and sisters to the sea creatures. Allusha keeps her promise, but when the children come to the cracks in the sea, the Quallupilluit are not there, for they are dancing with Allusha's father and mother in the house.

Murray, B. 2004. *Thomas and the Metis Sash*. (S. Dawson, illustr.; R. Flamand, trans.). *Li saennchur fleshii di Michif: Thomas and the Metis Sash*. (Michif Children's Series). Winnipeg, MB: Pemmican Publications.
In each of the books in this series, Thomas is introduced to another aspect of his Métis cultural heritage. In this story, Thomas and his classmates

finger-weave a two-coloured belt in art class. When Thomas takes his blue and white belt home to show his parents, his mother says it reminds her of her Métis sash, which she takes out to show him. Thomas then takes the sash to school, where he shares the sash and his mother's explanations of it with his classmates and art teacher.

Nanji, S. 2000. *Treasure for Lunch*. (Y. Cathcart, illustr.). Toronto: Second Story Press.

Although Shaira is thrilled when her grandmother comes to stay with her while her parents are away, her Grandmother packs her tasty goodies for her school lunch that she is ashamed to eat in front of her friends. Shaira burries the bhajias and the kebabs in the snow. When the snow begins to melt, her buried treasure is exposed. In this story, Nanji addresses cultural embarrassment and celebration.

Oberman, S. 1994. *The Always Prayer Shawl*. (T. Lewin, illustr.) Honesdale, PA: Boyds Mill Press, Caroline House; distributed by St Martin's Press.

This story is about the importance of tradition and the certainty of change. When Adam grew up in Russia in the early 1900s, the revolution forced his family to flee to North America. Before he left, his grandfather gave him a prayer shawl, which became of tremendous significance. Events come full circle when Adam's grandson assures him that their "always prayer shawl" and their name will continue through the generations.

Patton, A., and W. Burton. 2007. *Fiddle Dancer*. (S.F. Racette, illustr.; N. Fleury, trans.). Saskatoon: The Gabriel Dumont Institute.

While visiting his grandfather Nolin attends a community dance and discovers his grandfather's talent as a jigger (dancer). Nolin learns about his Métis cultural heritage, and eventually, in spite of his apprehension, he also learns how to dance. The story highlights the importance of Elders as role models, and the special bond between grandparents and grandchildren. The book is written in English and Michif-Cree.

Pawagi, M. 1998. *The Girl Who Hated Books*. (L. Franson, illustr.). Toronto: Second Story Press.

Meena's parents love books, but Meena hates them. That's especially bad because there are books all over the house – mostly stacked to the ceiling. When Meena's cat leaps up on top of one of the tallest towers, Meena tries to rescue him. Instead, she knocks the books over and out of the pages fly Humpty Dumpty, Ali Baba, Peter Rabbit, and other literary characters, who convince Meena about the power of books. Meena's cultural heritage is hinted at in the illustrations of the book, but never referred to specifically in the text.

Pendziwol, J. 2004. *Dawn Watch*. (N. Debon, illustr.). Toronto: Groundwood Books.

During a night-time sail across Lake Superior, a girl wakes up to take watch with her father. The air is crisp and cold and Dad points out the Big Dipper and Little Bear and muses that the North Star has guided sailors for thousands of years. Together they watch the sun rise and finally see land in the distance. The lyrical, first-person narrative quietly captures the wonder of the universe during a late-night journey.

Pendziwol, J. 2005. *The Red Sash*. (N. Debon, illustr.). Toronto: Groundwood Books.

The story is set in the early years of the nineteenth century, and is told through the eyes of a young Métis boy living just outside Fort William. One day the boy helps rescue a white trader whose canoe is destroyed in a storm on the lake. The clear, mixed-media illustrations capture the people and the place, contrasting the harsh storm in the wilderness with the final rendezvous at the fort, where the voyageurs (including the boy's father), the traders, and the local community dance and celebrate together.

Quinlan, P. 1994. *Tiger Flowers*. (J. Wilson, illustr.). Toronto: Lester Publishing.

When Joel's uncle dies of AIDS, Joel does not know how to deal with his grief. He is reassured when he talks to his mother and she tells him that she also feels sad and lonely. When he goes to the tree-house that he and his uncle had built, Joel picks a tiger lily (his uncle's favourite flower) to give to his sister Tara, who is also grieving the loss.

Ruurs, M. 1996. *A Mountain Alphabet*. (A. Kiss, illustr.). Toronto: Tundra Books.

One of many alphabet books set in Western Canada, this book contains hidden animals, plants, and a letter of the alphabet in each painting. Notes at the end of the book make for an informative as well as an aesthetic reading experience. Grizzly bears, loons, mountains goats, moose, and people populate this alphabet book.

Sanderson, E. 1990. *Two Pairs of Shoes*. (D. Beyer, illustr.). Winnipeg: Pemmican Publications Inc.

Maggie receives a pair of dress shoes from her mother for her birthday. They were shoes she had wanted for a long time. When she goes to show them to her grandmother, who is blind, grandmother tells her to open a special box. In the box is a pair of beautiful beaded handmade moccasins. Maggie is told that she now has two pairs of shoes and that she must learn when and how to wear each pair.

Sauriol, L. 2004. *Les trouvailles d'Adami*. (L. Franson, illustr.). Quebec: Les éditions soleil de minuit.

An Inuit boy moves south to the city with his mother, and compares what he sees out of his window with his memories of the north – until he is drawn out of his basement hideaway to make friends with his next-door neighbour.

Setterington, K. 2004. *Mom and Mum Are Getting Married!* (A. Priestley, illustr.). Toronto: Second Story Press.

The upcoming wedding of Rosie's two mothers, Mom and Mum, is seen through the eyes of an excited eight-year-old. Perhaps she can get to be a bridesmaid or at the very least flower girl. Disappointed when these two suggestions are nixed, Rosie is ready to take on her role when the wedding day rolls around. All goes famously, with rings exchanged, petals scattered, and celebratory bubbles floating around the happy couple.

Skirving, J. 2006. *P Is for Puffin.* (O. Archibald, illustr.). Chelsea, MI: Sleeping Bear Press.

This Newfoundland and Labrador picture book focuses on the history, peoples, traditions, and landscapes of the province, depicted in verse, illustration, and informational text. This alphabetic tour highlights the natural beauty of different parts of the province and many of its unique cultural aspects.

Skrypuch, M.F. 1996. *Silver Threads.* (M. Martchenko, illustr.). Toronto: Penguin Books Canada.

Based on historical events, this is the story of a couple who escape poverty and hardship in Ukraine to move to the Canadian frontier. Tragedy strikes when Ivan is imprisoned as an "enemy alien" when the First World War breaks out. Anna struggles alone to keep their property and valuables, but hope comes from an unexpected source.

Spalding, A. 1999. *Me and Mr. Mah.* (J. Wilson, illustr.). Victoria, BC: Orca Book Publishers.

Ian moves with his mother from a prairie wheat farm to the city, where he becomes friends with their neighbour, Mr Mah, who enjoys tending his vegetable garden. When Ian discovers that Mr Mah keeps a box of memories of his past in China, they help each other by sharing their secret feelings of displacement.

Spalding, A. 2001. *It's Raining, It's Pouring.* (L.E. Watts, illustr.). Victoria, BC: Orca Book Publishers.

Little Girl watches the rain and thunder through her window. Little Girl is determined to stop the rain so she can play. Appealing to the readers' imagination and drawing on magic realism, *It's Raining, It's Pouring!* takes the reader on a journey with Little Girl up into the clouds to help Old Man get out of bed so that he can go back to taking care of the weather.

Spalding, A., and A. Scow. 2006. *Secret of the Dance.* (D. Gait, illustr.). Victoria, BC: Orca Book Publishers.

In 1935, Aboriginal cultural practices in Canada, such as the potlatch, were forbidden. This is the story of an eight-year-old boy's family, who held a forbidden potlatch in faraway Kingcome Inlet. The boy slipped from his bed to witness the event. In the Big House masked figures danced by firelight to the beat of the drum, and there the boy recognized a man whose life's work had been to uphold the law. Now, this man had a secret that could have sent the boy's family to jail.

Steffen, C. 2003. *A New Home for Malik*. (J. Stopper, illustr.). Calgary: Calgary Immigrant Woman's Association.

This is the story of a five-year-old boy who has just moved to Calgary from Sudan. Everything is new and different for him. Readers follow Malik as he meets new friends, learns a new language, and experiences Canada's four seasons for the first time.

Thien, M. 2001. *The Chinese Violin*. (J. Chang, illustr.). Vancouver: Whitecap Books.

In this immigration story, a young girl and her father leave everything familiar behind when they move to Canada from China. The only memento they bring with them is a Chinese violin. As they face the challenges of starting new lives in a new place, the music of the violin connects them to the life they left behind – and guides the girl to a musical future.

Trottier, M. 1995. *The Tiny Kite of Eddie Wing*. (A. Van Mil, illustr.). Toronto: Stoddart Kids.

Eddie thinks of nothing but kites and kite flying, but because his family is too poor to buy him a kite, Eddie has to make do with his imagination and his dreams. When he flies an invisible kite over the hilltops, Old Chan, who organizes the annual Festival of Kites, helps to make Eddie's dream come true.

Trottier, M. 1997. *Heartsong = Ceòl cridhe*. (P. MacAulay-Mackinnon, illustr.). Sydney, NS: University College of Cape Breton Press.

Told in English and Gaelic, this story tells of a fiddle passed down through four generations. From father to son, from that son to his daughter, from that daughter to her daughter, and from her daughter to a new toddler in the family – and all the events it attended throughout those years.

Trottier, M. 1999. *Flags*. (P. Morin, illustr.). Toronto: Stoddart Kids.

This is a story of innocence and friendship between Mary, a child visiting her grandmother for the summer during the Second World War, and Mr Hiroshi, a Japanese man living next door. When Mr Hiroshi is taken away from his home to a camp, Mary tries to keeps her promise to look after his garden until he returns.

Uegaki, C. 2003. *Suki's Kimono*. (S. Jorisch, illustr.). Toronto: Kids Can Press.

On her first day of first grade, Suki chooses to wear her Japanese kimono to school. It is a beloved gift from her grandmother. Her older sisters

object and the children on the playground initially laugh. Fortunately
for Suki, her day ends in triumph, with her teacher and classmates won
over by her impromptu dance performance as well as by her courage and
independence.

Ulmer, M. 2001. *M Is for Maple: A Canadian Alphabet.* (M. Rose, illustr.).
Chelsea, MI: Sleeping Bear Press.
From British Columbia to Newfoundland, this alphabet book shares
some of Canada's symbols, history, people, and culture. In rhymes and
informative text, details of Canada's past and present are described, from
the Northern Lights to Mounties and the cities of Toronto, Victoria, and
Quebec.

Van Camp, R. 1997. *A Man Called Raven.* (G. Littlechild, illustr.). San Francisco:
Children's Book Press.
This contemporary story, set in the Northwest Territories, blends the past
and the present to tell of Chris and Toby's learning from a strange raven
man. Drawn from the animal legends and folklore heard by the author, who
grew up as part of the Dogrib Nation, the story emphasizes the importance
of having respect for nature.

Van Camp, R. 1998. *What's the Most Beautiful Thing You Know about Horses?*
(G. Littlechild, illustr.). San Francisco: Children's Book Press.
In Fort Smith on a day so cold the ravens refuse to fly, Van Camp cannot go
outside. Instead, he asks his family and friends, "What's the most beautiful
thing you know about horses?" The people of the Dogrib Nation in the
Northwest Territories have little experience with horses. The many answers
Van Camp receives (including one from the book's illustrator) form the
basis for this text that reveals secrets about horses and about the people in
Van Camp's life.

Waboose, J.B. 1997. *Morning on the Lake.* (K. Reczuch, illustr.). Toronto: Kids
Can Press.
In this series of three linked stories, an Ojibway grandfather and his young
grandson set out one misty morning in a birchbark canoe. They watch a
pair of loons, climb a rocky cliff, and then go deep in the woods, where they
eventually see a pack of timber wolves. Grandfather's wisdom and courage
are transmitted to the boy, and he is able to overcome his fear of the wolves
and stand his ground in the gaze of the pack leader.

Waboose, J.B. 2000. *Sky Sisters.* (B. Deines, illustr.). Toronto: Kids Can Press.
This story about two young Ojibway sisters sees them set out across the
frozen north where the Sky Spirits dance. They suck glistening icicles while
walking, meet a rabbit and a white-tailed deer, hear a coyote's call, and
spin together atop a hill until they fall down dizzy in the snow. The story

honours the mystery in the sky that is the Aurora Borealis and tells of the bond between sisters, generations, humans, and nature.

Ye, T. 1999. *Share the Sky*. (S. Langlois, illustr.). Toronto: Annick Press.
Fei-Fei lives in China with her Grandpa, who makes the kites she loves to fly through the sky with her elder cousin. When a letter from North America tells Fei-Fei it is time for her to rejoin her parents, she learns of the courage it takes to face a strange new life, of the tolerance and understanding one needs to deal with different ways and customs, and of the love of family.

Yee, P. 1996. *Ghost Train*. (H. Chan, illustr.). Toronto: Douglas & McIntyre / Groundwood.
The book draws on a poignant Chinese ghost-story tradition to recount hard historical facts about the dangers encountered in building Canada's railways. When a young woman travels to Canada to locate her father who is working on the railway, she quickly learns that he has died. With his spirit guiding her, she creates a beautiful painting to take back to China in his memory and honour.

Yee, P. 2002. *The Jade Necklace*. (G. Lin, illustr.). New York: Crocodile Books.
This story opens in China, where Yenyee's father gives her a jade pendant carved like a fish. When a typhoon blows up while he's out at sea, she throws the necklace into the water to bargain for his life. Still, he drowns, leaving her family penniless. The girl eventually accepts a job with a merchant family and accompanies them to the New World. After rescuing her charge from near drowning, she miraculously finds the lost jade pendant, and begins to accept her new home.

References

Agbo, S. (2003). Changing school–community relations through participatory research: Strategies from First Nations and teachers. *Canadian Journal of Native Studies, 23*(1), 25–56.

Alfred, G.T., & Corntassel, J. (2005). Being Indigenous: Resurgence against contemporary colonialism. *Government and Opposition, 40*(4), 597–714. http://dx.doi.org/10.1111/j.1477-7053.2005.00166.x

Aoki, T., Pinar, W., & Irwin, R. (2005). *Curriculum in a new key: The collected works of Ted Aoki*. Mahwah, NJ: Lawrence Erlbaum Associates.

Arizpe, E., & Styles, M. (2003). *Children reading pictures: Interpreting visual texts*. London, UK: Routledge Falmer.

Atwood, M. (1972). *Survival: A thematic guide to Canadian literature*. Toronto: Anansi.

Au, K. (1993). *Literacy instruction in multicultural settings*. Fort Worth, TX: Harcourt.

Au, K.H., & Kawakami, A.J. (1994). Cultural congruence in instruction. In E.R. Hollins, J.E. King, & W.C. Hayman (Eds.), *Teaching diverse populations: Formulating a knowledge base* (pp. 5–23). Albany: SUNY Press.

Bainbridge, J., & Fayjean, J. (2000). Seeing oneself in a book: The changing face of Canadian children's literature. *English Quarterly, 32*(1–2), 55–62.

Bakhtin, M.M. (1981). In Holquist, M., & Emerson, C. (Trans. & Eds.) *The dialogic imagination*. Austin: University of Texas Press.

Bamford, A. 2003. *The visual literacy white paper*. Report for Adobe Systems Incorporated. Sydney, AU: University of Sydney. Retrieved December 15, 2009, from http://www.adobe.com/uk/education/pdf/adobe_visual_literacy_paper.pdf (no longer available).

Banks, J.A. (2001). *Cultural diversity and education: Foundations, curriculum and teaching* (4th ed.). Needham Heights, MA: Allyn & Bacon.

Banks, J.A., Cookson, P., Gay, G., Hawley, W.D., Irvine, J.J., Nieto, S., Schofield, J.W., & Stephan, W.G. (2001). Diversity within unity: Essential principles for teaching and learning in a multicultural society. *Phi Delta Kappan, 83*(3), 196–203.

Bannerji, H. (2000). *The dark side of the nation: Essays on multiculturalism, nationalism and gender*. Toronto: Canadian Scholars' Press.

BC Ministry of Education. (1998). Shared learnings: Integrating BC Aboriginal content K–10. Victoria, BC: Ministry of Education.

Bearne, E. (2004). Multimodal texts: What are they and how do children use them? In J. Evans (Ed.), *Literacy moves on: Using popular culture, new technologies and critical literacy in the primary classroom* (pp. 16–30). London: David Fulton Publishers.

Bell, L.A. (1997). Theoretical foundations for social justice education. In M. Adams, L.A. Bell, & P. Griffin (Eds.), *Teaching for diversity and social justice: A sourcebook* (pp. 3–15). New York: Routledge.

Bergeron, B.S. (2008). Enacting a culturally responsive curriculum in a novice teacher's classroom: Encountering disequilibrium. *Urban Education, 43*(4), 4–28. http://dx.doi.org/10.1177/0042085907309208

Bérci, M. (2007). The autobiographical metaphor: An invaluable approach to teacher development. *Journal of Educational Thought, 41*(1), 63–89.

Beynon, J. (2004). *From teacher to teacher educator: Collaboration within a community of practice*. Vancouver, BC: Pacific Educational Press.

Bhabha, H. (1994). *The location of culture*. New York: Routledge.

Bogdan, R., & Biklen, S.K. (2007). *Qualitative research for education: An introduction to theories and methods* (5th ed.). New York: Pearson Education.

Boler, M. (1997). The risks of empathy: Interrogating multiculturalism's gaze. *Cultural Studies, 11*(2), 253–273. http://dx.doi.org/10.1080/09502389700490141

Bradford, C. (2001). *Reading race: Aboriginality in Australian children's literature*. Melbourne, Vic.: Melbourne University Press.

Bradford, C. (2007). *Unsettling narratives: Postcolonial readings of children's literature*. Waterloo, ON: Wilfrid Laurier University Press.

Brenna, B. (2011). Characters with disabilities in contemporary novels for children: A portrait of three authors in a framework of Canadian texts. *Language and Literacy, 13*(1). Retrieved October 30, 2011 from http://ejournals.library.ualberta.ca/index.php/langandlit/article/view/9781.

Brindley, R., & Laframboise, K. (2002). The need to do more: Promoting multiple perspectives in preservice teacher education through children's literature. *Teaching and Teacher Education, 18*(4), 405–420. http://dx.doi.org/10.1016/S0742-051X(02)00006-9

Britzman, D. (1998). *Lost subjects, contested objects: Toward a psychoanalytic inquiry of learning*. New York: SUNY Press.

Britzman, D. (2003). *Practice makes practice: A critical study of learning to teach.* New York: SUNY Press.

Brown, M.W. (1977). *The important book.* New York: HarperCollins.

Bruner, J. (1986). *Actual minds, possible worlds.* Cambridge, MA: Harvard University Press.

Burke, A. (2009). Inspiring aesthetic response through the multimodality of picture books. In C. Clark & T. Messinheimer (Eds.), *Perceptions of literacy and reading* (pp. 27–41). London, UK: Pied Piper Press.

Burke, A. (2002). Using the out in picture books to develop characters in dramatic role. (Unpublished master's thesis). Memorial University of Newfoundland, St John's, NL.

Burke, A., & Peterson, S. (2007). A multidisciplinary approach to literacy through picture books and drama. *English Journal, 96*(3), 74–85. http://dx.doi.org/10.2307/30047299

Burns, R. (2009). Comprehension and incorporation in teacher candidates' reading about diversity. *Journal of Reading Education, 34*(2), 19–24.

Cadiero-Kaplan, K. (2002). Literacy ideologies: Critically engaging the language arts curriculum. *Language Arts, 79*(5), 372–381.

Cajete, G. (1994). *Look to the mountain: An ecology of Indigenous education.* Skyland, NC: Kivaki Press.

Canadian Museum of Civilization (2006). *The last best west: Advertising for immigrants to Western Canada.* Retrieved December 15, 2009 from http://www.civilization.ca/cmc/exhibitions/hist/advertis/ads1-01e.shtml.

Carson, T., & Johnston, I. (2001a). Cultural difference and teacher identity formation: The need for a pedagogy of compassion. *JPCS: Journal for the Psychoanalysis of Culture and Society, 6*(2), 259–264.

Carson, T., & Johnston, I. (2001b). Desires and resistances in multicultural education: Preparing teachers for classrooms of cultural diversity. In R. Golz & R.W. Keck (Eds.), *Humanisierung der Bildung Jahrbook* (pp. 115–123). New York: Peter Lang.

Cervetti, G., Pardales, M.J., & Damico, J.S. (2001). A tale of differences: Comparing the traditions, perspectives, and educational goals of critical reading and critical literacy. *Reading online.* Retrieved October 25, 2010 from http://www.readingonline.org/articles/cervetti.

Chamberlin, J.E. (2003). *If this is your land, where are your stories? Finding a common ground.* Toronto: Alfred A. Knopf.

Chui, T., Tran, K., & Badets, J. (2004). *The ethnic boundary in Atlantic Canada: A legacy of the region's immigration history.* Ottawa: Statistics Canada.

Clandinin, D.J., & Connelly, F.M. (1996). Teachers' professional knowledge landscapes: Teacher stories. Stories of teachers. School stories. Stories of schools. *Educational Researcher, 25*(3), 24–30.

Cochran-Smith, M. (1995). Color blindness and basket making are not the answers: Confronting the dilemmas of race, culture, and language diversity in teacher education. *American Educational Research Journal, 32*(3), 493–522.

Cochran-Smith, M. (2000). Blind vision: Unlearning racism in teacher education. *Harvard Educational Review, 70*(2), 157–190.

Cochran-Smith, M. (2004). *Walking the road: Race, diversity, and social justice in teacher education.* New York: Teachers College Press.

Cochran-Smith, M., & Lytle, S. (1999). Relationships of knowledge and practice: Teacher learning in communities. *Review of Research in Education, 24*(3), 249–305.

Connelly, F.M., & Clandinin, D.J. (1988). *Teachers as curriculum planners: Narratives of experience.* New York: Teachers College Press.

Cook-Lynn, E. (1996). *Why I can't read Wallace Stegner and other essays: A tribal voice.* Madison: University of Wisconsin Press.

Curtis, C.P. (1995). *The Watsons go to Birmingham – 1963.* New York: Bantam Doubleday Dell.

Cushner, K., McClelland, A., & Safford, P. (2003). *Human diversity in education: An integrative approach* (4th ed.). New York: McGraw-Hill.

Darling-Hammond, L. (2006). Constructing 21st-century teacher education. *Journal of Teacher Education, 57*(3), 300–314. http://dx.doi.org/10.1177/0022487105285962

Davis, R.D., Ramahlo, T., Beyerbach, B., & London, A.P. (2008). A culturally relevant teaching course: Reflecting pre-service teachers' thinking. *Teaching Education, 19*(3), 223–234. http://dx.doi.org/10.1080/10476210802250265

Deloria, P.J. (1998). *Playing Indian.* New Haven, CT: Yale University Press.

Deloria, V. (1969). *Custer died for your sins.* New York: Avon Books.

Deloria, V. (1997). Anthros, Indians, and planetary reality. In T. Biolsi & L.J. Zimmerman (Eds.), *Indians and anthropology: Vine Deloria Jr. and the critique of anthropology* (pp. 202–222). Lincoln: University of Nebraska Press.

Delpit, L. (1995). *Other people's children: Cultural conflict in the classroom.* New York: The New Press. http://dx.doi.org/10.2307/358724

Dietrich, D., & Ralph, K.S. (1995). Crossing borders: Multicultural literature in the classroom. *Journal of Educational Issues of Language Minority Students, 15,* 17–38.

Dion, S. (2007). Disrupting molded images: Identities, responsibilities, and relationships – teachers and Indigenous subjects materials. *Teaching Education, 18*(4), 329–342. http://dx.doi.org/10.1080/10476210701687625

Donald, J. (Ed.). (1991). *Psychoanalysis and cultural theory: Thresholds.* London: Macmillan Education.

Dong, Y.R. (2005). Bridging the cultural gap by teaching multicultural literature. *Educational Forum, 69*(4), 367–382. http://dx.doi.org/10.1080/00131720508984709

Doxtater, M. (2004). Indigenous knowledge in the decolonial era. *American Indian Quarterly, 28*(3), 618–633. http://dx.doi.org/10.1353/aiq.2004.0094

Dudek, D. (2011). Multicultural. In P. Nel & L. Paul (Eds.), *Keywords for Children's Literature* (pp. 151–160). New York, London: New York University Press.

Duffy, G.G., Webb, S.M., & Davis, S. (2009). Literacy education at a crossroad: Can we counter the trend to marginalize quality teacher education? In J.V. Hoffman & Y. Goodman (Eds.), *Changing literacies for changing times: An historical perspective on the future of reading research, public policy, and classroom practices* (pp. 189–197). New York: Routledge.

Eastern School District Newfoundland and Labrador (n.d.). Vision statement and goals. Retrieved March 20, 2010 from http://www.esdnl.ca/aboutesd/mission/

Edwards, G., & Saltman, J. (2010). *Picturing Canada: A history of Canadian children's illustrated books and publishing*. Toronto: University of Toronto Press.

Eigenbrod, R. (2005). *Travelling knowledges: Positioning the im/migrant reader of Aboriginal literatures in Canada*. Winnipeg: University of Manitoba Press.

Eisner, E. (2002). *The educational imagination: On the design and evaluation of school programs* (3rd ed.). Upper Saddle River, NJ: Pearson Education.

Ellsworth, E. (1997). *Teaching positions: Difference, pedagogy, and the power of address*. New York: Teachers College Press.

Feiman-Nemser, S. (2001). From preparation to practice: Designing a continuum to strengthen and sustain teaching. *Teachers College Record, 103*(6), 1013–1055. http://dx.doi.org/10.1111/0161-4681.00141

Fleras, A. (2010). *Unequal relations: An introduction to race, ethnic, and Aboriginal dynamics in Canada* (6th ed.). Toronto: Pearson Canada.

Fontaine, P. (1999). Foreword. In J. Hylton (Ed.), *Aboriginal self-government in Canada* (pp. ix–x). Saskatoon, SK: Purich Press.

Francis, D. (1992). *The imaginary Indian: The image of the Indian in Canadian culture*. Vancouver, BC: Arsenal Pulp Press.

Freebody, P., & Luke, A. (1991). Literacies programs: Debates and demands in cultural contexts. *Prospects, 5*(3), 7–16.

Freire, P. (1983). *Pedagogy of the oppressed* (M.B. Ramos, Trans.). New York: Continuum. (Original work published 1970).

Freire, P. (1998). *Teachers as cultural workers: Letters to those who dare teach* (D. Macedo, D. Koike, & A. Oliveira, Trans.). Cambridge, MA: Westview Press.

Frye, N. (1995). *The bush garden: Essays on the Canadian imagination* (2nd ed.). Concord, ON: Anansi. (Original work published 1971).

Fuller, M.L. (1994). The monocultural graduate in the multicultural environment: A challenge for teacher educators. *Journal of Teacher Education, 45*(4), 269–277. http://dx.doi.org/10.1177/0022487194045004005

Fultz, L.P. (2003). *Toni Morrison: Playing with difference*. Urbana: University of Illinois Press.

Galda, L., & Short, K.G. (1993). Visual literacy: Exploring art and illustration in children's books. *Reading Teacher, 46*, 506–516.

Galway, E. (2008). *From nursery rhymes to nationhood: Children's literature and the construction of Canadian identity*. London, UK: Routledge.

Gangi, J.M. (2004). *Encountering children's literature: An arts approach*. San Francisco, CA: Pearson.

Gardner, J. (1971). *Grendel*. New York: Knopf.

Gardiner, J.R. (2003). *Stone Fox*. New York: HarperCollins.

Garmon, M.A. (2004). Changing preservice teachers' attitudes/beliefs about diversity: What are the critical factors? *Journal of Teacher Education, 55*(3), 201–213. http://dx.doi.org/10.1177/0022487104263080

Gay, G. (2000). *Culturally responsive teaching: Theory, research and practice*. New York: Teachers College Press.

Gee, J.P. (2001). Identity as an analytic lens for research in education. In W.G. Secada (Ed.), *Review of Research in Education, 25*, 99–125. Washington, DC: American Educational Research Association. http://dx.doi.org/10.2307/1167322

Ghosh, R., and Tarrow, N. 1993. Multiculturalism and teacher educators: Views from Canada and the USA. *Comparative Education, 29*(1), 81–92.

Giroux, H. (Ed.). (1991). *Postmodernism, feminism and cultural politics: Redrawing educational boundaries*. Albany: SUNY Press.

Grant, C. (Ed.). (1992). *Research and multicultural education: From the margins to the mainstream*. Bristol, PA: Falmer Press.

Greene, M. (1965). Real toads and imaginary gardens. *Teachers College Record, 66*(5), 416–425.

Grigg, C. (2003). The painted word: Literacy through art. In M. Styles & E. Bearne (Eds.), *Art, narrative and childhood* (pp. 127–136). Staffordshire, UK: Trentham Books Ltd.

Groening, L.S. (2004). *Listening to old woman speak: Natives and alterNatives in Canadian literature*. Montreal: McGill-Queen's University Press.

Grossman, P., Valencia, S., Evans, K., Thompson, C., Martin, S., & Place, N. (2000). *Transitions into teaching: Learning to teach writing in teacher education and beyond*. CELA Research Report #13006. Albany, NY: National Research Center on English Learning and Achievement.

Grumet, M. (1991). Curriculum and the art of daily life. In G. Willis & W.H. Schubert (Eds.), *Reflections from the heart of educational inquiry: Understanding curriculum and teaching through the arts* (pp. 74–89). New York: SUNY Press.

Gunderson, L. (2007). *English-only instruction and immigrant students in secondary schools: A critical examination.* Mahwah, NJ: Lawrence Erlbaum Associates.

Gunew, S. (2003). *Haunted nations: The colonial dimensions of multiculturalism.* New York: Routledge.

Hammett, R.F., & Bainbridge, J. (2009). Preservice teachers explore cultural identity and ideology through picture books. *Literacy, 43*(3), 152–159. http://dx.doi.org/10.1111/j.1741-4369.2009.00522.x

Harste, J.C., Leland, C., Schmidt, K., Vasquez, V., & Ociepka, A. (2004, January/February). Practice makes practice, or does it? The relationship between theory and practice in teacher education. *Reading Online, 7*(4). Retrieved February 5, 2010 from http://www.readingonline.org/articles/art_index.asp?HREF=harste/index.html.

Heath, S.B. (1983). *Ways with words: Language, life and work in communities and classrooms.* Cambridge, UK: Cambridge University Press.

Heffernan, L. (2004). *Critical literacy and writer's workshop: Bringing purpose and passion to student writing.* Newark, DE: International Reading Association.

Higgins, J. (2008). Mi'kmaq organizations and land claims. *Newfoundland and Labrador Heritage* website. Retrieved September 15, 2009 from http://www.heritage.nf.ca/aboriginal/mikmaq_claims.html

Hodgkin, K., & Radstone, S. (2003). Introduction. In K. Hodgkin & S. Radstone (Eds.), *Contested pasts: The politics of memory* (pp. 1–21). London, UK: Routledge.

Howells, R. (2003). *Visual Culture.* Cambridge, UK: Polity Press.

Howrey, S.T., & Whelan-Kim, K. (2009). Building cultural responsiveness in rural, preservice teachers using a multicultural children's literature project. *Journal of Early Childhood Teacher Education, 30*(2), 123–137. http://dx.doi.org/10.1080/10901020902885661

Hoy, H. (2001). *How should I read these?: Native women writers in Canada.* Toronto: University of Toronto Press.

Hughes, P. (1998). Exploring visual literacy across the curriculum. In J. Evans (Ed.), *What's in the picture? Responding to illustrations in picture books* (pp. 115–131). London: Paul Chapman Publishing Ltd.

Innu Nation. (n.d.). Welcome to Innu.ca. Retrieved from http://www.innu.ca/ January 27, 2013.

Iseke-Barnes, J. (2008). Pedagogies for decolonizing. *Canadian Journal of Native Education, 31*(1), 123–148.

Iser, W. (1980). *The act of reading: A theory of aesthetic response*. Baltimore, MD: Johns Hopkins University Press.

James, C.E., & Shadd, A.L. (2001). *Talking about identity: Encounters in race, ethnicity, and language*. Toronto: Between the Lines.

Jewitt, C. (2008). Multimodality and literacy in school classrooms. *Review of Research in Education, 32*(1), 241–267. http://dx.doi.org/10.3102/0091732X07310586

Joe, R. (1998). I lost my talk. In D.D. Moses & T. Goldie (Eds.), *An anthology of Canadian native literature in English* (pp. 113–114). Toronto: Oxford University Press.

Johnson, L. (2002). "My eyes have been opened": White teachers and racial awareness. *Journal of Teacher Education, 53*(2), 153–167. http://dx.doi.org/10.1177/0022487102053002007

Johnston, I. (2003). *Remapping literary worlds: Postcolonial pedagogy in practice*. New York: Peter Lang.

Johnston, I. (2006). Exploring the entanglements of cultural identity and teacher identity formation in multicultural and anti-racist education. In D. Zinga (Ed.), *Navigating multiculturalism, negotiating change* (pp. 160–168). Cambridge: Cambridge Scholars Press.

Johnston, I., Bainbridge, J., & Shariff, F. (2007). Exploring issues of national identity, ideology and diversity in contemporary Canadian picture books. *Papers: Explorations into Children's Literature, 17*(2), 75–82.

Keene, E.O., & Zimmerman, S. (1997). *Mosaic of thought: Teaching comprehension in a reader's workshop*. Portsmouth, NH: Heinemann.

Kiefer, B.Z. (1995). *The potential of picture books: From visual literacy to aesthetic understanding*. Englewood Cliffs, NJ: Merrill.

Kiefer, B.Z. (2010). *Charlotte Huck's children's literature*. New York: McGraw-Hill.

King, T. (1998). *Coyote sings to the moon*. Toronto: Key Porter Kids.

King, T. (2003). *The truth about stories: A native narrative*. Toronto: House of Anansi Press.

King, T. (2004). *Coyote's new suit*. Toronto: Key Porter Books.

Kosnik, C., & Beck, C. (2009). *Priorities in teacher education: The 7 key elements of pre-service preparation*. New York: Routledge.

Kress, G. (2003). *Literacy in the new media age*. London, UK: Routledge. http://dx.doi.org/10.4324/9780203164754

Labrador Métis Nation (2007). *Labrador Métis Nation*. Retrieved September 14, 2009 from http://www.labradormetis.ca/home/3 (no longer available); retrieved June 19, 2012 from NunatuKavut (2012). *About NunatuKavut*. http://www.nunatukavut.ca/home/about.htm.

Ladson-Billings, G. (1995a). Toward a theory of culturally relevant pedagogy. *American Educational Research Journal, 32*, 465–491.

Ladson-Billings, G. (1995b). But that's just good teaching! The case for culturally relevant pedagogy. *Theory into Practice, 34*(3), 159–165. http://dx.doi.org/10.1080/00405849509543675

Ladson-Billings, G. (1997). *The dreamkeepers: Successful teachers of African-American children.* San Francisco, CA: Jossey-Bass.

Ladson-Billings, G. (2001). *Crossing over to Canaan: The journey of new teachers in diverse classrooms.* San Francisco, CA: Jossey-Bass.

Langer, J.A. (1995). *Envisioning literature: Literary understanding and literature instruction.* New York: Columbia University Teacher's College.

Lapp, D., Flood, J., & Fisher, D. (1999). Intermediality: How the use of multiple media enhances learning. *Reading Teacher, 52*(7), 776–780.

LaRocque, E. (1996). When the other is me: Native writers confronting Canadian literature. In J. Oakes & R. Riewe (Eds.), *Issues in the North* (Vol. 1, pp. 115–134). Edmonton: Canadian Circumpolar Institute.

Larrick, N. (1965, September 11). The all-white world of children's books. *Saturday Review, 48,* 63–65, 84–85.

Lee, S., & Dallman, M.E. (2008). Engaging in reflective examination about diversity: Interviews with three preservice teachers. *Multicultural Education, 15*(4), 36–44.

Lester, J. (1998). *From slave ship to freedom road.* New York: Dial Books for Young Readers.

Lewis, A.E. (2001). There is no race in the schoolyard: Color-blind ideology in an almost all-White school. *American Educational Research Journal, 38*(4), 781–811. http://dx.doi.org/10.3102/00028312038004781

Lewis, C. (2000). Limits of identification: The personal, pleasurable, and critical in reader response. *Journal of Literacy Research, 32*(2), 253–266. http://dx.doi.org/10.1080/10862960009548076

Lewis, D. (2004). A word about pictures. In T. Grainger (Ed.), *The Routledge Falmer reader in language and literacy* (pp. 199–216). London: Routledge Falmer.

Lewison, M., Flint, A.S., & Van Sluys, K. (2002). Taking on critical literacy: The journey of newcomers and novices. *Language Arts, 79*(5), 382–392.

Liggett, T., & Finley, S. (2009). "Upsetting the apple cart": Issues of diversity in preservice teacher education. *Multicultural Education, 16*(4), 33–38.

Liston, D., Whitcomb, J., & Borko, H. (2006). Too little or too much: Teacher preparation and the first years of teaching. *Journal of Teacher Education, 57*(4), 351–358. http://dx.doi.org/10.1177/0022487106291976

Loh, C. (2009). Reading the world: Reconceptualizing reading multicultural literature in the English language arts classroom in a global world. *Changing English, 16*(3), 287–299. http://dx.doi.org/10.1080/13586840903194755

Loyie, L. (2002), *As Long as the Rivers Flow.* Toronto: Groundwood Books.

Lukens, R. (2002). *A critical handbook of children's literature* (6th ed.). New York: Longman.

Mahoney, J. (2010, March 9). Canada's visible minority population to nearly double by 2031. *Globe and Mail*. Retrieved March 13, 2010 from http://www. theglobeandmail.com/news/national/canadas-visible-minority-population-to-nearly-double-by-2031/article1494651/#interactive (no longer available).

Manderson, D. (2003). From hunger to love: Myths of the source, interpretation and constitution of law in children's literature. Benjamin N. Cardozo School of Law, Jacob Burns Institute for Advanced Legal Studies, *Research Paper no. 64*. Retrieved February 10, 2009 from http://papers.ssrn. com/sol3/papers.cfm?abstract_id=375260.

Manguel, A. (1993). Introduction. In C. Stephenson (Ed.), *Countries of invention: Contemporary world writing* (pp. viii–xi). Toronto: Addison-Wesley Publishers Limited.

Manning, E. (2003). *Ephemeral territories: Representing nation, home and identity in Canada*. Minneapolis: University of Minnesota Press.

Maracle, L. (1990). *Sojourner's truth & other stories*. Vancouver: Press Gang Publishers.

McCarthy, C. (1998). *The uses of culture: Education and the limits of ethnic affiliation*. New York: Routledge.

McDaniel, C.A. (2006). *Critical literacy: A way of thinking, a way of life*. New York: Peter Lang.

McKenzie, A. (2003). The changing faces of Canadian children: Pictures, power and pedagogy. In A. Hudson & S. Cooper (Eds.), *Windows and words: A look at Canadian children's literature in English* (pp. 201–218). Ottawa: University of Ottawa Press.

McNair, J.C., & Colabucci, L. (2007). "Let's get smart about art": Developing visual literacy with picture books. *Journal of Children's Literature, 33*(1), 10–13.

Merriam, S.B. (1998). Case studies as qualitative research. In S.B. Merriam (Ed.), *Qualitative research and case study applications in education*. San Francisco, CA: Jossey-Bass.

Milner, H.R. (2005). Stability and change in prospective teachers' beliefs and decisions about diversity and learning to teach. *Teaching and Teacher Education, 21*(7), 767–786. http://dx.doi.org/10.1016/j.tate.2005.05.010

Momaday, S. (1966). *House made of dawn*. New York: Harper & Row.

Morrison, T. (2002, May 27–29). Grendel and his mother. In T. Morrison, The foreigner's home: Meditations on belonging, *Alexander Lecture Series*. Congress of the Social Sciences and Humanities, University of Toronto, Toronto.

Mukherjee, A. (1998). *Postcolonialism: My Living*. Toronto: Tsar Publications.

Munsch, R. (1984). *Millicent and the wind*. Toronto: Annick Press.

Ndura, E. (2004). Teachers' discoveries of their cultural realms: Untangling the web of cultural identity. *Multicultural Perspectives, 6*(3), 10–16. http://dx.doi .org/10.1207/s15327892mcp0603_3

Nieto, S. (2000). *Affirming diversity: The sociopolitical context of multicultural education* (3rd ed.). New York: Addison Wesley Longman.

Nodelman, P. (1988). *Words about pictures: The narrative art of children's picture books*. Athens: University of Georgia Press.

Nodelman, P. (1999). Decoding the images: Illustration and picture books. In P. Hunt (Ed.), *Understanding Children's Literature* (pp. 69–80). New York: Routledge.

Nodelman, P. (2008). At home on native land: A non-Aboriginal Canadian scholar discusses Aboriginality and property in Canadian double-focalized novels for young adults. In M. Reimer (Ed.), *Home Words: Discourses of children's literature in Canada* (pp. 107–128). Studies in childhood and family in Canada. Waterloo, ON: Wilfrid Laurier University Press.

Nodelman, P., & Reimer, M. (2000). Teaching Canadian children's literature: Learning to know more. *Canadian Children's Literature, 26*(2), 15–35.

Nodelman, P., & Reimer, M. (2003). *The pleasures of children's literature*. Boston: Allyn and Bacon.

Norton, D.E. (2009). *Multicultural children's literature: Through the eyes of many children*. Boston, MA: Pearson Education, Inc.

Patton, M.Q. (2002). *Qualitative research and evaluation methods*. Thousand Oaks, CA: Sage Publications.

Phelan, A.M. (2005). A fall from (someone else's) certainty: Recovering practical wisdom in teacher education. *Canadian Journal of Education, 28*(3), 339–358. http://dx.doi.org/10.2307/4126474

Philips, S. (1983). *The invisible culture: Communication in classroom and community on the Warm Springs Indian Reservation*. New York: Longman Inc.

Phillips, D.K., & Larson, M.L. (2009). Embodied discourses of literacy in the lives of two preservice teachers. *Teacher Development, 13*(2), 135–146. http:// dx.doi.org/10.1080/13664530903043962

Pratt, M.L. (1992). *Imperial eyes: Travel writing and transculturation*. New York: Routledge.

Pratt, P. (1991). Arts of the contact zone. *Profession, 91*, 33–40.

Raggatt, P.T. (2006). Multiplicity and conflict in the dialogical self: A life-narrative approach. In D. McAdams, R. Josselson, & A. Lieblich (Eds.), *Identity and story: Creating self in narrative* (pp. 15–35). Washington, DC: American Psychological Association. http://dx.doi.org/10.1037/11414-001

Reimer, M. (Ed.). (2008). *Home words: Discourses of children's literature in Canada*. Studies in childhood and family in Canada. Waterloo, ON: Wilfrid Laurier University Press.

Richardson, V. (1994). Conducting research on practice. *Educational Researcher,* *23*(5), 5–10.

Robertson, J. (1997). Teaching about worlds of hurt through encounters with literature: Reflections on pedagogy. *Language Arts, 74*(6), 457–466.

Roessingh, H., & Kover, P. (2003). Variability of ESL learners' acquisition of cognitive academic language proficiency: What can we learn from achievement measures? *TESL Canada Journal, 21*(1), 1–21.

Rosenblatt, L.M. (1978). *The reader, the text, the poem: The transactional theory of the literary work.* Carbondale: Southern Illinois University Press.

Rosenblatt, L.M. (1982). The literary transaction: Evocation and response. *Theory into Practice, 21*(4), 268–277. http://dx.doi.org/10.1080/00405848209543018

Rosenblatt, L.M. (1983). *Literature as exploration* (4th ed.). New York: Modern Language Association of America.

St Denis, V. (2007). Aboriginal and anti-racist education: Building alliances across cultural and racial identity. *Canadian Journal of Education, 30*(4), 1068–1092. http://dx.doi.org/10.2307/20466679

Saldanha, L. (2000). Bedtime stories: Canadian multiculturalism and children's literature. In R. McGillis (Ed.), *Voices of the other: Children's literature and the postcolonial context* (pp. 165–176). New York: Garland Publishing.

Santomé, J.T. (2009). The Trojan horse of curricular contents. In M. Apple, W. Au, & L.A. Gandin (Eds.), *The Routledge international handbook of critical education* (pp. 64–79). (E. Cavieres, Trans.). New York: Routledge.

Santoro, N. (2009). Teaching in culturally diverse contexts: What knowledge about "self" and "others" do teachers need? *Journal of Education for Teaching, 35*(1), 33–45. http://dx.doi.org/10.1080/02607470802587111

Saul, J.R. (2008). *A fair country: Telling truths about Canada.* Toronto: Viking Canada. http://dx.doi.org/10.7202/044173ar

Schissel, B., & Wotherspoon, T. (2003). *The legacy of school for Aboriginal people: Education, oppression and emancipation.* Toronto: Oxford University Press.

Seale, D., & Slapin, B. (1992). *Through Indian eyes: The Native experience in books for children.* Philadelphia, PA: New Society Publishers.

Sendak, M. (1957). *Very far away.* New York: Harper.

Seppänen, J. (2006). *The power of the gaze: An introduction to visual literacy* (A. Ahonen & K. Clarke, Trans.). New York: Peter Lang.

Serafini, F. (2009). Understanding visual images: What to respond to? Attending to aspects of picturebooks. In J. Evans (Ed.), *Talking beyond the page* (pp. 10–26). London: Routledge.

Sfard, A., & Prusak, A. (2005). Telling identities: In search of an analytic tool for investigating learning as a culturally shaped activity. *Educational Researcher, 34*(4), 14–22. http://dx.doi.org/10.3102/0013189X034004014

Shor, I. (1996). *When students have power: Negotiating authority in a critical pedagogy*. Chicago: University of Chicago Press.

Siegel, M. (2006). Rereading the signs: Multimodal transformations in the field of literacy education. *Language Arts, 84*(1), 65–77.

Simpson, J. (2008, April 26). Warning: The boom out West is both a lure and a trap. *Globe and Mail*, p. A27.

Sipes, L. (2007). *Storytime: Young children's literacy understanding in the classroom*. New York: Teachers College Press.

Sleeter, C.E. (2001). Preparing teachers for culturally diverse schools: Research and the overwhelming presence of Whiteness. *Journal of Teacher Education, 52*(2), 94–106. http://dx.doi.org/10.1177/0022487101052002002

Smagorinsky, P. (2002). *Teaching English through principled practice*. Upper Saddle River, NJ: Pearson Education, Inc.

Smith, E.B. (2009). Approaches to multicultural education in preservice teacher education: Philosophical frameworks and models for teaching. *Multicultural Education, 16*(3), 45–50.

Stake, R. (1995). *The art of case study research*. Thousand Oaks, CA: Sage Publications.

Statistics Canada (2008). *Aboriginal Peoples in Canada in 2006: Inuit, Métis and First Nations, 2006 census: Inuit*. Retrieved November 16, 2009 from http://www12.statcan.ca/census-recensement/2006/as-sa/97-558/index-eng.cfm?CFID=67189&CFTOKEN=57844413

Stephens, J. (1992). *Language and ideology in children's fiction*. New York: Longman.

Sterling, S. (1992). *My name is Seepeetza*. Vancouver: Groundwood Books.

Sterzuk, A. (2008). Whose English counts? Indigenous English in Saskatchewan schools. *McGill Journal of Education, 43*(1), 9–19. http://dx.doi.org/10.7202/019570ar

Stewig, J.W. (1995). *Looking at picture books*. Fort Atkinson, WI: Highsmith Press.

Strong-Wilson, T. (2006). Touchstones as sprezzatura: The significance of attachment to teacher literary formation. *Changing English, 13*(1), 69–81.

Strong-Wilson, T. (2007). Moving horizons: Exploring the role of stories in decolonizing the literacy education of white teachers. *International Education, 31*(1), 114–131.

Strong-Wilson, T. (2008). *Bringing memory forward: Storied remembrance in social justice education with teachers*. New York: Peter Lang.

Tan, S. (2010). Picture books: Who are they for? Retrieved December 24, 2010 from http://www.shauntan.net/essay1.html.

Taylor, L. (2007). Reading desire: From empathy to estrangement, from enlightenment to implication. *Intercultural Education, 18*(4), 297–316. http://dx.doi.org/10.1080/14675980701605170

Todd, S. (2003). *Learning from the other: Levinas, psychoanalysis and ethical possibilities in education*. Albany: SUNY Press.

Toohey, K., & Derwing, T.M. (2008). Hidden losses: How demographics can encourage incorrect assumptions about ESL high school students' success. *Alberta Journal of Educational Research, 54,* 178–193.

Vizenor, G. (1994). *Manifest manners: Postindian warriors of survivance*. Hanover, NJ: Wesleyan University Press.

Vygotsky, L.S. (1978). *Mind in society: The development of higher psychological processes*. Cambridge, MA: Harvard University Press.

Wagamese, R. (2006). *Keeper'n me*. Toronto: Anchor Canada. (Original work published 1994).

Ward, A. (1989). Communicative inequality: The participation of native Indian and non-native children in instructional dialogue in a cross-cultural kindergarten class. Unpublished PhD dissertation, University of Victoria, Canada.

Wenger, E. (1998a). Communities of practice: Learning as a social system. *Systems Thinker, 9*(5), 11–22.

Wenger, E. (1998b). *Communities of practice: Learning, meaning, and identity*. Cambridge, UK: Cambridge University Press.

Werner, W. (2008). Teaching for hope. In R. Case & P. Clark (Eds.), *The anthology of social studies: Issues and strategies for elementary teachers* (pp. 171–175). Vancouver: Pacific Educational Press.

Wilder, L.I. (1953). *Little house on the prairie*. New York: HarperCollins.

Wilhelm, J.D. (2009). The power of teacher inquiry: Developing a critical literacy for teachers. *Voices from the Middle, 17*(2), 36–39.

Williams, D. (1996). *Deformed discourse: The function of the monster in medieval thought and literature*. Montreal: McGill-Queen's University Press.

Wilson, T. (2000). *Ravenwing: A white teacher's experiences of teaching and living within a First Nations community. Unpublished teacher narrative*. Victoria, BC: University of Victoria.

Winch, G., Johnston, R.R., Holliday, M., Ljungdahl, L., & March, P. (2001). *Literacy: Reading, writing, and children's literature*. Melbourne, AU: Oxford University Press.

Winters, C., & Schmidt, G. (2001). *Edging the boundaries of children's literature*. Boston, MA: Allyn & Bacon.

Wolf, D., & DePasquale, P. (2008). Home and native land: A study of Canadian Aboriginal picture books by Aboriginal authors. In M. Reimer (Ed.), *Home words: Discourses of children's literature in Canada* (pp. 87–105). Studies in childhood and family in Canada. Waterloo, ON: Wilfrid Laurier University Press.

Wright, J. (1980). *Education of minority students: Problems and challenges. The minority student in public schools*. Princeton: Educational Testing Service.

Author Biographies

Joyce Bainbridge, professor emeritus of the University of Alberta, has, for the last thirty years, conducted research and taught university courses in language and literacy education, with a specialization in children's literature and children's writing. In 2000 she was awarded the Alberta Teachers' Association Educational Research Award for her study of teachers' responses to Canadian children's literature. Her textbook *Constructing Meaning* (co-authored with Rachel Heydon) is used widely across Canada.

Beverley Brenna is an assistant professor in curriculum studies at the University of Saskatchewan, where her research interests include literacy, children's literature, and special education. She is the principal investigator for a SSHRC project exploring patterns and trends in North American children's books featuring characters with disabilities, and she has other studies exploring teaching reading comprehension strategies in the context of graphic novels. She has published nine fiction books for children and young adults, and her international awards include the Dolly Gray Award for Children's Literature. More about her published work can be found at http://www.beverleybrenna.com.

Anne Burke is associate professor of children's literature and literacy education at the Faculty of Education, Memorial University of Newfoundland. She teaches children's literature and digital literacies. Her research focuses on the performativity of multimodality in picture books, children's digital reading and authoring practices, assessment of new literacies, and virtual play worlds for the young child. She is the author of *Ready to Learn: Using Play to Build Literacy Skills* (Pembroke,

2010), and co-editor with Roberta Hammett of *Assessment of New Litera-cies: Perspectives from the Classroom* (Peter Lang, 2009). Recently she co-edited *Children's Virtual Play Worlds: Culture, Learning, and Participation* (Peter Lang, 2013) with Jackie Marsh. She has researched and written widely in the areas of multimodality, multiliteracies, and new literacies.

Mary Clare Courtland is a professor in the Faculty of Education, Lake-head University, where she teaches undergraduate courses in literacy and children's literature and graduate courses in curriculum and lit-eracy, as well as a PhD research symposium. Her research interests include literacy teacher education and literacy for practising teachers, with an emphasis on Canadian children's and young adult literature to promote readers' understandings of diversity and social justice. Mary Clare recently co-edited with Trevor Gambell (2010) a text entitled *Lit-erature, Media and Multiliteracies in Adolescent Language Arts* (Pacific Educational Press).

Ismel González, PhD candidate and contract lecturer at Lakehead Uni-versity's Faculty of Education, has conducted research in modern lan-guages and cultures, teaching and learning, and literacy. He has also taught university courses in curriculum and instruction in English as a second language and English language learners, and literacy education in the content areas in the intermediate/senior division.

Roberta Hammett is professor of education at Memorial University of Newfoundland, where her research focuses on literacies, including their intersections with digital technologies, multiculturalism, identities, gender, secondary English education, teacher education, and teacher professional development. She co-edited *Assessing New Literacies: Per-spectives from the Classroom* (Peter Lang, 2009) and four other books that relate to her fields of research. Her teaching centres on intermediate and secondary English education, new literacies, digital technologies, and qualitative and action research. Hammett successfully completed several grant-supported research studies and organized two funded national conferences.

Ingrid Johnston is a professor of English education in the Depart-ment of Secondary Education in the Faculty of Education, University of Alberta. Her research and teaching interests focus on postcolonial literary theories and pedagogies, young adult literature, picture books, and Canadian literature, with a focus on issues of social justice. She has published *Re-mapping Literary Worlds: Postcolonial Pedagogy in Practice* (Peter Lang, 2003), with a Chinese translation, in 2007; a co-edited book on curriculum studies; and a recent co-authored book (with Jyoti Mangat) entitled *Reading Practices, Postcolonial Literature, and Cultural Mediation in the Classroom* (Sense Publishers, 2012).

Heather Phipps is a doctoral student in the Faculty of Education at McGill University. Her research interests include early childhood education, children's literature, identity, language, and community in culturally and linguistically diverse classrooms.

Farha D. Shariff completed her PhD from the University of Alberta with a focus on secondary education. In 2011 she was awarded the Doctoral Dissertation Award for her research in the literary experiences of second-generation South Asian youth as they explored contemporary postcolonial fiction. She has taught university courses in secondary English language arts education as well as elementary social studies education.

Teresa Strong-Wilson, associate professor at McGill University, has conducted research and taught education or interdisciplinary courses or seminars in the child/children's literature, curriculum, doctoral formation, early childhood education, Indigenous education, literacy, memory, and teachers and social justice. From 2009 to 2012, she was a research fellow in McGill's Institute for the Public Life and Ideas (Memory and Echo). She is senior co-editor of the *McGill Journal of Education*. On the topic of memory and teachers, she is best known for her work on touchstones: e.g., *Bringing Memory Forward: Storied Remembrance in Social Justice Education with Teachers* (Peter Lang, 2008); *Memory and Pedagogy* (ed. Mitchell, Strong-Wilson, Pithouse, and Allnutt) (Routledge, 2011); and, most recently, *Envisioning New Technologies in Teacher Practice* (Strong-Wilson et al.) (Peter Lang, 2012).

Angela Ward, a professor at the University of Saskatchewan, has worked as a teacher and teacher educator in cross-cultural settings across Canada and internationally. For the last twenty-five years she has researched language and literacy in K–12 classrooms and shared her understandings with many generations of teacher candidates. She is especially committed to enhancing the educational experiences of

Aboriginal students. Angela has contributed chapters to recent books on field experiences (Ralph, Walker, and Wimmer, eds, *The Practicum in Professional Education: Canadian Perspectives* [2010]; Falkenberg and Smits, eds, *Field Experiences in the Context of Reform of Canadian Teacher Education Programs* [2010]). She has also written books and articles on Aboriginal education.

Lynne Wiltse is an associate professor at the University of Alberta who teaches courses in the areas of language and literacy and children's literature. Previously, she taught in the School of Education at Thompson Rivers University in Kamloops, BC. Her research interests include minority language education, multicultural children's literature, sociocultural theory, teacher education, and qualitative methodologies. In 2005 her doctoral study won the Qualitative Dissertation Award and was published as a monograph, *Cultural Diversity and Discourse Practices in Grade 9.*

Index